THE LOCAL ECONOMIC
IMPACT OF WAL-MART

THE LOCAL ECONOMIC IMPACT OF WAL-MART

Michael J. Hicks

CAMBRIA
PRESS

YOUNGSTOWN, NEW YORK

Copyright 2007 Michael J. Hicks

Library of Congress Cataloging-in-Publication Data
Hicks, Michael J.
    The local economic impact of Wal-Mart / Michael J. Hicks.
        p. cm.
    Includes bibliographical references and index.
    ISBN 978-1-934043-38-7 (alk. paper)
    1. Wal-Mart (Firm)—Economic aspects. 2. Chain stores—United States—Economic aspects. 3. Retail trade—United States—Economic aspects.
I. Title.

HF5465.U64W354 2007
381'.1490973—dc22

2007005150

To Janet:
For being all that you are, and most especially
for putting up with me.

And to Morgan Grace, Nathan Michael
and John Thomas:
It is my solemn promise never to read this book
to you at bedtime!

TABLE OF CONTENTS

LIST OF FIGURES

List of Figures

LIST OF TABLES

FOREWORD

Good economists are seldom popular with the political class. This is not a shortcoming unique to democratic systems. Dictators like good economists even less. Why is this?

As a rule, politics doesn't educate. It obfuscates, pontificates, and prevaricates. It often seeks to advance the interests of the few at the expense of the many. It is a playground for the short-sighted and the demagogic. Economics, on the other hand, tells us a great deal about how material life can be improved through the operation of entrepreneurship and markets. It informs us that there are laws beyond those that legislatures pass, and consequences for ignoring them.

The good economist is the one who takes the discussion of economic matters to the lofty level it deserves. When others spout clever sound bites, unsubstantiated charges, and snake-oil remedies, it's the good economist who raises his hand and calmly declares, "Wait a minute! Let's look at the facts. Let's separate the wheat (truth, logic, and evidence) from the chaff (nonsense, false assumptions, and panaceas)."

Perhaps it was inevitable that the one company virtually all of us have patronized, Wal-Mart, would become a political football. Any firm that makes its way to the top spot on the Fortune 500 list, as

Wal-Mart did for the first time in 2002, is bound to attract attention and indeed, praise and admiration from some and envy and hostility from others. More than a few people have come to assume that bigness in business automatically implies a woeful trail of victims; some of those folks then make a nice career out of convincing the victims that they need their help. All too often, emotion drives the debate at least as much as information.

Michael Hicks, however, is interested in facts. He asks the right questions and provides the answers that thorough research suggests. He surveys the weight of evidence and analysis in the existing literature, and adds some informed insights of his own. This is what good economists are supposed to do. There are no wild claims or hidden agendas here. This book is a triumph of empiricism over mysticism.

As an occasional patron of big box retail stores like Wal-Mart, I could never quite relate to many of the routine attacks on them. With each visit, I park in an ample parking lot. I'm greeted by employees who smile, say hello, ask to help if I seem to need assistance, and thank me as I walk out the door. If I'm unhappy with price or service (I can't remember the last time I was), I know I can get a quick refund and shop elsewhere. My search costs as a consumer are usually lowered by buying there and it seems my wallet benefits as well — no doubt because competition makes big box retailers pass on their natural economies of scale in the form of lower prices. The sheer volume of Wal-Mart's trade alone suggests that the number of people who vote for Wal-Mart with their dollars is far greater than the number of those who vote for President and the Congress.

Even as an economist myself, I still learned much from this book that I didn't know. For instance, Wal-Mart's influence on labor markets is surely less than most would expect, in part because it employs less than one percent of the U.S. workforce. The company receives comparatively little in the way of subsidies in spite of the misguided generosity of state and local governments who try to pick winners and losers in the marketplace. The anti-Wal-Mart campaigns of today are eerily reminiscent of the Luddite crusades against chain stores seven decades ago — proof of the old adage that the more things change, the more they remain the same. The 1975 law against resale price maintenance agreements probably gave a huge, unintended boost to big box retailers at the same time it hurt smaller, more traditional stores. And it's quite likely that other big box retailers have more to fear from an efficient, aggressively competitive Wal-Mart than do locally-owned mom-and-pop shops.

But as Michael Hicks himself explains, economics — and indeed, this book — is less about a particular firm than it is about the markets in which it operates and the market forces which both propel and discipline the behavior of all firms. A lay reader will assuredly find the text challenging while professional economists will appreciate the extensive references to the often technical findings of their peers. Friends as well as critics of Wal-Mart will find things they like and things that they don't. No one will argue that Hicks doesn't take command of the subject.

Corporate mortality in free (or relatively free) markets is markedly high. The average person lives longer than most companies do. Competition, after all, is a dynamic, ongoing, leap frog process whereby today's leader can become tomorrow's follower, or even disappear altogether. Bigness is hardly a guarantee of permanence. Indeed, the vast majority of the firms on the Fortune 500 list 40 years ago are no longer with us. It should be sobering to even Wal-Mart's most severe critics that not even their behemoth nemesis can safely behave as though markets don't matter.

Nothing clarifies and informs quite like facts — backed up with solid evidence and sound reasoning. Accordingly, the literature of good economics has another worthy addition with this volume by Michael Hicks.

Lawrence W. Reed
President
Mackinac Center for Public Policy
Midland, Michigan

PREFACE

The genesis of this book lies in my longstanding frustration with the quality of the debate about Wal-Mart's impacts. Since early 1999, which marked the beginning of my study of Wal-Mart, I have struggled against a general misperception to explain what serious researchers do, and do not know about Wal-Mart and local economies. Now, as was the case then, the claims about Wal-Mart, both for the good and the bad were widely made, but often without benefit of data or analysis. I have long believed that an honestly constructed book on the matter was overdue. This is my attempt at such a book.

My interest in Wal-Mart's local impacts came about quite by accident, resulting from a heated local policy debate surrounding a new Wal-Mart store in rural West Virginia. (I was then an economics professor at Marshall University and Director of Research of the University's Center for Business and Economic Research). My interest in Wal-Mart's local impact has continued as time permits, and has resulted in a number of papers and talks on the matter. I do not bring strong preconceptions about Wal-Mart's specific impacts, and have published work that Wal-Mart's critics and admirers alike claim as evidence in support of their cause. I hope this is some proof of my objectivity on the issue.

Most of this book was written in late 2005, through the summer of 2006. I mention this because these months have been among the most fruitful periods of new research on Wal-Mart, and new studies emerge with remarkable frequency. A number of the papers I cite in this book are unpublished and forthcoming papers, a fact which reflects the freshness of the questions at hand. Still, the review of existing studies and new empirical analysis in this book is much broader in scope than is elsewhere available.

One feature of this book that bears comment is the ease with which academics researchers including myself, criticize existing studies. This will be unfamiliar to many readers. I want to be clear that this criticism is largely the mechanism we use to guide further exploration, not censure one another. Or as Isaac Newton asks in the preface to *Principia* "... the defects I have been guilty of ... be not so much reprehended as kindly supplied, and investigated by new endeavors of my readers." To give weight to this point, you will find I share criticism others have of my research (even agreeing in some instances).

Recently, a number of conscientious researchers of Wal-Mart have been criticized for having their research directly, or indirectly sponsored by Wal-Mart or their foes. This includes several researchers I specifically thank in the acknowledgments (whose work both criticizes and lauds Wal-Mart). I am personally skeptical that these economists would trade off their reputations for these payments; it just doesn't pay off, and being economists they are all highly rational. More to the point, I cannot find any sign of bias in their work, even when I disagree with their findings. (That is not true of course, of many recent popular books on the matter, and I often call their objectivity into question). Yet, it is still useful to make a full disclosure: I have no pecuniary link to Wal-Mart other than as a consumer (I once calculated diaper expenses topped $1,500 per year!). I am affiliated with two public universities and a well-known think tank. It is almost certain that researchers at both institutions have done work sponsored by both Wal-Mart and its foes. I don't know what they might be, and have no financial connection to them. In short, any bias I demonstrate in this book is due to far baser motivations than my simple mercenary inclinations.

Finally, I welcome comments on this book. It is my earnest hope that others will explore the issues I have included in this book, and alert me to other pressing questions regarding Wal-Mart's local impact. Any errors in this book are sadly of my own doing.

Opinions expressed within this book are those of the author, and do not represent the official opinion of the Air Force Institute of Technology, the U.S. Air Force, the Department of Defense, the Mackinac Center for Public Policy or Marshall University.

ACKNOWLEDGMENTS

Nobody writes a book by themselves, and many colleagues have assisted in the development of this work. I wish to thank Kent Sowards at Marshall University, for superb guidance and assistance with the data and Brie Salmons at Marshall University for overseeing the excellent map production. Kristy Wilburn, formerly of Marshall University, is guilty of pushing me into thinking about Wal-Mart. I wish to thank also Cal Kent at Marshall University, Mark Burton at the University of Tennessee and my colleagues at the Air Force Institute of Technology, especially Jeff Smith, for their insights, support and friendship through this process.

A number of fellow Wal-Mart researchers have helped me along the way, sometimes inadvertently. I wish to thank, in no particular order, Ken Stone, Richard Vedder, Emek Basker, Russell Sobel, Nicole Kazee, Kevin Brancato, Chris Holling and Arin Dube for sharing data and thoughts on these matters. My work has also benefited from more than a dozen anonymous referees, editors at seven journals, many members of the media and participants at the 2005 Global Insight Wal-Mart Conference.

I also wish to thank the very excellent editorial staff at Cambria Press. They have been tough taskmasters, but anytime you don't find an error in this book it is entirely their fault.

In the end, it is my family who has been most responsible for urging me along with this project, and bearing the burdens of my distraction. My parents John and Wanda Hicks have been a constant source of encouragement on this and everything else. I thank George and Helen Thomas for supplying me with diversion and support, and especially for providing a place for my family to hide while I wrote about Wal-Mart. Most especially I am thankful for Janet without whom I could not have written this book, nor done anything else of consequence.

THE LOCAL ECONOMIC
IMPACT OF WAL-MART

INTRODUCTION

> Motorists may buy at your service station but damn you because they think you are a monopoly. They may go out of their way to save a few pennies at your chain store and then denounce you for paying low wages ... without enlightened public opinion based upon self interest, a business with a million customers can be crucified by a militant minority.
>
> Don Franscisco, 1936

Wal-Mart stores are an omnipresent feature of American life. This ubiquity has spawned both highly positive and strongly negative responses. Consumers appreciate Wal-Mart for its convenience, low prices, and extensive selection. Individuals from nine of 10 American households have shopped at a Wal-Mart in the past few months, far more than have voted in any U.S. election. Furthermore, the average American household spends an astonishing $2,300 / year at the store.[1] These families have clearly revealed their preference for the price, quality, and convenience of Wal-Mart. The retailer is also familiar to critics. Among the complaints lodged against Wal-Mart are condemnation of its impact on local wages, retail competition, sprawl, income equality, health care and its potential for speeding the rate of globalization. Policymakers, mostly in state legislatures and local governments, also fret about Wal-Mart and its impact on tax revenues and expenditures.

This book is an effort to objectively examine these issues, and I take seriously the expressions of interest by critics and advocates alike. In this book, I examine the existing research critically and try to expose flaws as fully as necessary. My work here is partially theoretical but primarily empirical. I seek to answer the positive, not normative, questions about Wal-Mart's impact. I attempt to ascertain what the company's impact is, not what it should be, although normative issues are discussed in the summary.

In evaluating the range of potential impacts of Wal-Mart, I do not mean to provide blanket intellectual cover for all the company's critics or its advocates. The loudest arguments in the public square consist of emotional rather than thoughtful analysis. Because of this, I attempt to largely steer clear of some of the fringe debates and touch only lightly on these issues.

It is also useful to explain at the outset that this is not really a book about Wal-Mart, Inc. Economists study markets, not individual firms. This book is instead about those markets in which Wal-Mart operates and how the company affects and is affected by them. Consequentially, my analysis does not speak to many issues that are directly related to the firm. For example, I do not emphasize its marketing efforts, use of radiofrequency identification, supply chain innovations, or allegations of gender discrimination or antiunion behavior except where

---

[1] See Fishman (2006) regarding the household shopping data. The per family expenditure data are those reported by Wal-Mart and elsewhere and are correct in that it is the store's annual sales divided by the number of households in the United States.

there is a clear market component to these facets of the firm. This does not mean that these things are not important issues. On the contrary, they are so important that I leave the analysis to researchers in management and law who specialize in these areas.

The pieces of Wal-Mart's story that I do analyze remain very exciting elements of the U.S. and increasingly global economy. In fact, these issues are so important that there is an explosion of research and educational issues related to the subject. Furthermore, there are a surprising number of courses on Wal-Mart across the academic spectrum. One anti-Wal-Mart group even developed a curriculum that is being taught at over 25 colleges and universities nationwide. Constance Hays, writing in the *New York Times* in 2003, relates that the study of Wal-Mart has become a "Topic A" in business schools.[2]

To analyze the relationship between Wal-Mart and the markets in which it operates, I have organized the book into five sections, which focus on the most salient local issues surrounding the opening and operation of a Wal-Mart store. In Section I, to establish a context for the study, I discuss the history of chain stores and the transition to big-box stores, which are now such a common mechanism for bringing goods—and increasingly services—to consumers. I follow this with a mapping of Wal-Mart's locations and a discussion of the measurement of impacts used in the book. This is followed by an analysis of how Wal-Mart locates its stores.

Section II considers Wal-Mart's impact on labor markets, the markets for goods and services, and the aggregate local economy. The chapters analyze questions regarding how Wal-Mart impacts the private sector, areas that have been a prime target of inquiry over the past 15 years. Wal-Mart's impact on local tax revenues and expenditures and on antipoverty and health care programs—the latter an obvious policy frontier—is the focus of Section III. Section IV deals specifically with social impacts of Wal-Mart. By this, I mean factors such as sprawl, union participation rates, poverty, income inequality, and local

---

[2] See www.walmartwatch.com for the curriculum.

philanthropy. Finally, in Section V, I review the legal environment surrounding Wal-Mart and evaluate the political economy of the anti-Wal-Mart legislation. I conclude the study with research and policy recommendations to state and local leaders who are considering Wal-Mart's entrance into a community.

In addition to critically examining over 200 relevant studies, I contribute completely new statistical analyses in each section. Thus, this book contains a dozen brand new empirical studies embedded within a critical review of the existing research. Many of my findings echo existing work by others (or my previous research), but a larger proportion of this research is being presented for the first time here. The methods are, however, not new, and the techniques of analysis are, in virtually every instance, familiar to economists.

Consistent with the objective of this book, I include substantial technical detail regarding the estimation of Wal-Mart's impact. This technical component should be clear to academic researchers and graduate students who are familiar with scholarly research in econometrics or statistics. Readers who have a less technical background may react to the statistical details with less joy than my economist colleagues. To assist those who are less well versed in econometrics, each equation and graph is accompanied with a clear description of the link between Wal-Mart and the effect discussed. Most readers will find that the depiction of Wal-Mart's effects presented in the fashion that I offer in this book more clearly illuminates, rather than masks, relationships between the retailer and the markets in which it acts.

In the end, this book tackles the most salient questions about Wal-Mart's local impact—Where does Wal-Mart locate stores? What happens to the local retail economy? What stores close, and which new stores open? Will prices drop? What happens to tax collections when Wal-Mart comes to town? How much will Wal-Mart cost local taxpayers? Will Wal-Mart cause us to pay more for antipoverty programs? Will Wal-Mart close mom-and-pop stores? Will local charities suffer? What will happen to sprawl in our county?—in addition to many, many more. Before addressing these issues, however, I explore some important history of chain stores and big-box stores in the United States.

THE HISTORY AND MEASUREMENT OF WAL-MART

Placing the experience of Wal-Mart into historical context is an important part of any study which purports to explain its impact today. Thus, an understanding of the development and growth of chain stores, as well as the antipathy towards them provides a solid start to the economic and policy questions surrounding Wal-Mart today.

Beyond a history of chain stores and the newer big-box variety is the very real concern over the methods of estimating Wal-Mart's impacts on local communities. Much of the research that informs public policy and makes headlines is technically rigorous, thoughtful, unbiased and helpful. But, for every solid analytical effort, local policy makers are likely to confront dozens of studies or reports of dubious methodology and intent. So a first step is to review the statistical methods and techniques appropriately used to explain Wal-Mart's impact. This is also a good venue to explain how to interpret the statistics within this book.

Finally, Wal-Mart's method of choosing location, and the very real study concerns that emanate from this decision warrant considerable analysis. Any study which purports to explain Wal-Mart's impact on a local community must first face the very real possibility that the retailer is systematically making location choices for new firms. This very real possibility has the unfortunate, but unavoidable consequence of misleading researchers. For, if Wal-Mart always chooses to locate in growing counties, then growth will occur subsequent to Wal-Mart's arrival, whether or not the retailer had any meaningful effect. The reverse is also true, and this question is at the very heart of how we measure the retailer's impact.

To explain these three fundamental issues surrounding Wal-Mart, in this section I offer a chapter on the history of chain stores. Chapter 2 focuses on the data sources and measuring Wal-Mart and Chapter 3 provides much detail on how Wal-Mart enters markets.

CHAPTER ONE

THE CHAIN STORE
HISTORICALLY CONSIDERED

The modern chain store predates Wal-Mart by more than a century. Thus, the growth of Wal-Mart from 1962 through the early part of the 21st century must be viewed within the context of a long history of nationwide chain stores.

The modern chain store in the United States is generally considered to have developed at about the time of the Civil War with the opening of Gilman & Hartford's store in New York. This store eventually grew into the Great Atlantic & Pacific Tea Company, the precursor of the present day A&P. These merchants pioneered the method of opening multiple stores on the template of the original store design. The company quickly grew and became the Great American Tea Company, with 25 retail establishments by the end of the Civil War. These stores were turned over to the heirs of the original owners and expanded to 100 stores by 1880. This growth slowed somewhat, and by the turn of the century only 200 A&P stores were opened. However, by 1920 this

Table 1.1
Chain Store Entrance, 1900–1910

Year	Stores
1900	D. Pender Grocery Co., Hook Drugs, Daniel Reeves (acquired by Safeway), Dockum Drug Stores (now with REXALL Drugs)
1901	United Cigar Stores, H. L. Green (originally F&W), Grand-Silver, Lane Bryant, A. L. Duckwall, Walgreen
1902	J.C. Penney, Schulz Brothers
1903	Morris Stores
1904	
1905	Peoples Drug Stores
1906	W. T. Grant Co
1907	Louis K. Liggett, Mading's Drug Stores, Fisher Brothers
1908	A. S. Beck, Katz & Besthoff (now Rite Aid)
1909	Western Auto Supply, Gallaher Drug, Hested Stores

Source: Lebhar (1952) with author's updates.

number grew to 4,600, and A&P experienced a zenith of over 15,500 stores by 1930 (Lebhar, 1952).

The first decade of the 20th century appears to be the threshold for the development of the chain store. Godfrey Lebhar's excellent reference of chain stores provides a snapshot of successful chain entrance of that decade. See Table 1.1.

The rapid growth of chain stores during the early 20th century speaks to their popularity with consumers. It also speaks to some inherent economic benefit in operating chain stores. The most likely explanation for the rise in chain stores was the presence of economies of scale. The quaint language of one of the first chroniclers of chain stores provides a noneconomic explanation: "In buying, the chain store undoubtedly enjoys whatever advantage inheres in the factor of quantity" (Nichols, 1940, p. 100). He further explains:

> Large orders help to cut down overhead expenses for
> the manufacturer; production can be standardized and

economical machine processes introduced. Then again, the large order enables the manufacturer to anticipate his production schedule and he, in turn, is able to buy his raw material on a large scale and at a substantial saving. (p. 101)

The leading chronicler of chain stores in the 20th century provides a clear description of the role of local and firm scale economies. Lebhar explains that, although individual stores can operate with large volumes of goods,

> Most of the advantages the chains enjoy may be traced directly to the fact that the business is conducted through more than one unit because most of those advantages come from *volume*, and the volume the chains are able to attain depends mainly upon the number of stores they operate. (Lebhar, 1952, p. 7)

This passage foretells some of the current research on Wal-Mart, which is modeled as interaction between economies of scale of the individual establishment (store size) and the interaction of either scale economies in transportation and oversight or scale economies in international trade.[1]

The growing transportation and information networks in the United States during the early 20th century were fertile fields for this type of retail innovation. By the time Wal-Mart's founder, Sam Walton, was born in 1918, chain stores had become ubiquitous. Indeed, Springfield, Missouri, the place that Walton describes in his earliest memories, was home to a number of chains. In 1923, a Springfield native became president of United Cigar stores, which was one of the largest chains in the nation.[2] Virtually any consumer in the United States would

---

[1] These are Holmes (2006) and Basker and Van (2005), respectively.
[2] Reported by Grosenbaugh (2006) from a story in Springfield's *The Leader* about James Dixon originally of Springfield.

FIGURE 1.1   Selected 20th-Century Chain Stores

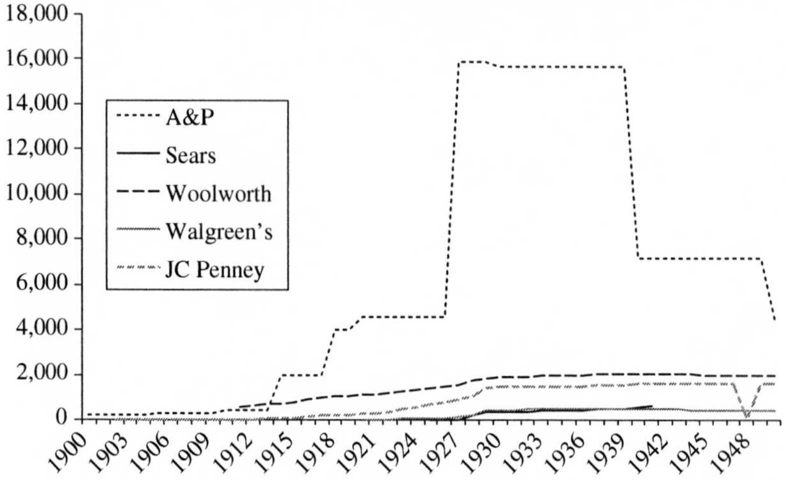

Data from Lebhar, 1952.

have seen and shopped in at least one variety. At least one current researcher, Bethany Moreton, argues that Wal-Mart has its roots in Ozark agrarian culture. That may be so (and her study is a fine read), but Sam Walton and all his contemporaries who later patronized him had already digested a steady diet of chain stores (see Moreton, 2006). A graph of the explosive growth of chain stores is given in Figure 1.1.

Considering Wal-Mart within the context of earlier chain store growth is important to better understand its role in transforming the retail trade sector. Wal-Mart stores (and the supercenters) are popularly depicted as enjoying historically record expansion. This is a poor characterization. To illustrate, I compare the growth of several similar stores across time. By collecting their start date to a single point, I can show how the leading chain stores grew relative to each other in different decades of the 20th century. As surprising as it may be, neither the rate nor level of Wal-Mart's growth is outside the historical norms. Figure 1.2 presents a clear illustration of Wal-Mart's relative growth (by number of store locations) compared with that of earlier

FIGURE 1.2   Selected Chain Store Growth Rates

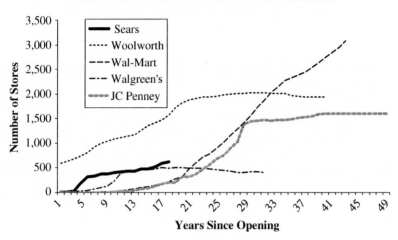

Data are normalized to date by author. Wal-Mart data from Wal-Mart's 2005 data release. The remaining data are from Lebhar, 1952.

chain stores. What makes Wal-Mart different is its increasingly strong growth in later life. Notably, this graph omits A&P, which had over 15,000 stores at its peak in the 1940s.

Interestingly, retail itself has declined in relative importance throughout all of the 20th century for which we have reliable data. Perhaps the first widespread concern with the retail sector occurred shortly after World War I. Lawrence Mann, a well-known economist of the period, began an article in the field's premier journal with the statement "No important field of business statistics has been so neglected ... as retail and wholesale merchandising" (Mann, 1923, p. 609). By the end of the decade, the federal government began collecting data on employment and wages by industry. The retail sector mattered most at the outset of the collection effort and has declined as a share of total income ever since (Figure 1.3).

This declining share of retail trade is fairly consistent with the inexorable productivity growth in this sector. Of interest is the drop in the retail share during World War II, when consumer goods were

FIGURE 1.3   Retail Share of Total Personal Income, 1929–2004

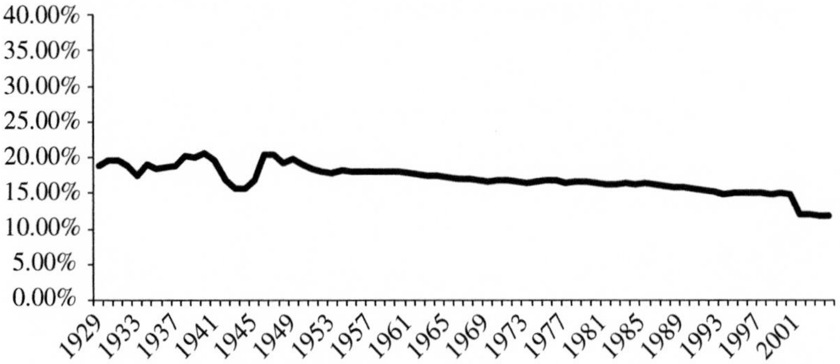

Source: Bureau of Economic Analysis.

heavily rationed. This was followed by an almost instant rebound after the war. The sharp reduction in 2001 reflects an accounting change whereby the North American Industrial Classification System displaced the Standard Industrial Classification System, resulting in a reclassification of some of the wholesale and retail sector activities into transportation and services. Consumers today buy more goods and services than their grandparents but spend a declining share of their income on retail goods.[3]

Mann's study measured total retail sales and value added in the sector. He estimated markups of roughly 25% (from which the costs of retail were deducted). Mann's research also noted the emergence of chain stores. He reports that "there are at present about 3,000 depart-ment stores, 100 mail order houses, and 1,000 chains in the United States which together operate about 100,000 stores and handle over 25 per cent of the total retail business" (Mann, 1923, p. 615). A later comparison of the retail sector in Canada and the United States esti-mated general merchandise operating costs of 25% to 27% of total

---

[3] The proponents of consumerism as a dominant cultural force face some daunting evidence in these data.

FIGURE 1.4   Economies of Scale

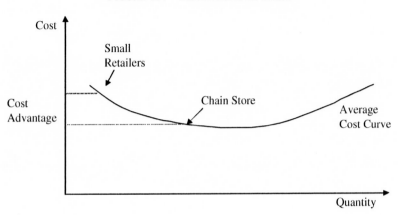

revenue (Whitely, 1936). Mann also concluded that "the department store and mail order house offer the consumers advantages in selection of goods from a larger stock, while the chain store usually offers goods at lower prices than independent dealers" (p. 616). This is in reference to the cost advantages of scale and is depicted in Figure 1.4.

Scale economies occur when a firm reduces its average cost as it produces more goods and services. When the size of the firm (in terms of total sales) determines cost efficiency, small retailers suffer from higher per unit costs than large retailers (especially chain stores). Mann noted this relationship. In addition to the 100,000 large chain stores that provided about 25% of retail trade, Mann counted 1.2 million small retailers and predicted that

> Their relative importance will probably continue to decrease, but there is no probability that they will all be forced out of business, as they usually have the advantage of convenience of location as compared with department stores and mail order houses, give more personal service (including credit and delivery) than chain stores, and are receiving closer cooperation from wholesale dealers who look upon the large-scale retailer as a common enemy. (Mann, 1923, pp. 615–616)

This passage could be found in any recent management book on Wal-Mart or in the popular writings about the firm. Fishman (2006) dedicated at least two chapters to supplying modern anecdote to the final sentence in this passage.

In 1928 *The Nation* published an article entitled "Chain Stores: The Revolution in Retailing" by Merryle Rukeyser.[4] His writing captured the essence of the process. He noted that the struggle between chain stores and existing retail "is waged less on the issue of size than on that of efficiency" (Rukeyser, 1928, p. 568). He believed that

> In the future chain-store managers will have to show increasing subtlety and business genius, for chain will compete against chain, thus neutralizing the obvious advantages in quantity buying. The retail business in the future will go increasing to the best-managed chains and the genuinely talented independent merchants, who have emulated chain-store efficiency and tempered it with a better grasp of local idiosyncrasies. (Rukeyser, 1928, p. 570)

Commerce in general was frenetically growing through the 1920s, and chain stores were a large part of this growth, but the stock market crash of 1929 and the nation's plunge into the Great Depression brought forth a fervor of anti-chain store sentiment.

THE WAR ON THE CHAINS 1930–1941

Fear and loathing of chain stores were not a creation of the Great Depression, but it was during this period that a confluence of events—from antipathy toward big business and the resurgence of the 19th-century progressive movement—combined to bring the anti-chain store sentiment to national prominence. History Professor Carl Ryant, writing in 1973, relates that early opponents of mail order catalogs—the precursor to the chain in much of rural America—spread

---

[4] He is the father of the late well-known Wall Street pundit Louis Rukeyser.

rumors that the founders of Montgomery Ward and Sears & Roebuck were African-American. He further notes that as a result of this and other anti-chain campaigning in the south, Sears & Roebucks' 1903 catalog contained a promise to mail goods in unmarked wrappers (Ryant, 1973). Godfrey Lebhar, the first real chronicler of chain stores, describes the challenges that the founder of the United Cigar Stores faced from being fictitiously linked to the "tobacco trust."[5] Lies, rumor mongering, and distortions—in short, the stuff of a modern political campaign—were among the tactics used by opponents to keep mail order firms and chains distant from consumers.

Despite the happy economic climes of the 1920s, the anti-chain store movement began to take shape. A leading researcher of the political economy of the time, Thomas Ross, marks 1927 as the start of the movement, but it was not until the stock market crash of 1929 that the explosion of sentiment affected the nation in general. By 1930, and virtually every year thereafter until the eve of America's entry into World War II, debating clubs at high schools and colleges argued about chain stores, including such topics as "Resolved: That Chain Stores Are Detrimental to the Best Interests of the American Public" (Ryant, 1973, p. 209). By 1940 a review of all existing debate manuals for college and high school students found them to uniformly contain debate notes on chain stores (Lebhar, 1952, p. 143–144). By 1941 students had other matters to debate, but the 1930s saw a remarkable explosion of anti-chain store legislation, which was motivated by a wistful remembrance of a quieter time. Richard Schragger, a law professor at the University of Virginia, argues that the broad appeal of the anti-chain store movement gathered together such disparate voices as progressives (Brandeis and LaFollette), populists such as Louisiana's colorful Huey Long, New Dealers (like then Senator Hugo Black),

---

[5] George Whelan, the founder of United Cigar Stores, generated a particularly pernicious affect on society since his chain of tobacco stores did away with the then usual wooden Indian, which, in an early form of joint advertising, adorned the front of virtually every tobacconist. A chain store killed Kawliga (see Lebhar, 1952, pp. 114–116).

unions, agrarians, farmers, the Ku Klux Klan, and African-American leaders, not to mention incumbent retailers (see Schragger, 2005, p. 3; see also Lebhar, 1952). This odd admixture was remarkably effective at motivating legislative change. It also bears an uncanny resemblance to the present-day critics of Wal-Mart, with perhaps a little less fringe participation.

In 1927, 13 state legislatures saw bills regulating chain stores either by restricting the legal number (Maryland) or specific type (drug stores in Pennsylvania) of chain or imposing graduated license taxes (GLTs) on subsequent stores in a single state. The first to see litigation was Maryland's law, which limited chain stores to five and levied a $500 fee on each of the second through fifth stores. The case against the state was brought by the Keystone Grocery and Tea Company in the circuit court of Allegheny County. The law was struck down in April 1928 by Judge Albert Doub, whose stinging rebuke of the legislature provides a distant echo to today:

> The plaintiff is engaged in an innocent, ordinary, useful and necessary business, permitted and authorized by the laws of this State and every other State. It has made substantial investments in merchandise, stock, legal obligations and commitments for leases and intangible property. One store in the city of Cumberland may pay a tax of twenty dollars [a tax levied on all retailers based on amount of inventory carried] while the chain store will be required to a pay a license tax of five hundred and twenty dollars. ...It is impossible to declare that both of them will receive, if this Act is to be enforced, the equal protection of the laws as required by the Fourteenth Amendment of the Constitution (Lebhar, 1952, pp. 117–119, in *Keystone v. Huster*).

Judge Doub was particularly strong in his ruling and went further in clearly articulating the benefits to commerce. However, anti-chain legislation continued. The banner year was 1933, during which time state legislatures and assemblies proposed 225 and passed 13 anti-chain laws. See Figure 1.5.

FIGURE 1.5   State-Level Chain Store Tax Proposals

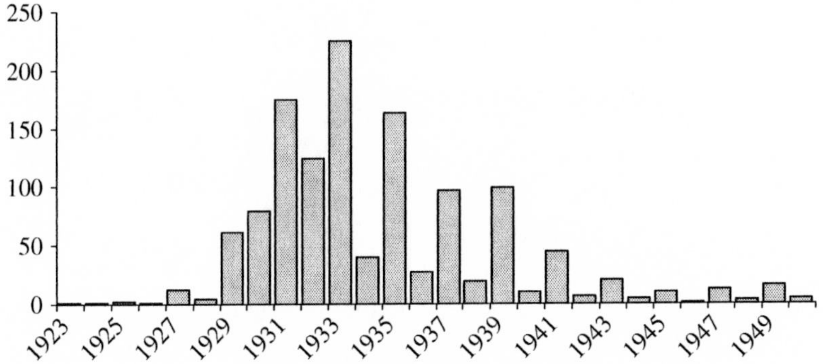

250 ─
200 ─
150 ─
100 ─
50 ─
0 ─

1923 1925 1927 1929 1931 1933 1935 1937 1939 1941 1943 1945 1947 1949

Source: Lebhar, 1952, from Retailers Manual of Taxes and Regulations, 1951.

The chain stores resisted this wave of legislation in the courts and in the court of public opinion. The American Retail Federation (ARF)—a new industry group—hired as a representative a well-known executive, Clarence Sherrill, from Kroger Grocery and Baking Company. Sherrill was a retired army colonel and so well known for revolutionizing supply chains that his persona was fictionalized in the portrayal of a soldier between the world wars by novelist Anton Myrer.[6] Famous before his military retirement, one adoring biographer *in Time Magazine* said of his time as an engineering officer that "efficiency has played a large part in Colonel Sherrill's efficiency scheme; he has learned how to squeeze the eagle [which then adorned the dollar] until it can be heard squealing down at the treasury."[7] He became much better known after his work at the ARF in lobbying for an end to mitigate the effects of the anti-chain store movement. A speaker's bureau, advertisements, and placards appeared supporting chain stores and answering their critics. In fact, the strategies used by Wal-Mart in

---

[6] Col. Sherrill had seen heavy fighting, having served as chief of staff to the 77th Infantry Division in World War I. The fictionalized account of an army officer appears in Myrer's novel *Once an Eagle*.

[7] *Time Magazine*, December 14, 1925.

response to their critics could have been taken right out of Colonel Sherrill's playbook.

My favorite example of this advertising campaign is a mock letter to the editor of a newspaper from a manager of a Thom McAn store, Mr. W. R. Webb of Amarillo, Texas. The letter accompanies a picture of Webb in a tidy suit, with his wife and infant daughter, Anita, who, we find out later, was recently adopted. His letter, which drips with mockery, notes the suffering of his independent competitor, who just built himself a new $5,000 home, and the hard-heartedness of his employer—a Wall Street boss—who just authorized flood relief charity to a hard-struck community. He notes his salary, Christmas bonus, and vacation, his ability to pay off debts, buy furniture, join a good fraternal order, and adopt a baby. He explains how he was unemployed for 3 years before Thom McAn hired him and how he now plans to build a home. He ends by asking the paper to print the letter in big type because it would "serve the chain stores right if everybody who traded with them knew all about them" (Nichols, 1940, p. 222). Some of this had to mitigate the anti-chain store fervor, but it did not turn the tide in favor of the chain stores.

Professor Richard Schragger provides much insight into what he calls the localist movement of the times, dominated by a "producerist" ideology. He argues that the weakening of the anti-chain store movement was partially due to a shift to a more inclusive "consumerist" movement associated with the New Deal. Women and African-Americans, he argues, would find voice in this movement that they could not in the existing world of "small dealers and worthy men" who owned and operated the incumbent retailers (Schragger, 2005, p. 10, citing McCraw, 1984).

Before the chain store tax died, it lived well. The legislation, which survived court scrutiny, emerged as a GLT. The GLT assessed a cumulative, often increasing fee on chains within a particular state. For example, the first store paid no GLT, the second, $10; the third, $20; the fourth, $40. The top rate was in Texas, with $750 per store over 50. These were prohibitive amounts at the time, with one store's taxes in the most extreme cases equaling the annual salary of one employee, and this at a time when the average chain store was employing perhaps a dozen workers, with a profit of only $950/year (Lebhar, 1952; Ross, 1986).

A modern study of the chain store tax unveiled some important insights into the movement. Professor Thomas Ross describes the political economy of the chain tax movement across the states. His study carefully describes some of the anomalies of the political conditions. He especially notes that it is apparent that, in many instances, the laws passed by the legislature were purposefully unconstitutional. They were for political show and nothing more. This argument, which is clearly within the framework of the economic theory of regulation, describes how self-interested politicians use political activity to maximize their support. I revisit his argument later in a more modern context.

Ross (1986) describes the chain store tax as an effective mechanism for politicians to garner support. Intriguingly, he questions the high failure rate of anti-chain store regulation in the courts. His empirical model was designed to answer the questions:

> To the extent that legislators have any foresight about the constitutionality of the laws they pass, one has to wonder what it means to pass bills that are struck down. Kentucky, for example, passed a number of chain tax bills, but none of them survived. What were these legislators doing? They had a number of Supreme Court approved models to work from, yet all their attempts failed. (Ross, 1986, p. 131)

Ross further cites Virginia, in which both the Senate and Assembly passed laws, with the Senate's mirroring one already struck down. The Senate, despite a vote to withdraw from the Assembly and Conference committee, failed to withdraw the legislation, and it failed to pass in a common form that could be brought to the governor for signature.

Ross tested the relationship between the introduction or passage of a law and state-level conditions that might support its passage. The empirical model tested (a) the decision to pass a bill, (b) pass one that survived court scrutiny, and (c) failure to pass a bill. He evaluated in a statistical model the influence of big chain retailers, grocers, and the political structure of the state. He found that dominance of groceries, not other general merchandise, was the leading influence fostering adoption of effective chain store taxes. Furthermore, he notes that although the taxes did not significantly affect nongrocery chain entrance, they did limit grocery penetration significantly. He concludes that "as there is considerable evidence that the grocery chains were a procompetitive force leading to lower food prices, these taxes could well have served to raise food prices" (Ross, 1986, p. 137). This is eerily familiar to the current debate about Wal-Mart.

It is tempting to give credence to the interest group voices that clashed in the localist and producerist versus consumerist notions advanced by Schragger. Perhaps it was the growing discontent of the farm lobby or the realization by manufacturers that chain stores helped their business. However, other factors emerged to crush the advance of the state-level chain store taxes. The first was the ultimately ineffective efforts at the federal level to rein in chain stores; the second was a world war.

Representative Wright Patman, whose home state of Texas had already enacted the toughest chain store GLT, brought that state's fervor to the federal policy scene. Joining forces with Samuel Robinson, they crafted legislation that prohibited price discrimination across retailers that could not be justified by actual cost savings. This modification of the Clayton Act is widely regarded by economists as among the greatest misadventures of antitrust legislation. The effects of the passage appear to have been limited, and the great critic of Patman, Godfrey Lebhar, gives its impact but little notice. It is highly unlikely today that most retail store managers involved in buying have even the faintest knowledge of Wright Patman.

Rebounding from his victory in the Robinson-Patman Act, Patman proposed a federal GLT that was higher than Texas' prohibitive rate. The proposed federal fee was so onerous that *Business Week* editorialized "Would you believe it, if you were to, that a congressman, and an influential congressman at that, had proposed that the Federal Government tax the F.W. Woolworth Co. about $9,000,000 a year?"

(Lebhar, 1952, p. 242). The proposal was much debated (with over 2,000 pages of congressional testimony). Patman argued that chains concentrated power in a few banks, destroyed local communities and depressed farm prices, led to monopolization of retail markets, and limited worker opportunities. It is difficult to assess across time and with so few easily accessible records, but it appears Patman struggled with facts and analysis. He argued that chains led to the bank failures of the Great Depression and farm losses exceeding $3 billion. He even went so far as to blame the Great Depression, from which the economy had emerged by 1937 only to slump again into recession, on chain stores and stated that prosperity merely awaited the passage of his bill, now known as "The Death Sentence Bill." Few Americans charged the chain stores with the Great Depression, and bank failures apparently were more common in places less densely populated by chain stores. President Franklin Roosevelt's Secretary of Agriculture publicly opposed the bill, and the *Congressional Record* was filled with letters from agricultural interests heralding their connection to chain stores. The bill died in committee, but chain stores benefited greatly from a public airing of the quality of Patman's arguments (see description by Lebhar, 1952).

The anti-chain store movement was dealt a blow with the advent of World War II. In the United States, far more urgent matters collected the attention of public officials, and rationing of consumer goods (and some limited wage and price controls) muted the debate. This is probably the only instance in history in which a war actually led to less economic regulation (although only in this narrow sphere). The postwar years saw large population shifts, the development of the interstate highway system, and a new form of retail store.

THE BIG-BOX FORMAT

In 1962, Sam Walton opened his first new store. In that year also stores opened that would eventually be known as Kmart, Woolco, and Target. Wal-Mart's growth lagged far behind these other retailers until the 1970s.

From the end of World War II through the early 1970s, the number of retail establishments changed only modestly, between 1.7 and 1.9 million stores. America, on the other hand, changed a great deal. The rapid development of the interstate highway system, housing of returning veterans, and their baby-boom progeny ushered in a rapid expansion of suburban dwellings. To be sure, small towns and cities also saw growth, but it was in the fringe of cities, recently called suburban, that most of the growth took place. Cars played a role in linking rural areas for some time, and in a series of recent papers Todd Neumann at the University of Arizona used car ownership as a method for controlling for the competitiveness and entrance patterns of retailers over several decades (Neumann, 2004, 2005).

An excellent contemporary study (Douglas, 1962) estimated the cost structure of retailers, with a focus on the potential presence of scale economies. Among the findings of this study are that retail is a decreasing cost industry (i.e., firms enjoy a cost advantage the larger they become). I have graphed some of the tabular data from this study to make the point. Preserving Douglas' size category of firm (from very small progressively to the largest), I plot two series of data. The profit rate across all retail firms (using 1956–1957 tax records) reveals what will become a familiar story in this book: Retailing is a low-profit-rate industry. However, the dollar of profit per dollar of invested asset or the profitability returns on size grows robustly as the firm grows in size. This is evidence of scale economies, although because this is corporate, not establishment, data, it is not possible to determine whether the source of the scale economies is through more efficient supply chains or larger individual stores. See Figure 1.6.

These data reveal that many of the smallest categories of firms were simply not viable. The expansion of the interstate highway system reduced transportation costs for retail firms and reduced travel and search costs for consumers. The former permitted the exploitation of scale economies in supply chains, which Wal-Mart has famously enjoyed. The latter permitted the exploitation of scale economies at the firm level, a far more important issue. For retailers who were established in those places that enjoyed what Lawrence Mann called in 1923

FIGURE 1.6   Profits and Profitability of Assets of Retail Firms by
Size Category (1956–1957)

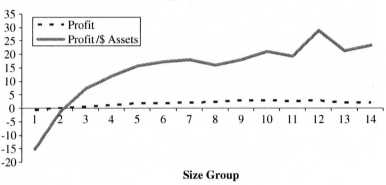

Size Group

The size categories ranged from up to $25,000 in assets to $250,000, with the range doubling in size for each successive group. *Source*: Douglas, 1962.

"convenience of location," rents were high, physical structures were small, and often parking was limited. These were in urban centers in big cities or small towns and, by 1970, were inconvenient places for motorists. They also suffered much higher costs because of their small size than did a larger retailer. The economic conditions that favored a large retailer located outside a city or town (with lower rents and larger facilities) were in place.

The purely economic factors associated with the growth of big-box retailing do not require much elaboration. But it is important to reiterate they are economic factors that were exploited by a number of firms. Sam Walton's vision did a better job than any of his contemporaries, but nothing quite as remarkable as the A&P store of half a century earlier. However, there is more to the story.

FEDERAL LAW AND THE GROWTH OF CHAIN STORES

Prior to 1975, it was common for manufacturing firms to establish a minimum price below which retailers could not sell their products. The economic consequences of resale price maintenance (RPM) laws on prices have been vigorously debated, especially with respect to their anticompetitive outcomes. However, one important study draws the link between these RPM agreements and the structure of the retail industry.

The Consumer Goods Pricing Act of 1975 ended the practice of resale price maintenance. Professor David Boyd, then at Denison University, provided a strong argument supporting the notion that this legislation led to the expansion of retailers and the rapid demise of smaller stores. Boyd's argument focuses on the value customer service provides retail consumers. He argues that the knowledge of specific retail items (e.g., the relative quality of a stereo system) is part of the value consumers receive from customer service. The RPM agreements in the industry that were common before 1975 resulted in a diffusion of this knowledge across retail stores. All stores had incentives to provide this service because there was far less price dispersion in retail markets. However, after the passage of the Consumer Goods Pricing Act of 1975, a firm seeking to be the low-cost seller could largely ignore the need to maintain knowledgeable sales staff on hand, sparing the expense. Thus, a consumer could obtain the information about the item at a retailer whose staff was knowledgeable (and, therefore, better compensated) and then simply make the purchase at the low-cost retailer. Boyd labels this "retail free riding."[8]

Although Boyd carefully acknowledges that RPM agreements can be used for anticompetitive purposes, including collusion between firms and price discrimination, his tightly woven argument proves particularly persuasive. It seems at least highly likely that the growth of this retail free riding may well be one of the spawns of big-box retail.

Some research into the expansion of the big-box format suggests that shifting consumption patterns (or at least preferences for retailing format) have played a large role in the growth of big-box stores. One researcher directly tested this hypothesis along with the more traditional structural arguments (growth of scale economies at the establishment

---

[8] As of this writing, Wal-Mart is experimenting with subject knowledge experts in some departments.

and supply chain levels). In a study drawn from his doctoral dissertation in geography, Scott Munroe modeled the structure of the retail industry using a multi-equation approach that accounted for individual firm costs and location of firms relative to each other, which represented their slice of overall demand. The equations accounted specifically for the size of stores (including consumer preferences for size), consumer travel costs, consumer preferences for comparison and multipurpose shopping (combined venues and malls), variation in the cost of land based on location, operating costs, scale economies, and reduction of costs as a result of firm clustering. By combining these two equations into an individual model, Munroe was able to vary the size of the impacts and the distance of the firms from each other to better appreciate which factors dominated the results (Munroe, 1999).

The type of experimentation he used is based on extending theories that have already been heavily tested and largely accepted. The uniqueness in his work is in his combination of factors that could plausibly explain the growth in the big-box format. His report yielded enormous insight, including the very strong result that operating costs and scale economies were the major factors on the final size and spatial distribution of firms: the big-box phenomenon.

In the final analysis, all signs point toward scale economies in retail, which combine at the establishment and supply chain levels. This may echo the simple size findings that Edna Douglas estimated in 1962, or they may be reflected in some of the newest work by Professor Thomas Holmes at the University of Minnesota, who is exploring the interaction of economies of density, or the benefits that accrue to firms of dense distribution of their facilities over their supply chain networks.

In the end, Wal-Mart has become an important, if controversial, fixture in the economic landscape of the United States. In singling out Wal-Mart as a force to be studied, I like to keep in mind some observations from Professor Stanley Hollander, who wrote the following in 1962:

> New types of retailing frequently start out with crude facilities, little prestige and a reputation for cutting prices and margins. As they mature, they often acquire

> more expensive buildings, provide more elaborate
> services, impose higher margins, and become vulnerable
> to new competition. (Hollander, 1960, p. 38)

This insightful piece, written on the eve of Sam Walton's headlong plunge into entrepreneurship, is labeled the "wheel of retailing" by one marketing professor.[9] Economists might call it the Schumpeterian "creative destruction." Whatever it is called, its process has been argued to have unleashed dynamic change in many American communities. How big that change has been, if at all, is an empirical question. That is where I now turn my attention.

---

[9] Attributed to Malcom McNair, by Hollander (1960).

CHAPTER TWO

MEASURING WAL-MART

Explaining how Wal-Mart affects a local economy is contingent on having some idea of the county location selected by Wal-Mart and the timing of its entrance. Much of the early research on Wal-Mart was limited by the absence of data on where new stores were located and the dates of their establishment. Many of the early studies used business listings such as the Yellow Pages or news accounts to obtain this information. These data limitations are a prime reason why so many early studies used data of a limited geographic scope. Although more recent studies used broader geographic samples, I argue that the narrow geographic focus of some of these early studies is a strength, not a weakness. However, until recently there were no national studies to which policymakers could turn to study the impact of Wal-Mart on a comparative local or regional basis.

In 2005, four different individuals or groups of researchers published papers that contained new nationwide data on Wal-Mart stores. Two of the research groups received a formal data release from Wal-Mart at about the same time. One group, from the Public Policy Institute of California (PPIC), was given access to the timing and location of all Wal-Mart stores to prepare an independent research study. Another group, the highly respected consultancy Global Insight, received the data for use in a study funded by Wal-Mart but overseen by a nonpartisan group of senior economists.

I was one of the researchers who presented papers at the Global Insight Conference on Wal-Mart but I received my data directly from a Wal-Mart employee whom I had to beg and cajole. This employee conceded to sharing a file of data that contained all the same data that Wal-Mart eventually released to Global Insight and the researchers at PPIC, except that my data also included the county in which Wal-Mart was located. This employee did not really reveal any secret information; he just saved me about 3,000 hours of tedious data collection.

By far the most ambitious data collection effort was performed by University of Missouri economist Emek Basker, whose paper was published in 2005 (but had been widely available since about 2002 as a working paper). Her work compiled new Wal-Mart locations from a series of Rand McNally maps published from the early 1970s that showed new locations and store numbers. She matched many of these data with news reports of Wal-Mart's openings in what must have been a miserably tedious process that only a graduate student would bear. At the time of her writing, these data were the most complete available, and they remain an important source of information. However, later data releases revealed quite a few errors in timing of new stores entrances in her data.

In November 2005 Wal-Mart made a public data release of new stores so that researchers had access to good administrative data. It is still a laborious process to prepare and the data are fuzzy on some issues (e.g., when an existing store was transformed into a supercenter), but it was easier to work with these data than cross-check maps or check old Yellow Pages.

The other relevant data are much more easily obtained by researchers. The decennial census provides very accessible data on county or sub-county levels such as zip codes and census tracts regarding literally thousands of variables ranging from ethnicity to proportion of residents with indoor toilets. I use these data in one of my studies on income distribution because it is the best available source for this.

The federal government also collects data on detailed employment, income, and transfer payments (Medicaid, Social Security) by industrial sector at the county level. These data are available from the Bureau of Economic Analysis, Regional Economic Information System. These data date back to 1969, with state-level aggregations reaching in some cases back to 1929. There are weaknesses in these data, but they are the best available and widely used by researchers of all sorts.

The U.S. Census Bureau also collects data on the number of firms by size and industry at the county level. All of these data can be quickly downloaded on the World Wide Web and are the most commonly used for research questions involving jobs, wages, and market structure (number and size of firms) by industry. Unfortunately, in 2000, the United States changed the system slightly to better correspond with Mexico's and Canada's accounting systems. Although this was an improvement, it also means that many of the comparable data, especially in the retail sector, are quite poor. Fortunately, one can statistically account for this, and it is only a problem for some types of research questions.

State and local governments often collect their own data, especially on retail sales taxes or similar items for local use only. I use these data when available. Also commercial firms, notably Dun & Bradstreet, collect a significant amount of data on firms. These data are not terribly expensive, but historical records are difficult to compile and are plagued with errors. For example, some Wal-Mart stores in my 2001 study of West Virginia had reported latitude and longitude values placing them far out into the Atlantic Ocean. I was able to actually find one of these stores safely nestled in the hills of West Virginia.

The data used in this book are then almost entirely available from public sources, and researchers with even modest experience on regional issues will have seen them in countless studies. However, there is more to measuring Wal-Mart's impact than simply knowing the location of its stores and the timing of their entrance.

ASSESSING WAL-MART'S IMPACTS

Most early studies simply measured the presence of a Wal-Mart in a county or city, a yes-or-no question. The earliest study by Professor Ken Stone in 1989 examined Wal-Mart's impact by comparing what happened in cities with and without a Wal-Mart in Iowa. His technique, as I explain later, has a real weakness in that it fails to account for preexisting trends that would distort his findings. However, one main contribution of this study is that it treated Wal-Mart as a separate phenomenon that should be measured. Several intervening studies did much the same thing, often using some rather basic statistical techniques to evaluate Wal-Mart's impact. The method of measuring Wal-Mart did not advance much from this point.

In 2001, Kristy Wilburn and I, then at Marshall University's Center for Business and Economic Research, measured Wal-Mart's impact on 55 West Virginia counties from 1989 through 2000 using what is known as a *presence dummy variable* that reflected whether Wal-Mart was present in a county (Hicks and Wilburn, 2001). For those cases in which Wal-Mart had entered a county a second time, we simply added another variable to the county, making this a presence / count variable. We were also the first to systematically measure the impact of Wal-Mart in an adjoining county using a similar method. This is a common technique economists use to measure such things, but this approach has some drawbacks. Most importantly, it does not consider the possibility that the impact of Wal-Mart may develop slowly over time.

During this time, Emek Basker at Massachusetts Institute of Technology was working on a similar problem but used a data set that included a much larger geographic area. Basker measured Wal-Mart's impact using a polynomial distributed lag of Wal-Marts per capita in over 1,700 U.S. counties. This measure permitted her to estimate the rate at which the impacts materialized.[1]

---

[1] A later study derived from this dissertation is more accessible despite the publication lag. See Basker (2005a).

Lester Hadsell, an economist studying the impact of Wal-Mart on local tax rates in New York, used a variable similar to my presence / count and a variable that accounts for the number of years Wal-Mart had been present in a county. This study was derived from a doctoral dissertation that Hadsell completed in the late 1990s, and he was unaware of the work that Emek Basker or Kristy Wilburn and I were performing (see Hadsell, 2002).

David Neumark, Junfu Zhang, and Stephen Ciccarella, three economists then working at the Public Policy Institute of California and University of California–Irvine, presented a paper at the Global Insight conference in November 2005 that is, to date, probably the most extensive study of Wal-Mart and labor markets. These authors used two measures of Wal-Mart's exposure: number of years each store in a county had been open (similar to Hadsell's method) and number of stores in a county weighted by the number of years they have been open in each year.

Other studies, such as one by Arin Dube, Barry Eidlin, and Bill Lester (2005) at University of California–Berkeley's Institute for Industrial Relations, used methods similar to that of Hicks and Wilburn (2001) to measure impacts, but other methods of estimating Wal-Mart exposure, such as Wal-Mart's share of retail employment (Hicks, 2005a) were also developed. These measurements of Wal-Mart's impact represent only a small number of the mechanisms that may be used to explain the economic effects of this retailer, but they are a shared component of virtually all studies. Before discussing the actual measures of Wal-Mart's impact, it is helpful to understand what economic theory might say about the potential impact of a retailer like Wal-Mart.

ECONOMIC THEORY AND WAL-MART'S IMPACT

The theoretical treatment of Wal-Mart in all of these studies is based on standard economic theory and heuristics. However, understanding how consumer demand changes after Wal-Mart's entrance may help explain some of the divergent results reviewed later. Three stylized descriptions of Wal-Mart effects may occur during retail market adjustment periods: income effect, clustering effect, and labor productivity effect.

The Income Effect

If Wal-Mart enters a market and significantly lowers prices, as Hausman and Leibtag (2004) and Basker (2005b) conclusively find, consumers may experience an income effect for retail goods. If the income effect is positive, as it almost certainly is, it is indeed plausible that consumer demand for retail goods will rise, leading to higher net employment and incomes in the retail sectors.[2]

The basis for this effect is captured by the well-known Hicksian decomposition of a price change into income and substitution effects.[3] In this basic model, a utility-maximizing consumer chooses consumption of two goods, X_1 and X_2, which are more easily thought of by viewing X_2 as retail goods and X_1 are all other goods. U_1 is the initial level of utility, which is tangent to the original budget constraint. A price reduction for the retail goods resulting from the entrance of Wal-Mart will shift the budget constraint outward and result in a new utility-maximizing tangency at U_2. Original consumption of the retail goods was X^A, and the new level of consumption is X^B.

This is the basic treatment of the impact on consumption of a price decrease for a normal good. The innovation of this decomposition is that the change in consumption is split between a substitution effect and an income effect. The substitution effect reflects consumers' changing pattern of consumption. As illustrated here, this is the increased consumption as consumers consume more (along the utility function)

---

[2] Singh, Hansen, and Blattberg (2004) performed a study on Wal-Mart's impact on a single incumbent retailer, finding that their revenues dropped primarily because of fewer visits, not changes in the market basket mixes of consumers. A comprehensive study (on all or most incumbent firms) should conclusively answer the income effect question but would be very costly.

[3] This was developed by Nobel Laureate Sir John Hicks, and although I am closely related to at least three John Hicks, none have (yet) received a Nobel Prize, and I can claim no relation.

from X^A to X^C. The income effect is decomposed as the amount represented by the increased consumption X^C to X^B. As illustrated, both effects are positive and imply that at a lower price more of good X_2 will be consumed. This process explains theoretically the increased consumption of lower priced Wal-Mart–related retail products when the firm enters a market. Indeed, as I later review, the estimates of price reductions resulting from Wal-Mart are not inconsistent with a 5% increase in sales, which is the upper bound of the employment impacts across studies, which I describe later. (See Figure 2.1.) This reasoning suggests Wal-Mart will have a positive impact on consumption, which is related to this increase in retail employment.

The Clustering Effect

A second theoretical explanation of Wal-Mart's impact is clustering. Economists often treat clustering as a supply-side effect resulting from some local input shared inadvertently. However, researchers concerned with retail have traditionally described the clustering phenomenon as a demand-side phenomenon, which is associated with a reduction

FIGURE 2.1   Hicksian Decomposition and the Income Effect

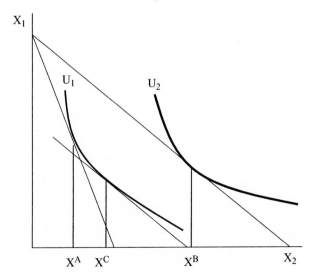

in consumer search or travel costs. For example, Nils Bohlin, a researcher at Stockholm University, modeled the cost-reducing benefits of marketing expenses for firms that are clustered (Bohlin, 2001). For our purposes, the effect could be supply side (inadvertently sharing marketing expenses) or demand side (lower consumer search / trip costs). The end result will be largely the same: clustering of retail activity.

The explanation for the clustering effect is straightforward. If Wal-Mart enters a market and attracts clusters of retail firms, then there could be considerable cross-county shopping with an increase in net employment, wages, and firms in a Wal-Mart county. This effect would likely be especially dominant when Wal-Mart first enters into an area. Clustering effects should dissipate as Wal-Mart enters adjoining counties, leading to greater retail saturation. However, a basic prediction is that surrounding counties will lose retail employment as the migration to clusters occurs.[4]

More formally, suppose two firms, i and j, enjoy lower production costs from being geographically close and producing similar goods or services (mathematically, their production function is $x(d_{i,j}^k d_{i,j}^p)$, in which $d_{i,j}^k$ is their geographical distance and $d_{i,j}^p$ their so-called product difference, or how similar their goods or services are. These firms will tend to then benefit from agglomerations A, such that $A_i = \Sigma \ \Sigma x(d_{i,j}^k d_{i,j}^p)$, which is the sum of the benefits of being physically close and producing similar goods (like retail goods and services).

However, the relationship could also be the reverse, such that firms suffer from being located nearby each other. For example, a strip bar and Christian bookstore will each suffer from being located nearby one another. In this case, the product of their interaction across space and product lines is negative and spatial distribution of firms will

---

[4] The real estate research literature describes this as demand externalities. See Eppli and Benjamin (1994). This is also highly consistent with the findings of Hicks and Wilburn (2001) and Basker (2005a). Singh, Hansen and Blattberg (2004) estimate the sales volume declines in a single incumbent retailer finding the basket mix remains unchanged, while average number of visits decline. They could not speak to net effect because of their examination of a single incumbent retailer.

increase. This has obvious implications for observed patterns of retail distribution.[5]

The Labor Productivity Effect

Third, Wal-Mart's much noted increase in labor productivity should lead to lower retail employment (as fewer workers produce more goods and service). Suppose a firm produces good X, with capital (K) and labor (L) inputs, and the demand for X is fixed in time period t. Then obviously $X_t = f(K,L)$ is the production function for the firm. It is clear that profits increase when the productivity of labor (X/L) increases *ceteris paribus* because wage costs are lower. If Wal-Mart is more productive than its competitors, its entrance into a market should reduce retail employment. Importantly, however, theory also strongly suggests that the effect of increased productivity is higher wages.[6]

These three effects suggest that, from a theoretical perspective, researchers looking at different times and locations may well find divergent results because of actual variations in the adjustment mechanisms to Wal-Mart even if the same methods are used. Konishi (2005) provides a game theoretic explanation of firm location decisions. In this model, retailers selling similar goods that locate proximally attract large numbers of consumers with expectations of low prices. This increases market size (total demand) but also results in price competition. Depending on the degree of competition and firm heterogeneity, his model argues that multiple spatial outcomes may result (multiple equilibria in the language of game theory). Given my argument, then, two technically competent studies may show conflicting findings but both be correct for their time and location, although the findings

---

[5] Basker (2005a) rejected retail agglomeration at the county level, while I found evidence of it.

[6] There is also pretty strong agreement among labor economists that firm and market characteristics influence wages as well. This would argue that a change in Wal-Mart's operating methods (e.g., labor mix) would potentially influence workers wages, although that is far from certain, as is the net employment impact.

clearly could not be generalizable across *all times* and *locations*.[7] Therefore, the choice of location and timing of the sample period may play a critical role in the estimation results of Wal-Mart's impact on labor markets. Furthermore, the type of endogeneity, a concern I discuss in the next section, may vary across regions and time. Therefore, I argue that it is useful to carefully target analysis to smaller geographic and temporal periods. I take this approach throughout the rest of this book.

Having reviewed how estimates were made and how the techniques of evaluating causation have varied, it is useful to examine what types of techniques are used to tease out Wal-Mart's impacts.

MEASURING THE IMPACT OF WAL-MART

It would be a happy situation for policymakers if a complete understanding of Wal-Mart's impact were a straightforward process. Unfortunately, it is not, and a good many researchers continue to treat Wal-Mart's impact as if it were a simple accounting exercise of jobs or businesses lost or gained after a Wal-Mart comes to town.

Three types of studies have emerged. The earliest were case studies, although new ones appear virtually every week. Case studies undoubtedly advance our understanding of some issues surrounding Wal-Mart, but they suffer from rather vast methodological limitations, which leave them unable to assign causation of effects directly to Wal-Mart or any other force for that matter. Case studies of Wal-Mart's impact often measure jobs or number of firms before and after Wal-Mart enters a market and cannot address or completely ignore other factors that affect the market during the time of examination. I include input–output models as part of this type of analysis. Input–output models are often requested or required as part of a legal requirement to explain Wal-Mart's specific impact on issues such as sales tax revenues from the store. Again, these might be useful,

---

[7] For divergent but technically rigorous studies, see Hicks and Wilburn (2001), Basker (2005a), Hicks (2005b), Hicks and Van (2005), Neumark, Zhang, and Ciccarella (2005), Dube, Eidlin, and Lester (2005) and Sobel and Dean (2006).

but they miss any existing trends and the possibility of determining effectively whether Wal-Mart's entrance into a retail market eliminates or creates new jobs.

Empirical studies, the second type, use some method of regression analysis to evaluate Wal-Mart's impact. Regression analysis is a statistical method that fits a line to a scatter plot of points called observations. In its simplest representation, two variables, X and Y, are plotted and a line is fit to these points. See Figure 2.2.

The slope of this line is an estimate of the change in Y when there is a one-unit change in X (based on the best fitting line). For our purposes, X could be the number of Wal-Mart stores in a county and Y the total retail sales. I have depicted a positive relationship (as X increases, so too does Y), but it could also be negative (or a downward slope). The relative importance of the size of the slope depends on the question being asked and graphically on the scale being used. Whether the line is statistically trustworthy or not depends on the spread of the points, or their *variance*. If the points are greatly spread out (and there are computational tests for this), then we say the line is not statistically reliable, or its slope is not different from zero (a flat line). This means that there is no effect. This determination has a subjective element, which I explain in each case where it matters.

FIGURE 2.2   The Basic Regression Line

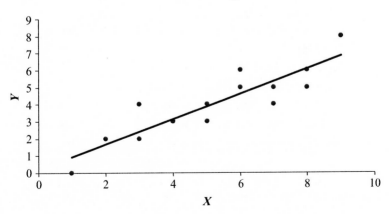

Most economic research wants to account for more than a single relationship such as, for example, Wal-Mart's impact on retail sales. We might also want to account for past values of retail sales, a trend, seasonality (if using monthly or quarterly data), or the influence of neighboring regions. The model then becomes a *multiple regression analysis*. The mathematics of the process essentially draws a line for each relationship (several *X* variables) to the *Y* variable. In this case, the slopes of the individual *X*s change meaning only modestly. Instead of simply representing the change in *Y* for a one-unit change in *X*, we measure the change in *Y* resulting from a one-unit change in *X*, holding all other *X* variables constant. Economists refer to this in Latin as *ceteris paribus*, which means holding all other factors constant.

Economists and statisticians often focus on much of the detail of these regressions. We pay particular attention to the error term, which is the sum of the squared vertical distances between the points on the scatter plot and the line we draw that best fits the equation. This gives the technique its name of ordinary least squares. We measure whether the error term enjoys a particular statistical distribution (often the normal or bell curve) and worry whether the variance of the errors is constant and unrelated to each other. Failure to account for these can lead to results that suffer from statistical bias or are unreliable. I only discuss these at length when a problem arises.

The data we use come in two basic formats: cross-sectional and time series. Cross-sectional models examine multiple units (e.g., counties) in the same time period (often a year). Time series models track a single unit (such as one county) across time. The bulk of the empirics in this book estimate cross-sectional, time series data, which, to choose one example, measure some facet of a county (e.g., retail sales) over many counties for several years.

Economists fret most about the appropriate variables to include in their model, a process called *model specification*. From this effort, researchers try to tease out causation from simple correlation. For the purposes of this book, two major challenges in this process emerge. Both problems have fairly straightforward, nontechnical descriptions. The first is that often two variables share a common trend but may not have a causal relationship. One unfortunate example is that my hairline and the U.S. population have both been rising steadily these past 20 years. The statistical relationship here is quite strong but causation is not. Economists test for trends in data using a test for stationarity. For the purposes of the current analysis, the presence of stationarity implies no worrisome trend with which one must deal. This is a straightforward problem to address, and given the relatively short time frame for many of the variables, stationarity is rarely a problem.

The second concern over the direction of the causal arrow is far more challenging and, in fact, remains unresolved. The gist of the problem is that if Wal-Mart is placing new stores in locations in which the economy is already growing, then the opening of Wal-Mart stores will be correlated with a growing economy. The reverse is also true: If Wal-Mart is placing new stores in economically declining communities, then statistics will show it is correlated with a declining economy. Correcting for this difficult problem is a recurrent theme in this book. It is known as the endogeneity problem.

Economists call the causal variables *exogenous* variables (or determined outside the model). The variable that is determined or estimated within the statistical model is known as an *endogenous* variable. The example just presented is a classic concern. If Wal-Mart is entering fast-growing counties, then the speed of the county's growth causes Wal-Mart to open a store. If we then estimate the growth rate of the county as a function of Wal-Mart's presence, we make the endogeneity error, which potentially leads to a biased estimate of Wal-Mart's impact. This is statistical bias, distinct from researcher prejudice.

To circumvent the endogeneity problem, researchers must find an instrument (either a variable or equation) that meets certain properties, which, unfortunately, cannot be mathematically confirmed. These are the third types of studies. The quality of the instrument is largely dependent on the theoretical argument used for it. As befits academia, there is much haggling over the quality of the instrument in the measurement, and it is always good sport by fellow researchers to critically review the choice of instrument. I do so here, including outlining the potential shortcomings of my own instruments, in the spirit of discovery, not to criticize or imply researcher prejudice.

The statistical technique used in these instances is often the two-stage least squares (2SLS) or some close cousin. Least squares is the statistical technique to choose the best fitting line to the scatter plot of points illustrated in Figure 2.2. This is accomplished by drawing a line that mathematically minimizes the vertical distance between the points on the scatter plot. The two stages refer to the first estimate using the instrument and the second estimate using the full equation. Each stage is calculated using a least squares approach, although there are other methods that are also appropriate.

Often researchers adjust the scale of their data to simplify interpretation or account for the possibility that the best fitting line is not straight (i.e., nonlinear). A common approach is to convert the scale of the variables by a logarithm. These are quite common across fields; for example, the Richter scale for measuring earthquakes is a logarithmic scale, or log scale for short. The benefit of the log scale is often in the interpretation of the model. For example, if I transform the variable that is impacted (the endogenous variable) into a log scale, then the slope, or β value, becomes the percentage change in Y when there is a one-unit change in X.

Some of the variables we are interested in take a discrete value (e.g., 1 or 0) or are a count variable $(1, 2, \ldots n)$. In these cases, the models are modestly more sophisticated, and the interpretation of the coefficients can mean that a one-unit change in X leads to a change in the probability that Y will happen. I make these situations clear in the text.

In the end, the empirics are critical but understanding all the nuances of the empirical methods is not. Some readers will be undergraduate or graduate students who have not yet been exposed to these methods or are in fields of study where they are infrequently used. Other readers may be policymakers grappling with the issues and do not have the leisure to carefully digest each statistical detail. Therefore, I follow the tradition in economics journals and carefully describe each piece of statistical work in straightforward prose. The data are publicly available. In the end, I am hopeful that readers and others will more fully explore the questions I ask and seek answer to in this book.

HOW TO INTERPRET THE STATISTICS IN THIS BOOK

The majority of the references to statistical analysis I use in this book are from existing published works. These references require minimal technical explanation because they have already been published in an accessible forum where this is emphasized. Thus, when reviewing a published source, I simply construct a general relationship with an equation of the type:

$$\text{Emp} = f(\text{Wal-Mart}, \text{Pop}) \tag{2.1}$$

which I describe as "employment is a function of the presence of a Wal-Mart and population." (Please note this is hypothetical but close to what the rest of the book offers.) This equation typically represents a statistical model in which a researcher has collected data on employment, population, and the presence of a Wal-Mart store across a number of counties, states, or cities over time. Once again, the usual inference in these types of models is that the causal arrow points from Wal-Mart and population to the employment level. The quality of the data and the appropriateness of the statistical relationship get to the heart of Wal-Mart's impact and whether the study's findings are to be believed. I discuss each study this critically, both technically and nontechnically, in the text, as I do the new research findings I present.

When I introduce my new research on Wal-Mart, I provide a little more technical detail. My intent is to make my work sufficiently transparent that it can be fairly evaluated and replicated by other researchers. Therefore, I discuss in more detail the data sources and the model considerations and provide an explicit statistical model such as:

$$\text{Emp}_{i,t} = \alpha + \beta_1(\text{Wal-Mart}_{i,t}) + \beta_2(\text{Pop}_{i,t}) + e_{i,t} \tag{2.2}$$

which I describe as "employment in county i, in year t is a function of a common intercept α, the presence of a Wal-Mart in county i, year t, and population. I also note that there is a white noise error term, e, which is the distance each point on the scatter plot deviates from the best fitting line. When economists use the term *white noise*, they are simply saying that the error term exhibits the right statistical distribution for the model (often the normal, or bell-shaped, curve). Much of the remaining technical detail will be explained in footnotes.

Importantly, in these types of statistical models, the components of interest are the estimated values of β which is the slope of the best fitting line. For example, the β_1 for Wal-Mart in this equation would typically represent the impact the retailer has on employment. To present these values, I display them in a table, which contains considerable additional information for the statistically savvy reader. See an example in Table 2.1.

In this table, I display the elements of Equation 2.2 that were statistically estimated. In this book, I show the coefficients in the order of the equation, so $\alpha = 2,200$, $\beta_1 = 55.4$, and $\beta_2 = 0.45$. Often only some of these variables are important for interpretation while the others are

TABLE 2.1
Hypothetical Impacts of Wal-Mart Explained

	Model 1
Intercept	–2,200
	(–0.41)
Wal-Mart	55.4**
	(1.91)
Population	0.45***
	(4.38)
Adjusted R^2	0.86
Durbin-Watson	1.87
Observations	430

control variables. Control variables are usually important for isolating the effect that we are trying to examine but are not of direct policy importance. For example, if I wanted to understand what educational factors determine whether a person 25 to 35 years of age holds a job in a given month, I would have to account for gender because these are prime childbearing years, which has an obviously critical impact on female labor force participation but no particular policy implications (at least in the United States).

In this hypothetical example, we are interested in whether the presence of Wal-Mart impacts employment, and Table 2.1 shows that the effect is 55.4 workers (the average across years and counties). I typically make mention of the control variables but do not linger over their interpretation unless it is important in understanding the issue at hand.

Underneath each coefficient, a t statistic is displayed, which is the well-known measure of statistical significance or certainty. The t statistic is roughly the ratio of the estimated slope to its variance. It is helpful to think of this as the *signal to noise ratio*. A signal to noise ratio of about 3:2 approaches the traditionally reported level of statistical significance. The asterisks beside the coefficient denote the level of statistical significance. Typically, *** denotes statistical significant at the 0.01 level, which means that the estimated statistical relationship could have occurred through chance in only 1 of 100 samples. Lower levels of statistical significance are denoted by fewer asterisks or occasionally other symbols. Each is noted in the text. Not infrequently, the work is not a sample but the total of the population. For our purposes, the meaning of the t statistic is the same. It is common to provide the statistical significance to each variable. However, it is critical to understand that a coefficient that is statistically significant to the 10% level and thus has a p value of 0.100 or smaller (e.g., 0.09999) is not really different from one that has a p value of 0.100001 for practical purposes. Also, a variable can be highly statistically significant and have no economic relevance. For example, if I found that there is great statistical certainty that Wal-Mart led to a net job creation of 1.4 jobs per county, I would not ascribe economic relevance to this finding. That is, I would describe the impact of Wal-Mart as essentially zero in this case despite finding statistical significance. Both of these processes involve some value judgment, and I will be as clear as possible in each case in which there is a close call to be made. All empirical research demands this type of judgment, and by including the underlying statistical results the reader can better evaluate whether the findings are not only statistically significant but also meaningful in a practical sense as well.

To further explain the model, I include a type of Durbin-Watson statistic, which is a measure of a type of statistical bias that occurs when error terms are related. This value should ideally be between about 1.3 and 2.2 and mostly is not a problem. I also report the number of observations (e.g., counties and years) to give some notion of how useful broadly extrapolating the results might be. I also include a standard goodness-of-fit measure: the adjusted R^2. This tells us roughly how much of the variability in the observed data is explained by my model. It does not really tell us how good the model is, only how well it fits the data. Other specific statistical pieces are included only where necessary.

As I think an objective reader will see, my intent is not to argue a particular case. I will provide results that will both comfort and distress Wal-Mart and its critics alike. In the end, I will make some clear conclusions based on my research and that of others. My real goal is to provide an accurate accounting of issues, not to take sides in the debate.

For those readers in disciplines that do not typically use these types of statistical tools, I have taken great effort to explain the results in plain prose. The detailed statistical modeling efforts of many researchers do, however, remain an important part of the process of understanding Wal-Mart's impact, and I have not attempted to dilute these efforts. They are especially important in the analysis of such a contentious issue and are a check on any possible bias in presentation. I now turn my attention to how Wal-Mart may choose a location and timing for a new store.

CHAPTER THREE

THE DIFFUSION
OF WAL-MART'S ENTRANCE

The pattern of Wal-Mart entering markets has become a famous description of expanding influence from the once humble Bentonville, Arkansas, to the far coasts of the United States. The expansion looks roughly like an expanding doughnut spreading out from Bentonville that some might pejoratively characterize as a virus.[1] The following maps clearly illustrate this progression.

It is easy to imagine that this pattern of entrance results in a surge of new Wal-Mart stores in a state over a very short period of time, perhaps 3 or 4 years. This pattern was especially apparent in the 1980s and 1990s. A second wave of openings is in full force, with

---

[1] David Neumark probably showed the first of these 'new store' maps at the November 2005 Global Insight conference on the economic impact of Wal-Mart.

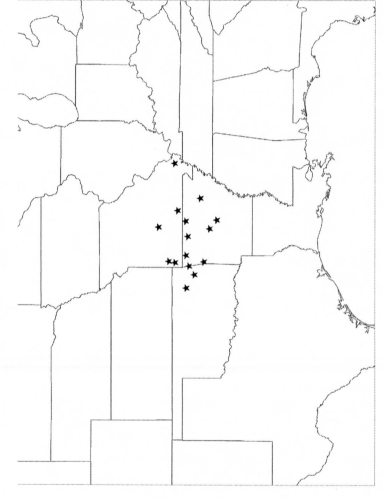

FIGURE 3.1   Wal-Mart Stores, 1962–1965

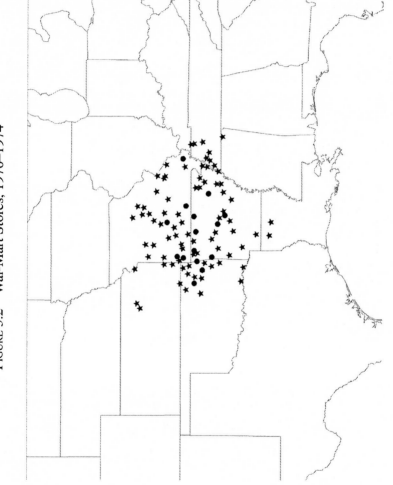

Figure 3.2   Wal-Mart Stores, 1970–1974

FIGURE 3.3   Wal-Mart Stores, 1975–1979

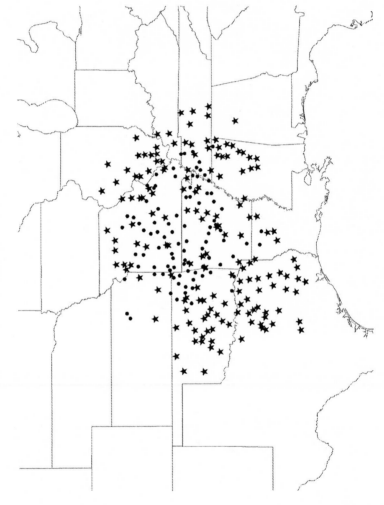

FIGURE 3.4 Wal-Mart Stores, 1980–1984

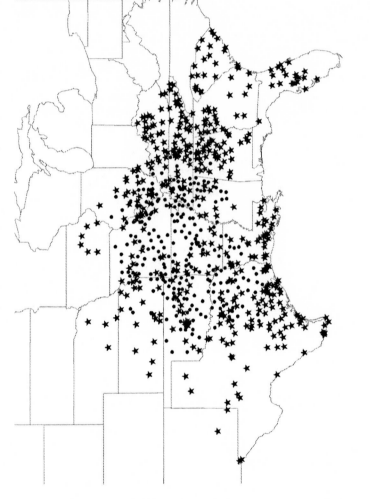

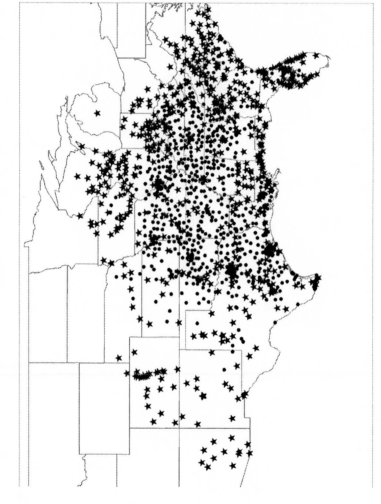

FIGURE 3.5   Wal-Mart Stores, 1985–1989

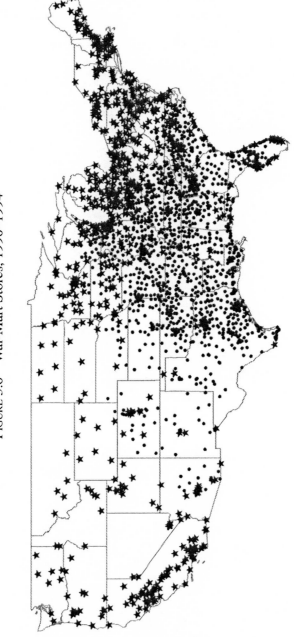

FIGURE 3.6 Wal-Mart Stores, 1990–1994

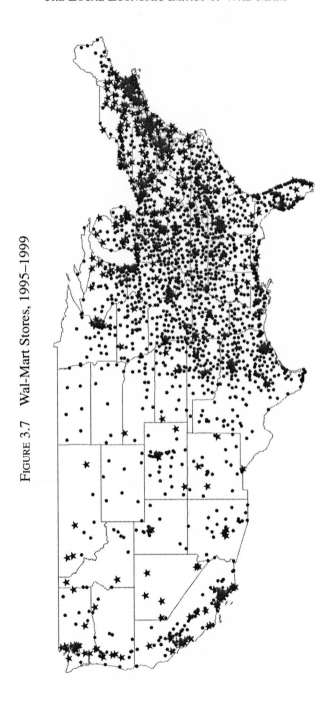

FIGURE 3.7   Wal-Mart Stores, 1995–1999

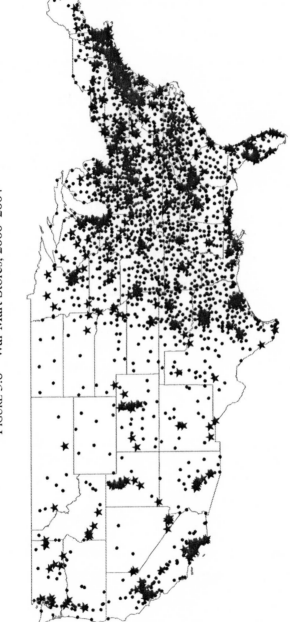

FIGURE 3.8   Wal-Mart Stores, 2000–2004

FIGURE 3.9   Wal-Mart's Entrance into Michigan (New Stores by Year)

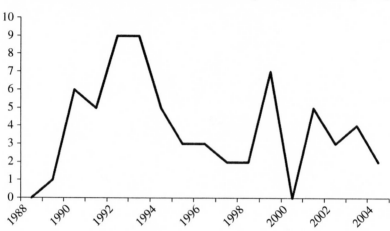

much of the newer stores being supercenters. Michigan's experience illustrates this phenomenon nicely. See Figure 3.9.

It is easy to understand how the dramatic and rapid entrance of so many Wal-Mart stores in a state can overwhelm residents with a feeling of an ever present and unstoppable Wal-Mart behemoth. The chain store growth I describe in Chapter 1 was much more geographically dispersed, and the relative paucity of automobiles and interstates meant that unless one traveled frequently from town to town, a consumer would not come across several chain stores of the same type in one day. Today, even a short trip of perhaps 150 miles along an interstate could reveal a half dozen or more Wal-Mart stores and as many other big-box rivals.

However, these spikes of retail openings are not new. Swedish economists Risto Laulajainen and Lars-Erik Gadde show that this pattern of retail expansion is very similar to that experienced as far back as the 1950s. There are clearly benefits from this type of entrance, which assists in the selection of the best locations. Laulajainen and Gadde argue that locational avoidance of competition from major competitors led to much of the entrance behavior of two large chain stores examined (Laulajainen and Gadde, 1986). Understanding how Wal-Mart views the entrance choice is important to much of the remaining discussion in this book.

SOME ECONOMIC ANALYSIS OF HOW WAL-MART LOCATES STORES

Models of economic activity that incorporate the effects of geography have become increasingly important in economic research. Modeling firm location decisions in a game theoretic framework is an important extension of this research effort. For economists concerned with empirical analysis, understanding the role of local conditions in market entrance and timing is critical in correctly estimating local effects. A good statistical model must explain how to isolate effects such as a Wal-Mart store entrance. Studies that do not exclude the possibility that Wal-Mart systematically enters markets with some common characteristic (such as country growth rate) cannot effectively isolate Wal-Mart's impact in the local market. This endogeneity concern is a repeated theme of this book.

Fortunately, studies of retail location decisions are common and date back at least 70 years.[2] Lebhar (1952) argued that using real estate experts for site selection is one of the factors of firm efficiency. One recent book with the subtitle "How to Beat Wal-Mart" devotes a chapter to retail location and lists proximity to customers and competition as the first two factors (Joseph, 2005, pp. 80–81).

Hernandez and Biasiotto (2001) argue that large chain stores use a portfolio management process for location decisions. They argue that the cost of land holdings and risk matter more to large chain stores than extending the value of the portfolio of assets. They build their argument heuristically using behavioral data from a survey of chain stores.

---

[2] See Ratcliff, R.U. (1939) Problem of Retail Site Selection, *University of Michigan Business Studies*. And Feltman, C.E(1938) Location Selection—The Basis of Successful Business, *Chain Store Age*, 93 Worth Street, New York, New York. Both are discussed in Nichols [1940].

In a very important study, Khanna and Tice (2005) examine the role of local prices, debt, and operating efficiency in a firm's location and market exit decision. They find that large retailers are more likely to enter markets during recessions, which they argue is a strategic approach to promote exit of highly leveraged incumbent firms. Their model is as follows:

$$prob(\text{Entrance}) = f(c, \text{Price Index, Debt,}$$
$$\text{Chain Efficiency and Size, Competition}) \quad (3.1)$$

where the probability of entrance (also exit for incumbent firms) is a function of chain and non-chain price indexes, chain size, financial efficiency, and local competition (a modified Hirschman-Herfindahl Index).[3]

The more recent economic focus on Wal-Mart has examined a rather broad range of issues. The first two econometric studies of Wal-Mart tested whether Wal-Mart entered markets based on income or population. Franklin (2001) performed a test of Wal-Mart super-centers in 100 metropolitan statistical areas (MSAs) in the 1990s. He did so through the use of the following multinomial logit model:

$$prob(WM \text{ entrance}) = f(c, \text{Household Income,}$$
$$\text{Population}) \quad (3.2)$$

where the probability of Wal-Mart's entrance is a function of median household income and population. He tested three models with median household income and population separately in the equation

---

[3] The Hirschman-Herfindahl Index is one of the two most commonly employed measures of market competition. It is calculated as the sum of the squared market shares of all the firms in a market. So, if one firm holds the entire market (a monopoly), then the HHI will be $100^2 = 10,000$, conversely, if ten firms each hold ten percent of the market, the HHI is $\Sigma 10^2 = 1,000$.

(with intercept) and one combined model. He found no statistical relationship between population and Wal-Mart supercenter entrance across these three specifications. He did find a small, but statistically strong negative correlation between Wal-Mart's entrance and median household income.[4]

Kristy Wilburn and I (2001) evaluated Wal-Mart's impact on the retail industry in 55 West Virginia counties from 1988 through 2000. In this study, we tested endogeneity estimating a model of store entrance where

$$prob(WM \text{ entrance}) = f(c, \Delta\text{Personal Income},$$
$$\Delta\text{Personal Income}_{t-1}) \quad (3.3)$$

such that the probability that Wal-Mart entered a county (or upgraded to a supercenter) was a function of current and lagged county growth in personal income. This study rejected any statistically meaningful relationship across several distributional assumptions.

In a more recent study, Global Insight (2005) examined the counties in which Wal-Mart had entered before 2004. An analysis of the 5-year average growth rate of the retail sector indicated that 45% of Wal-Mart counties were growing slower than the national average in the first 5 years before Wal-Mart's entrance and 55% were growing more rapidly. They also compared population growth and found a similar split. This led the researchers to conclude that there is no relationship between county growth or population levels and Wal-Mart's entrance decision.

More recently, I examined the entrance decision of Wal-Mart in Maryland as part of a comparison of endogeneity tests (Hicks, forthcoming-a). I found very modest evidence of growth-related factors in Wal-Mart's decision. Testing a panel model of Wal-Mart's entrance

---

[4] Interestingly, this negative relationship suggests that a study of Wal-Mart's impact that does not account for this pre-existing lower income would tend to understate the positive impacts of Wal-Mart on incomes.

on various potential explanatory variables, I found that only real personal income growth rates achieved traditional levels of statistical significance in explaining Wal-Mart's entrance decision. However, this estimate explained only 11% of the entrance decision. See Table 3.1.

Not all researchers—myself included—accept that endogeneity can be excluded as a concern. Basker (2005a) speaks directly to the endogeneity issue by using what was then the most extensive set of

TABLE 3.1
Wal-Mart Entrance Model

	Coefficient diagnostics		Model diagnostics	
	Coefficient (β from linear model)	t	R^2	F
Real earnings per worker	1.05	1.13	0.10	1.51*
Real per capita personal income	0.0005	0.77	0.09	1.47*
Real personal income	2.10E-06	1.26	0.10	1.62*
Real earnings	2.84E-06	1.29	0.10	1.74*
Population	1.69E-06	1.63	0.10	1.73**
Big-box stores per capita[a]	−2387	−1.06	0.11	1.67*
Pull factor	6.71	1.45	0.10	1.76**
Real per capita personal income growth rates (1 year)	−1.27	−1.58	0.11	1.83**
Real personal income growth rate (1 year)	−1.40*	−1.90	0.11	1.86***
Population growth rate (1 year)	−1.49	−1.28	0.10	1.60*
Change in pull factor, t to $(t-3)$	10.62	1.23	0.10	1.76*
Number of big-box retailers	−0.006	−0.95	0.21	2.05***
Total employment	1.79E-06	1.00	0.09	1.66*
Adjacent Wal-Mart or supercenter	−6.9E06	−0.003	0.09	1.76*
Existing Wal-Mart or supercenter	−0.014	−0.847	0.09	1.79*

Note. All values represent prior year entrance. Source: Hicks (forthcoming-a).
[a]Big-box stores are those retail stores having more than 100 employees.
***$p = 0.01$. **$p = 0.05$. *$p = 0.10$. † $p = 0.15$.

data available to researchers.[5] In this analysis, Basker exploited the lag between announced and actual opening as an instrumental variable to account for the retail market conditions when a store entered the area. Basker estimates the basic relationship as follows:

$$\frac{retail}{pop} = f(c,\phi,t) \tag{3.4}$$

where per capita retail employment is a function of an intercept (c) and county fixed effects (ϕ), time specific fixed effects (t), and an error term. However, she notes that this estimate will suffer endogeneity bias if the Wal-Mart entrance is correlated with the error term.[6] To correct for this, she used the date of planned entry to identify the equation. This means that she accounted for the growth rate in the planned opening period. This very clever approach also permits her data to eliminate systematic data error-related bias in her estimates of store opening dates, which were drawn from commercial maps with Wal-Mart locations noted. Basker limited her sample to those counties with similar characteristics to better control for endogeneity.

David Neumark, Junfu Zhang, and Stephen Ciccarella (2005) approached the endogeneity problem using an identification strategy that used information directly from Wal-Mart's location strategy. In their reading of Sam Walton's biography, they found his direct explanation of their growth strategy. They quote Walton:

> [Our growth strategy] was to saturate a market area by spreading out, then filling in. In the early growth years of discounting, a lot of national companies with distribution systems already in place—Kmart, for example—were growing by sticking stores all over the country. Obviously, we couldn't support

---

[5] Basker's 2005 work was an extension of her 2001 doctoral dissertation.
[6] Strictly, it is the covariance structure that is worrisome, but this will arise from the less technical relationship I describe here.

anything like that … We figured we had to build our stores so that our distribution centers, or warehouses, could take care of them, but also so those stores could be controlled. We wanted them within reach of our district managers, and of ourselves here in Bentonville, so we could get out there and look after them. Each store had to be within a day's drive of a distribution center. So we would go as far as we could from a warehouse and put in a store. Then we would fill in the map of that territory, state by state, county seat by county seat, until we had saturated that market area. … So for the most part, we just started repeating what worked, stamping out stores cookie-cutter style. (Walton, 1992, pp. 110–111, cited in Neumark, Zhang, and Ciccarella, 2005).

Developing an identification strategy offered the possibility of creating an equation that was simply the time and distance from the opening of the original store in Bentonville, Arkansas. On the surface, this is a deceptively simple technique, yet a remarkably brilliant instrument because it effectively isolates the Wal-Mart impact without any more detailed information about the retailer's entrance decision.[7] The equation they construct is simply

$$Y = f(d, d \times t) \tag{3.5}$$

where entrance decision is a function of distance of each new store from the original store in Bentonville (d), the number years since store i opened after the original in 1962 (t), which interacts with

---

[7] I have argued that Wal-Mart's entrance decision is largely affected by local developers who are paid to find suitable locations. This would eliminate some of the possibility that there is a clear and common entrance decision process distinct from the distance from Bentonville.

distance (*d*) calculated as their product.[8] Neumark, Zhang, and Ciccarella argue that the usefulness of this instrument diminished after Wal-Mart had successfully expanded to both coasts and, therefore, limited their analysis to the period before 1995.

Hicks (forthcoming) used a similar strategy of going specifically to the stores putative entry decision variables. In earlier work, I reported conversations among local developers affiliated with Wal-Mart. These conversations revealed that once Wal-Mart had chosen a county they retained local developers to locate individual stores within that county. However, in a 2005 radio broadcast about Wal-Mart's impact, Glenn Wilkins, Wal-Mart's regional public affairs director, stated that market size dictated Wal-Mart's choice of location. From this, I constructed an identifying equation that accounts for the total personal income in county *i* and *j* adjoining counties.

$$Y = f(PI_i, PI_j) \tag{3.6}$$

Panle Jia (2005) modeled Wal-Mart's entrance decision and controlled for endogeneity. Building potential profit functions for both existing small retailers and two chain stores, she constructed the equation

$$\Pi_i = f(X, \delta, \Gamma) \tag{3.7}$$

where individual firm profit in county *i* is a function of *X*, the local market demand, δ, the competition effect of multiple chain stores, and Γ, other local market attributes. By solving this type of equation for small stores and rival chains, she incorporated the information to

---

[8] They used a Haversine distance function, a later study by Dube, Eidlin and Lester employed a spherical distance function, and I have used both, a Euclidean distance (with spherical adjustments) and commercial mapping software distance which minimizes driving time using estimated speed limits. There is probably very little difference resulting from these choices, at least for what we measure.

be captured within the model by Basker, Neumark et al., Dube et al., and myself.

Thomas Holmes (2006) also specifically modeled firm economies of densities, which treats Wal-Mart's entrance decision as affected by the proximity of its other stores. This provides a clear endogeneity treatment within his model as it does in Jia's (2005) work.[9]

Russell Sobel and Andrea Dean (2006) at West Virginia University employed a technique known as a spatial autoregressive model. A spatial autoregressive model explicitly accounts for endogeneity as a routine part of evaluating economic activity across a spatial dimension. In so doing, the authors included lagged spatial error terms in their specification of the basic model. In another estimate, which I discuss later, I performed a comparison of results of the techniques of Neumark et al. and Basker in a spatial setting.[10]

The search for an understanding of Wal-Mart's timing and entrance decisions for endogeneity control also highlights the progression of research on this subject. Franklin and Hicks and Wilburn were all working independently on Wal-Mart in 1999–2001 and only became aware of each other's work as the papers were going into print. (I was able to cite Franklin's work on the final galley proof, but his was already at the printer.) Also, despite the publication lag for Basker (2005a), this work was largely completed as part of her 2001 doctoral dissertation. Publication lags of this magnitude are unfortunately quite common, especially in more highly regarded journals with more layers of peer review. Similarly, Dube, Eidlin, and Lester (2005) developed an identification strategy that was quite similar to that of Neumark, Zhang, and Ciccarella (2005). This research was performed almost simultaneously and without knowledge of each other's work.

---

[9] Unfortunately, as of this writing both Jia and Holmes are refining their papers, and much further discussion of them is probably premature. However, my best guess is that these and some similar work will be important future additions to the literature.
[10] Other research has incorporated some aspects of these instruments, including Hicks (2005a).

These studies represent considerable effort by a number of researchers over several decades. One problem with these efforts is that, in the end, there is little agreement in findings across methods. One possible improvement is to directly examine factors that influence the entrance decision.

SOME NEW EVIDENCE OF WAL-MART'S ENTRANCE BEHAVIOR

In addition to the fine work of researchers attempting to create an instrument that accounts for the endogeneity of Wal-Mart's entrance, an empirically based evaluation of the firm's location behavior is useful. Based on Sam Walton's biography, Wal-Mart expanded its stores from Bentonville to keep its stores close enough to ease managerial oversight and reduce supply chain costs. Thus, the company was faced with a decision regarding location of new stores that potentially involves the distance from existing stores and local economic conditions at a suite of potential new locations. Wal-Mart faces the problem described mathematically as

$$\min_{D} \left(M(D_{i-j}) \middle| Q_d(X_i, X_i - X) \right) \tag{3.8}$$

where the company minimizes its management costs as a function of distance from the new store i to the most proximal store j, subject to local demand. Local demand Q_d is explained as both a function of local conditions at store i and the difference in local demand conditions between store i and j, its closest neighboring store. This is a very general treatment of this type of optimization problem. There are several potential routes to construct the decision process. For example, Wal-Mart could be maximizing demand subject to a managerial control measure of distance. Wal-Mart could also be worried about transportation costs, so factors such as the presence of an interstate highway or proximity to a distribution center matter. Decision makers at Wal-Mart may approach the location decision at both the headquarters and the local levels. In this case, the distance constraint provides specific guidance to the local decision maker. Furthermore, the local decision maker might really be a real estate developer contracted locally (as I believe it often is), which also adds principal-agent problems to the issue. Knowing which way to model this would really require asking Wal-Mart and getting them to answer honestly. I have asked Wal-Mart's representatives on several occasions to provide me specific information on how they site their stores. Not surprisingly, I cannot get an answer to this question. If the decision-making process were a centralized, highly controlled activity, then sharing that information with me could cost them considerable money. If the decision-making process is decentralized, then there is no single answer for them to give. Based on my experience in hierarchical organizations, I suspect the store combines these features with a series of successive briefs on location decision and timing, culminating in briefings to a vice president for strategic planning or some similar position.[11] The criterion for new firms might even adjust along the briefing path, as it so often does in other settings, making a single, time-invariant entrance decision mechanism virtually nonexistent.

However, economists are more interested in what businesses do, not in what they say they are doing, although the two are frequently the same. However, in a fundamental way, the relationship between distance and local demand, insofar as it can be discerned from the data, should indicate what variables influence the local location decision that is dependent on some proximity control. These decisions may or may not be time invariant. For example, the population density of the counties Wal-Mart enters has apparently grown with time. There is also dependence between the population density of counties Wal-Mart enters across time, even when they are entering states on opposite sides of the conterminous 48

---

[11] I am an Army Reserve officer, and have served on staffs at every level from a Rifle Battalion to a United Nations Command.

states.[12] Although a part of this could be due to overall population growth, it is more likely that Wal-Mart has actually adopted a *hierarchical diffusion in reverse order,* meaning that they are slowly shifting their focus from rural areas toward more urban markets, backfilling these locations. This notion was first advanced by Swedish economist Risto Laulajainen (1987) and expanded on by Graff (1998, 2006). There is also purely visible evidence of this behavior, as is shown in Figure 3.10.

In contrast, there is only modest evidence that the distance between stores has changed materially since Sam Walton added his second store, shrinking perhaps in the most recent decade or two. The evidence that I derive for this is based on geospatial mapping of Wal-Mart discount and supercenters from 1962 through 2004, which shows the distance of each new Wal-Mart from its closest existing neighbor.[13] The mean

FIGURE 3.10   Population density of Wal-Mart counties by store number

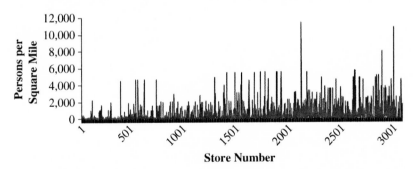

---

[12] I conducted a Portmanteau type test suggested by Brock, Dechert, Scheinkman and LeBaron (1996), which assesses the correlation of population density across time (using the store number as the sequencing variable, since that was how they were actually planned). I found that the size of the counties entered by Wal-Mart was correlated across over 90 consecutive entrances in the sample. This suggests that population density is playing a role in the entrance decision.

[13] This work was supervised by my colleague Brie Salmons at Marshall University. Roughly 40 stores were dropped from the empirical analysis for some obvious reasons (the first store had no predecessor), and some less obvious reasons (stores could not be mapped due to faulty addresses).

distance of each new store from its closest previously planned neighbor is 27.2 miles and the median distance is 16.8 miles. The long-distance jumps to Hawaii and Alaska partially account for the difference between the mean and the median. However, even eliminating these from the sample, there is still a skewing of the data, because Wal-Mart did occasionally open new stores more than 100 miles from existing stores. See Figure 3.11.

From these data I can begin to flesh out an empirical model to test the relationship between distance and local demand characteristics inherent in Wal-Mart's entrance decision. Using calculus to the very general theoretical function above permits me to optimize with respect to each of the variables.[14] This also yields a resulting empirical model in which the distance between a new Wal-Mart and its closest neighbor is a function of a local demand factors

FIGURE 3.11   Distance of Wal-Mart from closest neighboring store

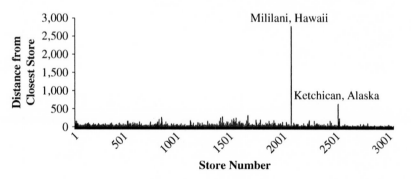

---

[14] I am intentionally being vague about this, to save space, and acknowledge that several different research approaches could yield very similar results (from game theory to Activity Based Costing). Data availability, not theory, is the big limitation here. I should note that the calculus I employ leading to this result assumes that managerial control is constant with respect to distance, and that there are no functional (as opposed to practical) relationships between the characteristics of regions i and j. These assumptions could be eased with little change in the functional relationship.

and the differences between demand factors in store i and its nearest neighbor, j. This provides the function

$$D_{i-j} = \alpha + X_i B + X_{i-j}\Phi + e \qquad (3.9)$$

where distance is a function of a fixed intercept, local demand variables X_i, and the difference in demand variables from store i and its most proximal neighbor, j. The change in notation from the earlier models reflects the fact that the demand variables are not clearly specified here and are actually a matrix of several variables. I must choose these variables, of which there may be many, from those available in existing data.

This empirical model permits me to estimate a simple ordinary least squares regression on distance and the demand variables. Because there is no clear guidance on the variables to be chosen (or the functional form of the model), I tested several variations of the dependent variable. I report the logarithm of distance (the well-known semi-log specification) and actual distance. For independent variables, I chose relative income, population density, and the proportion of residents residing in rural areas in the decennial census closest to the entrance date (except for the few before 1965 in which I used the 1970 U.S. Census data). I also eliminated the first new Wal-Mart in Alaska and Hawaii from consideration. Results appear in Table 3.2.

These results were very insensitive to the choice of demand variables. The results are quite interesting but require some interpretation. The first demand variable suggests that Wal-Mart places a new store 5 miles closer to an existing store for each increase of 1,000 persons per square mile in the new county. Per capita incomes seem to matter little either in magnitude or in terms of statistical significance. Also the relative consumer income in the new county relative to the closest Wal-Mart county did not affect the distance chosen for new store construction. Finally, the greater the percentage of rural population in the new county, the longer the distance from an existing store. Also, the more rural the closest store, the closer the new Wal-Mart. What then does all this mean?

TABLE 3.2

Influence of Demand Variables on Distance From Nearest Wal-Mart

	Distance	Log (Distance)
Intercept	20.21293***	2.300181***
	(17.23)	(45.39)
Persons per square mile	-0.005199***	-0.000187***
	(-8.16)	(-6.53)
Per capita personal income 1969	0.023448†	0.000136
	(1.42)	(0.33)
Ratio of total personal income county *i* to *j*	0.005907	0.000490
	(0.20)	(0.35)
Percent rural population in county *i*	20.64791***	1.738410***
	(9.55)	(18.47)
Percent rural population in county *j*	-13.70006***	-0.955101***
	(-4.38)	(-10.97)
Adjusted R^2	0.08	0.19
Durbin-Watson	1.71	1.67
Observations	2,984	2,984

***$p = 0.01$. **$p = 0.05$. *$p = 0.10$. †$p = 0.15$.

All things being equal, new stores are located farther away as the region is less densely populated and has less consumer demand. If a nearby Wal-Mart is in a more rural area, newer stores tend to be closer. I interpret these results as empirical evidence that Wal-Mart is following the entrance pattern argued by Laulajainen (1987) and Graff (1998, 2006) and described by Sam Walton in his biography.

This pattern tentatively supports an entrance decision that is influenced by local market demand. Thus, I have used these types of instruments in response to the interview with a Wal-Mart official. However, there are still some gaps in this analysis. First, testing these relationships with respect to cost (Holmes, 2006) or competition (Jia, 2006) might expand our understanding of the entrance decision. Also, and perhaps more importantly, although we know where Wal-Mart has located, we do not know the counties they passed over in their decision making. In the end, the endogeneity question will not likely be easily resolved. The entrance decision discussed here also impacts which theory discussed in Chapter 2 might best explain Wal-Mart's local impact. Let us turn our attention to that question.

SECTION II

THE COMMERCIAL IMPACTS

Understanding the role of Wal-Mart in local economies must begin with an evaluation of its impact on commercial economic activity. I do this by first assessing the impact of Wal-Mart on local labor markets, primarily in retail and wholesale. I then examine the markets for goods and services in those sectors in which Wal-Mart should have some effect. Finally, I evaluate Wal-Mart's impact on economic activity beyond retail and wholesale: the aggregate local economy. To begin, I review the literature on Wal-Mart's commercial economic impact. This is done in two parts, because the ability of the existing research to adequately address these issues is separated by the way individual researchers treat a central issue: the manner in which Wal-Mart makes entrance decisions for individual stores.

Simply, virtually all the early studies failed to recognize or examine whether Wal-Mart chose locations in a way that would bias a statistical study of the impact of Wal-Mart on growth: the endogeneity problem. Starting in about 2001, several studies emerged that treated this issue.

It is their findings, with fresh extensions, that form the core of this analysis.

In Chapter 4, I consider the newer studies of labor market impacts. I then provide new evidence of labor market impacts in two states. Chapter 5 evaluates Wal-Mart's impact on the market for goods and services. These impacts focus on the retail sector, including goods that are both competing and complementary to those offered for sale by Wal-Mart. In this I examine the current structure of wholesale and retail trade and the competitive effects of Wal-Mart on goods and its suppliers and describe why economists view competition as socially beneficial. This discussion includes examination of Wal-Mart's impact on consumer prices, including new analysis of price-level impacts in Florida. I conclude the chapter with new overall estimates of Wal-Mart's impact on retail sales dynamics in two states.

Chapter 6 includes an analysis of Wal-Mart's impact on the aggregate economy. I have two important reasons for including this. First, as a number of authors have noted, if the impact of Wal-Mart is simple reallocation of labor between sectors, then accounting for gross, not net, job flows poorly represents actual impacts (see Sobel and Dean, 2005). Second, many activist groups and at least one startlingly original theoretical paper have linked Wal-Mart's changing buying patterns with recent changes to international trade flows (see Basker and Van, 2005). It is important to review how Wal-Mart may impact manufacturing as a result. Importantly, though, at the time of this writing, no empirical studies convincingly make this linkage. I attempt to better explain this link by comparing the profit rate of Wal-Mart with those of its dominant domestic suppliers. Finally, I examine Wal-Mart in Iowa and Washington State and estimate the impact Wal-Mart has had on the stability of counties in these states. I end with a brief summary of findings regarding Wal-Mart's impact across labor markets, those for goods and services, and that of the aggregate local economy.

Chapter Four

The Labor Market Impacts of Wal-Mart

Wal-Mart influence on local labor markets is clearly one of the most important questions surrounding the retailer. Not surprisingly, estimates of Wal-Mart's impact largely began with concerns over retail employment across several subsectors. This interest also spread to Wal-Mart's impact on wholesale employment.

Empirical evaluations of Wal-Mart impact on local economies began with Ken Stone's (1989) study involving small towns and communities in Iowa. Stone offers mixed evidence of the impact, noting increased retail sales in cities with Wal-Mart. However, he found that the net effect on retail sales is less than the total sales of a new Wal-Mart, clearly suggesting that some existing retail trade is lost to a new Wal-Mart. The impact fades over time, and Wal-Mart stores locating outside small towns reduced retail businesses within the small towns, even if the overall impact was positive. Stone found in these (and later) studies mixed impacts on associated retail.[1] These studies suffer the inevitable problems with case studies in that they fail to control for preexisting or coincident factors, which may lead to spurious results.

Two nearly simultaneous studies by Franz and Robb (1989) and Ozment and Martin (1990) examined the impact of Wal-Mart on the structure of retail markets. Both studies report some modest positive impacts on wages, employment, and number of businesses within counties with Wal-Mart stores. The former study was primarily a survey, whereas the second tested data from publicly available sources. Importantly, Ozment and Martin also emphasized the possibility that Wal-Mart's choice of faster growing counties as potential new store sites distorts the results. This endogeneity concern continues to plague analysis of Wal-Mart entrance.

Later studies (Barnes, Connell, Hermenegildo, and Mattson, 1996; Ketchum and Hughes, 1997) examined Wal-Mart's impact while attempting to control for preexisting conditions in regions. Both studies examined retail sales and employment growth and found no evidence of increases in the number of retail firms. Barnes, Connell, Hermenegildo, and Mattson found a modest decline in the number of specialty retail stores at the county level. Other studies repeat many of these findings (see Artz, 1999; Artz and McConnon, 2001; Hornbeck, 1994; McGee and Gresham, 1995; Stone, Artz, and Myles, 2002; Mehta, Baiman, and Persky, 2004). Each of these studies suffers some common weaknesses (e.g., absence of convincing controls for underlying economic conditions; potential concern over selection bias or the subregions that were examined; failure to make statistical comparisons of impacts even when quasi-experimental comparisons have been used), thus undermining many of their conclusions. Also, some of these studies focus on issues other than employment. I believe it is important to mention the range of analyses that occurred in the late 1980s and 1990s.

---

[1] See Stone (1989, 1995, 1997). These studies restate many of the same findings but with further analysis of the cause and the interim changes to the state of the literature. Also see Stone, Artz, and Myles (2002), who also offer both policy guidance and recommendations for retailers coexisting with Wal-Mart.

Unfortunately, the absence of statistical analysis of these issues failed to remove ambiguity from the literature on Wal-Mart. See Table 4.1.

MODERN ESTIMATES OF WAL-MART'S IMPACT

The estimates that could be usefully considered as an accurate representation of Wal-Mart's impact must acknowledge endogeneity. Other studies simply cannot speak to Wal-Mart's impact.[2] This leaves very little available modern analysis.

The first of the econometric studies to empirically address endogeneity in Wal-Mart's entrance (Hicks and Wilburn, 2001) analyzed a panel of 55 counties in West Virginia from 1988 through 2000. The authors excluded endogeneity of the Wal-Mart entrance decision by testing entrance timing and location on contemporaneous and lagged per capita income growth. This is similar to the technique used by Franklin (2001), who examined the Wal-Mart supercenter impacts on the structure of grocery stores in metropolitan areas. Both studies concluded empirically that Wal-Mart entrance decisions are largely or wholly independent of regional growth conditions. Also these researchers offered anecdotal evidence that Wal-Mart is largely unconcerned with local economic conditions when making decisions to open new locations. This is fairly consistent with Graff's (1998) description of Wal-Mart's entrance strategy.

Wilburn and I in 2001 found that the entrance of a Wal-Mart store led to a modest increase in the number of retail establishments, a permanent retail employment increase of roughly 54 workers, and no impact on retail wages. We also found that entrance of a Wal-Mart store in a contiguous county reduces retail employment in that county (Hicks and Wilburn, 2001). However, this study has been criticized for failing to include an endogeneity test within the estimation framework

---

[2] These include Artz (1999); Artz and McConnon (2001); Barnes, Connell, Hermenegildo, and Mattson (1996); Franz and Robb (1989); Hornbeck (1994); Ketchum and Hughes (1997); McGee and Gresham (1995); Stone (1988, 1995, 1995a, 1997); and Stone, Deller, and McConnon (1992).

TABLE 4.1
Early Studies of Wal-Mart

Study	Impact	Location / Year	Types of Impact	Comments
Stone (1995)	Mixed, negative	1983–1993 Iowa cities	Study examined retail sales and pull factor in Wal-Mart host and surrounding towns; Wal-Mart expands trade areas for host towns but reduces retail pull factor in surrounding areas	Updated earlier work (Stone, 1989) with similar results. Also notes consumers shift buying patterns, a finding that anticipates Brennan and Lundsten (2002)
Franz and Robb (1989)	Positive	1969–1987 (26 states)	18 measures of population, wage, employment, and related industrial sector earnings	Compared Wal-Mart presence in 678 rural counties with 1,207 rural non-Wal-Mart counties. Those with Wal-Mart's enjoyed significant benefits. Study included econometric model of Wal-Mart presence
Ozment and Martin (1990)	None to small, positive	1978–1982, selected counties in Arkansas, Missouri, Oklahoma	Compares selected retail sales in counties with big-box retailers to those without. Finds benefits to consumers, some structural change in retail	Anticipates much of the future research on consumer benefits and fiscal impacts. Study notes the endogeneity concern

Barnes, Connell, Hermenegildo, and Mattson (1996)	Mixed across sectors	1988–1993 (14 north eastern counties)	Related retail sales of estimates of numbers of firms in retail subsectors and total population and incomes	Estimates pre / post-Wal-Mart levels of each variable. They found competing sectors suffered (very little), and those purported to benefit also showed little impact. Overall minimal impact
Arnold, Handelman, and Tiggert (1998)	N / A	1985–1995, in Atlanta, Chicago, Kingston	Conducted survey on consumers before and after Wal-Mart's entrance in three major cities. Finds consumer preferences adapt to Wal-Mart when it enters markets	Long-term analysis of preference adjustment toward big-box format and characteristics
Artz and McConnon (2002)	Mixed	1992–1995, Maine retail markets	Host towns see dramatic increase in gen. merchandise sales, mixed in other categories, whereas non-Wal-Mart towns saw little growth	Provides interesting data on sectoral differences in Wal-Mart's impact, largely consistent with other studies
Boarnet and Crane (1999)	Mostly negative	1993–1996 southern California	Reduced retail and food service wages and employment, lower levels of health care coverage, small positive tax revenue impacts	Examines levels of a very extensive number of potentially affected variables in region before and after Wal-Mart's entrance

(Continued)

TABLE 4.1 (*Continued*)

Study	Impact	Location / Year	Types of Impact	Comments
Brennan and Lundsten (2000)	N / A	1992, five small Minnesota towns	Survey of consumers in towns with Wal-Marts finds price is dominant shopping element, followed by variety, proximity, sales, and promotions	Identifies factors contributing to consumer preferences that benefit Wal-Mart
Hornbeck (1994)	Mixed	Review and synthesis of three studies	Argues for mixed policy for local communities, because opposing Wal-Mart could lead to greater losses with location of firm outside of towns	Examines Stone's Iowa study, Gruidl and Kline (1992), and Franz and Robb (1989)
McGee and Gresham (1995)	Positive in Wal-Mart host counties, losses adjacent	1982–1992, Iowa, Kansas, and Nebraska, 246 Wal-Marts and surrounding counties	Study examined sales conversion index (similar to pull factor) finding Wal-Mart stores drew commerce from surrounding counties	Argues for subcounty analysis of Wal-Mart's impacts
Davidson and Rummel (2000)	Positive in Wal-Mart towns, losses in adjacent cities	1990–1998, 43 Maine towns (13 with Wal-Mart stores)	Dramatic increases in retail sales in Wal-Mart host towns, small (< 10%) declines in neighboring towns	Study of retail sales specifically notes it did not account for endogeneity or controlling factors. Note absence of endogeneity tests or controls

Wilburn (1999)	Positive	1989–1999, 13 West Virginia Counties, 13 control counties	Notes modest increases in retail employment and number of firms in Wal-Mart host counties	Study was performed on a small, low-income region. Note absence of endogeneity tests or controls
Gruidl and Kline (1992)	Positive	1986–1989 southern Illinois counties	Short-term analysis of mass discounters (mostly Wal-Mart) finds that cities with Wal-Marts experience considerable retail sales growth, some from surrounding communities	Overall the region continued to see economic growth during this time, which contrasts with studies by Stone of a region in economic decline
Ketchum and Hughes (1997)	Small, positive	1990–1994 Maine counties	Studies retail, manufacturing, and service employment.. Finds no negative impacts, some evidence for positive impacts	Notes that retail growth in Maine was tepid before Wal-Mart's entrance and likely exogenous to Wal-Mart

(Curs, Stater, and Visser, 2004). Also the study region has been criticized because West Virginia is, in general, poorer and more rural than average (see www.preservationist.net/sprawl; Neumark, Zhang, and Ciccarella, 2005). The first criticism is appropriate only if endogeneity existed (hence, Hicks and Wilburn's tests to the contrary were incomplete). The second criticism is absolutely true in the sense that the results for West Virginia are probably generalizable to only a limited number of regions.

Basker (2005a) performed a similar analysis of a much larger sample of U.S. counties. She used a clever instrument—proxies of the planned entrance date for each store location—to control for endogeneity. Basker reports that an initial increase in retail employment dissipates to roughly a 55-worker increase after 3 years. This impact is also partially offset by a reduction in wholesale employment. Basker also found very modest impacts of Wal-Mart entrance on adjoining counties. The striking similarity of these employment findings to those of Hicks and Wilburn (2001) were noted by Villareal (2005), who compared the findings of the two existing studies at the time.

Basker's work has been criticized for its choice of instruments (Neumark, Zhang, and Ciccarella, 2005) and for its censoring of the sample (excluding sparsely populated counties, those with early Wal-Marts, and those with negative employment growth). This excludes virtually all of the counties with the most urgent and compelling policy concerns (Goetz and Swaminathan, 2006). This was a trade-off Basker made to ensure that her estimate was not confounded by endogeneity. Further, failure to control for interstate fiscal differences may offer a different endogeneity concern because the governments of states with high levels of local financing may actively seek Wal-Mart stores (Wassmer, 2004). Although painstakingly collected from Rand McNally maps, Basker's data were found later to contain significant errors compared with Wal-Mart's administrative data. Of greater import than these issues is the absence of a correction for spatial autocorrelation in the model, raising concern of spatial bias in the estimation results. In the end, it is important to note that these criticisms are aimed at the applicability of the findings, not the research process. Basker's research in this area is highly regarded, most especially by me.

Goetz and Swaminathan (2006) estimated the poverty impacts of Wal-Mart's presence. This study is important in that it addressed a major criticism of Wal-Mart in general and changing structural conditions, perhaps evidenced by the increase in the number of Wal-Mart stores nationwide. Using an instrumental variable estimation technique, which should account for some endogeneity concerns, the authors found that a new Wal-Mart entering a county between 1987 and 1998 had a marginal impact of 0.2% on the county poverty rate, and that stores that existed before 1987 increased the poverty rate by about half that amount. There are two major concerns with this study. First, the magnitude of the poverty impact of Wal-Mart estimated by these authors is small: 0.099% for existing Wal-Marts and 0.204% for new Wal-Marts. Also the assertion that the poverty result implies an externality of exchange at Wal-Mart is weak. Both this study and Basker (2005) used data that contained several errors in store timing dates (see Neumark, Zhang, and Ciccarella, 2005). I review this report again in a later section dealing specifically with social impacts of Wal-Mart.

Neumark, Zhang, and Ciccarella (2005) offer a novel identification strategy to overcome the endogeneity concerns. As mentioned, in their reading of Sam Walton's autobiography, Neumark et al. noted that Wal-Mart expansion was accompanied by a specific geographic concern regarding the distance from existing managerial infrastructure. (The authors also provide compelling visual illustration in their graphing of the expansion of Wal-Mart toward the coasts from Arkansas.) This pattern was also noted by Graff (1998) in his comparative study of location strategies of Wal-Mart and Kmart. Neumark, Zhang, and Ciccarella incorporate this strategy into their estimation using a time and distance function (from Bentonville, Arkansas) to identify the equation with which they test Wal-Mart's effect. Using national data received directly from Wal-Mart, these authors found that retail employment declines 2% to 4%, with significant geographic variability, and that payrolls per worker may also decline. This study has been editorially criticized by at least one economist for the implausibility of its finding that Wal-Mart is associated with significant nominal wage declines across the entire county labor market.[3] However, the extensive analysis used by these authors, including a number of sensitivity tests of the sampled counties, makes a compelling case. Perhaps most persuasive to me is that the effect of higher productivity attributed to Wal-Mart should lead to an eventual reduction in retail workers. Their results match the expected theory of Wal-Mart's national impact. Two issues in this study compel more questions. The first is that the size of the aggregate employment impact seems to point to endogeneity, although their very careful treatment of it seems to do as much as possible to preclude this. Second, I don't think a national study, even at the county level, speaks convincingly to the potential local impact, which likely varies by the type of effect that occurs within counties from among the three I described earlier. Larger studies average across these effects in different times and types of counties, which may be one reason why the estimates differ.

Global Insight (2005) conducted a national study of retail wages and employment and tested for exogeneity by comparing those counties in which Wal-Mart entered with those they did not. Global Insight failed to reject exogeneity in Wal-Mart's location decisions. Subsequently, this group used a structural model of county-level retail employment and wages, reporting net employment increases in the long run of about 100 workers and nominal wage declines of roughly 2%. Global Insight also found, as did Hausman and Leibtag (2004) and Basker (2005b), that Wal-Mart has a considerable price effect on grocery and other retail goods within the county in which it locates. They conclude that this effect led to a real wage increase for retail workers despite reductions in their nominal wages. Their work has been strongly criticized by Jared Bivens, Josh Bernstein, and Arin Dube in an Economic Policy Institute paper, most especially because of its sensitivity to changes in the structure of their model.[4]

---

[3] See Alan Reynolds (2005).

[4] Interpretation of the price findings is also more complicated than my discussion here; I extend this later.

Dube, Eidlin, and Lester (2005) tested Basker's data using a similar instrument to that of Neumark, Zhang, and Ciccarella on a model of rural and urban retail wages from 1992 to 2000. They found that wages for the retail sector in urban areas fall by less than 1% when a county is exposed to a Wal-Mart. However, in rural settings, retail wages may increase concomitant with a Wal-Mart entrance. This is also a very carefully crafted study, which provides one important support for my belief that impacts should be carefully scrutinized in smaller geographic areas.

Sobel and Dean (2006) tested the impact of Wal-Mart on the composition of small businesses using both detailed cross-sectional and spatial autoregressive estimates. The authors found no reduction in small businesses attributable to Wal-Mart, a finding similar to Basker's (2005) result. This study is particularly interesting in that it specifically addresses the impact on small businesses using spatial methods of analysis. I review it again later, when I specifically consider mom-and-pop stores.

In another study in which I compared the endogeneity corrections and tested exogeneity in Maryland, I found a reduction in retail trade and an increase in retail wages of more than $1.00/hr. This finding is very consistent with the productivity theory advanced in Chapter 2. See Table 4.2.

One clear conclusion can be drawn from these studies. Variations in the identification and treatment of endogeneity, specification of the model (its design), or the sampled time and location lead to different conclusions about Wal-Mart's impact on labor markets. Therefore, it is useful to provide another estimate of Wal-Mart's retail labor market impacts within the context of this work.

Before performing this estimate, it is important to reiterate why I focus analysis at the state or lower level (where data permit). Six of the studies presented in Table 4.2 are national studies, five of which test data at the county level. Two find positive retail employment impacts, two find negative retail employment impacts, one finds some mix of impacts, and another finds none at all. All are rigorous econometric analyses. One was paid for by Wal-Mart (but performed by very credible economists supervised by an outside body of solid researchers from both

TABLE 4.2
Newer Studies of Wal-Mart and Labor Markets

Author	Study Design	Findings	Consistent With Theories of
Hicks and Wilburn (2001)	Time space recursive panel model of 55 West Virginia counties, 1988–2000, annual data	Increase in employment by roughly 54 retail jobs, small increase in firms, no wage impact	Income effect, retail clustering
Basker (2005a)	IV panel of 1,700 larger U.S. counties, 1977–2000	Increase in employment by roughly 50 retail jobs, partially offset by loss of 10 wholesale jobs and small (1–3) reduction in retail firms	Income effect, retail clustering
Hicks (2005b)	Panel of 8 Pennsylvania counties with a Wal-Mart entrance in 2002. Estimate of labor market impacts using Quarterly Workforce indicators	A roughly 50-worker net increase in retail sector and a $0.50/hr increase in new hire wages	Income effect, retail clustering
Global Insight (2005)	Structural model of all U.S. counties, 1969–2003	Increase in employment, decrease in nominal wages	Income effect, retail clustering
Neumark, Zhang, and Ciccarella (2005)	IV panel of all U.S. counties, 1977–1995. Estimate of retail wage and employment and total earnings and employment at county level	Decline in retail employment of 2–4%, evidence of retail wage decrease, increase in overall employment, but decrease in overall real wages	Productivity increase
Dube, Eidlin, and Lester (2005)	IV of selected U.S. counties, 1992–2000	Wage decrease in urban retail markets after Wal-Mart entrance and possible wage increase in rural areas	Income effect, productivity effect

(Continued)

TABLE 4.2   (*Continued*)

Author	Study Design	Findings	Consistent With Theories of
Sobel and Dean (2006)	Cross-sectional and SAR test of U.S.	No Wal-Mart impact on small businesses	Income effect
Jia (2005)	Direct model of profit and entrance (with implied employment impacts)	Reduction of retail firms attributable to Wal-Mart	Productivity effect
Hicks (Forth-coming-a)	Panel of Maryland counties comparing endogeneity corrections	Increase in wages and total employment because of Wal-Mart, with a decrease in retail employment	Productivity effect

Note. SAR; IV, instrumental variable.

the political left and right). One was written by researchers at University of California–Berkeley's Institute for Labor Research and the remainder by professors (two of three groups also worked at university research centers). There is no pattern to their findings and no evidence of researcher bias. Indeed, the only vocal Wal-Mart critic has some mixed findings, and the only vocal Wal-Mart supporter finds no impact of the retailer. Why then are there such stark differences? There could be technical errors, as I have discussed. Alternatively, the choice of sampled times and regions (primarily because of data limitations or to sidestep endogeneity) means that these estimates could all be correct for place and time. Let me explain.

The ordinary least squares (OLS) estimate I discussed in Chapter 2 gives the average effect across the sample. Some counties have greater effects and others lesser effects. This is normal, and having larger or smaller impacts across counties is not a problem with the estimate. A problem arises when there is systematic variability in the effect (such as all rural counties are different from urban counties or when state fiscal policy differentiates the impact). Some of this variability is captured through other parts of the model such as an additional error term or intercept for each county, which captures non-time-varying influences (fixed effects). Other variability issues are captured through structural modeling (like the Global Insight effort).

I am most concerned that the geographic variability in the examined counties is not effectively capturing net trade dynamics. Further, only one of the studies described previously (Hicks and Wilburn, 2001) tests adjacent Wal-Mart impacts, which would certainly present an important additional consideration.

As a result of these concerns, I focus on effects at the state and county level (where data allow). This is an imperfect approach for several reasons. First, there are intrastate differences just as there are interstate differences, but they are almost certainly smaller. Second, the corrections for endogeneity available may not be well suited for smaller geographic areas, although some are intentionally designed to do this. So I choose instrumental variable approaches with this in mind, varying them to provide some comparative analysis where appropriate. Also, in providing several, more geographically focused estimates, I offer results from more studies, which have some instrumental variable variation, from which to better judge the overall local impact of Wal-Mart.

WAL-MART'S LABOR MARKET IMPACTS IN INDIANA

The retail sector in Indiana has enjoyed recent analysis regarding agglomeration, taxation, and infrastructure (Hicks, 2006a). This work found that the retail and the wholesale sectors have garnered an increasing share of the state's employment over the past three decades. This differs from national trends of a modestly declining retail sector. See Figure 4.1.

In addition, the mix of retail is not dissimilar from the national mix of retail activity. To make this case, note the differences between the Indiana retail data and the national average in terms of number of establishments (stores), sales, payroll, and employees presented in Table 4.3.

Indiana's retail has become very modestly less concentrated in the past two decades. I examine this by constructing a measure of

FIGURE 4.1   Retail Employment Share in Indiana 1969–2002

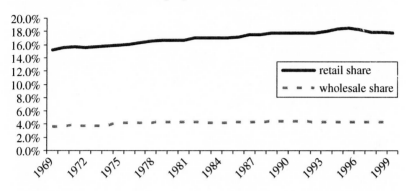

Source: Bureau of Economic Analysis, Regional Economic Information System, reported in Hicks, 2006b.

TABLE 4.3

Difference in Retail Trade Subsector Share, 2000 (Indiana–U.S.)

	Establishments	Sales ($1,000s)	Payroll ($1,000)	Employees
Motor vehicles / parts	1.9%	0.5%	−0.1%	−0.4%
Furniture / home furnishings	−0.1%	−0.6%	−0.4%	−0.4%
Electronics / appliance stores	0.0%	−0.6%	−0.5%	−0.3%
Building and garden equipment	1.7%	1.2%	1.8%	1.2%
Food / beverage	−2.0%	−2.7%	−2.8%	−2.9%
Health / personal care stores	−0.6%	0.0%	0.0%	−0.1%
Gasoline stations	0.6%	1.2%	1.0%	1.2%
Clothing / clothing accessories	−2.3%	−1.7%	−2.0%	−2.1%
Sporting goods	−0.1%	−0.7%	−0.6%	−0.8%
General merchandise	0.5%	1.9%	2.8%	3.9%
Miscellaneous retailers	0.4%	−0.3%	0.0%	0.0%
Nonstore retailers	0.1%	1.7%	0.9%	0.7%

Source: Bureau of the Census, County Business Patterns, reported in Hicks (2006b).

regional inequality across the retail share of employment. I use the well-known Gini coefficient, which is a measure of inequality. Here, I measure the relative share of retail in each county. A value of 0 means perfect equality in the retail share of total employment, whereas a value of 1 suggests that one county had all the state's retail employment. I then graph the maximum county value and minimum and median values since 1969. The calculations show that the maximum of the Gini coefficient declines, but there are almost no changes in the median of the Gini. Another inequality measure, Thiel's T, provides similar results, with very little change in the mean inequality but with some reduction in extremes. See Figure 4.2.

As with much of the nation, a significant change in the retail industry has been the growth of Wal-Mart stores across Indiana. Wal-Mart's expansion since 1962 has been a much heralded wave emanating from Bentonville, Arkansas, toward the coasts. Although the structure of the entrance decisions has been hotly debated, it is clear that the retailer enters a state proximally to regional distribution centers and fills the void between stores quickly, in perhaps 3 to 5 years. Wal-Mart's entrance at the state level is marked by a surge of stores, as can be seen in Figures 4.3 and 4.4.

FIGURE 4.2   Retail Gini Index, Indiana 1988–2004

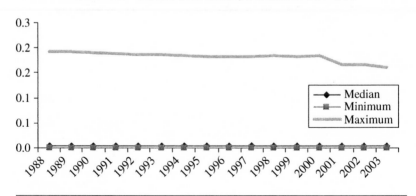

Source: Hicks, 2006b.

The cumulative impact of Wal-Mart's presence since 1983 illustrates the result of this burst of entrance, followed by the lower persistence of Wal-Mart stores entering in predominantly interstate-accessible counties, a pattern that differed from the early focus predominance of entrance into noninterstate counties. See Figure 4.5.

The patterns evidenced by higher retail trade shares and entrance by Wal-Mart accompany a decrease in spatial distribution differences in retail trade. This is probably best exemplified through an examination of Moran's I for retail employment in the state. Moran's I is a measure of local spatial autocorrelation. Spatial autocorrelation should be thought of as the degree of similarity of one county to its adjacent counties in terms of retail employment inequality. The equation takes the form:

$$M_i(\theta) = \frac{n \sum_{i=1}^{n} \theta_i \sum_{i=1}^{n} \widehat{W}\theta_j}{\widehat{W} \sum_{j=1}^{n} \theta_j^2} \tag{4.1}$$

where θ is the Gini index of retail employment. Moran's I is a straightforward estimate of the degree of local spatial autocorrelation

FIGURE 4.3   Wal-Mart's Annual Entrance in Indiana Counties

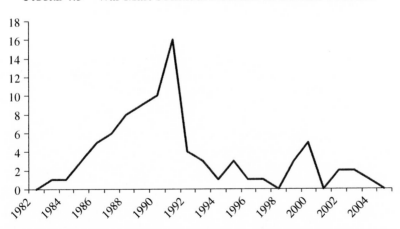

Source: Hicks, 2006b.

FIGURE 4.4   Wal-Mart's Entrance from 1988 to 2006

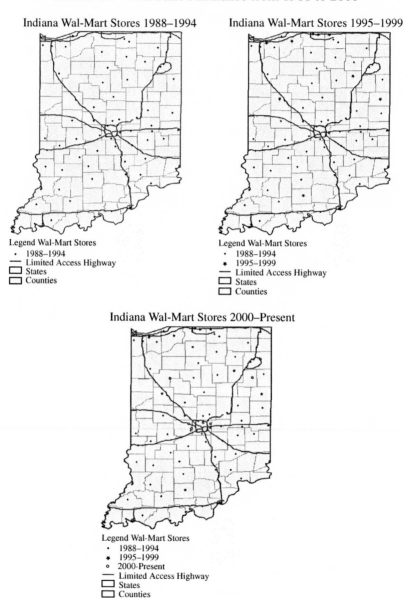

Source: Wal-Mart 2005 data release, GIS work by Brie Salmons, Marshall University.

FIGURE 4.5   Cumulative Wal-Mart Entrance in Indiana

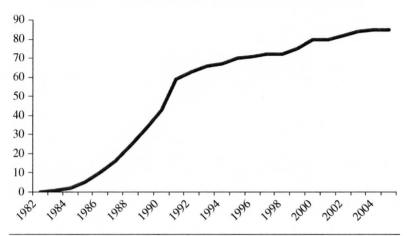

Source: Hicks, 2006b, from 2005 Wal-Mart data release.

in retail employment inequality in Indiana counties. A high Moran's I would imply a few large retail centers, with several adjacent areas with much less retail. This Moran's I was calculated annually for each year from 1988 to 2004. As is clear from Figure 4.6, Indiana has experienced a large reduction in spatial autocorrelation in retail unemployment.

One conclusion to be drawn from the evidence of spatial agglomerations and Wal-Mart entrance is that the increase in retail's share of employment results in more even geographic distribution in retail accessibility. This is consistent with, among other things, a general reduction in transportation-related transaction costs in retail shopping (at the intercounty level).

Another facet of this phenomenon is that the growth in the employment share of retail trade accompanies a decline in spatial inequality in employment in general. This should be an especially welcomed finding for rural areas. To understand the aggregate impact on retail employment, I turn to direct estimates.

The data I use are retail employment figures drawn from the Regional Economic Information system from 1988 (the year before

FIGURE 4.6   Moran's I of Retail Employment Inequality in Indiana

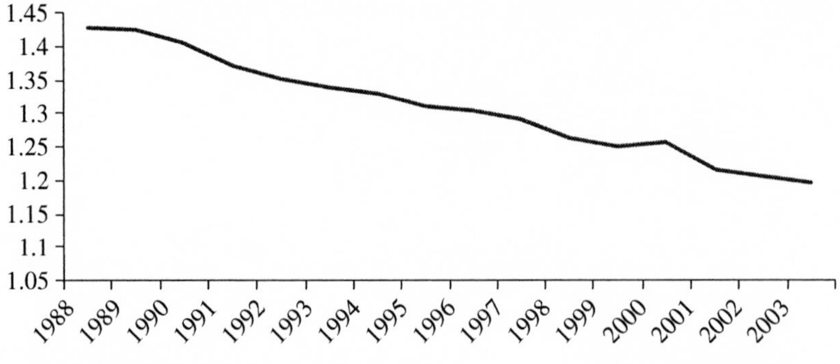

Source: Hicks, 2006b.

Wal-Mart's opening a store in Indiana) to 2004, the most recent data available. For Wal-Mart's entrance, I use data from two sources. The first is a data set supplied by a Wal-Mart employee, and the second is from Wal-Mart's 2005 data release. These data sets provide location and dates of openings for all U.S. Wal-Mart stores. Constructing a basic model of retail employment, I test the following model:

$$\ln(\widehat{Y}_{i,t}) = \alpha + \alpha_i + \beta_1\left(WM_{i,t}\right) + \beta_2\left(WM_{j,t}\right)$$
$$+ \Phi\widetilde{W}[\ln(\widehat{Y}_{j,t})] + \phi\ln(\widehat{Y}_{i,t-1}) + \varepsilon_t \tag{4.2}$$

where the dependent variable is the log of retail employment, explained by a common and region fixed-effect term, and a Wal-Mart presence variable (including superstores) in county i and another for the presence of a Wal-Mart in an adjoining county.[5]

---

[5] The model includes a spatial autocorrelation component $\Phi\widetilde{W}[\ln(\widehat{Y}_{i,t})]$ which includes the first-order contiguity matrix W of the dependent variable in surrounding contiguous counties j in time t. This first-order contiguity matrix is composed of a value of 1 for each county j, contiguous to county i, and 0 otherwise, thus measuring

I use two tests, one of which identifies this equation using a method developed around interpretation of Wal-Mart's entrance decision, as with Basker (2005). The second is an OLS version. The variables appear stationary through the use of the augmented Dickey-Fuller test. Importantly, the instrumental variable approach is estimated using a two-stage least squares estimate that includes a spatial lag in the first stage, thus eliminating spatial bias concerns (see Franzese and Hays, 2005). To illustrate how geographic variability may influence the findings, I separate the estimates into two groups (MSA and non-MSA counties, which I characterize as urban and rural, respectively). This approach was first used by Dube, Eidlin, and Lester (2005). Results appear in Table 4.4.

Although these results offer findings for a specific geographic region not earlier reported, the most interesting facet of this analysis is its evidence that geographic variability may matter as much as model specification in estimating impacts. In this model, in both the urban and rural samples and in the unreported full sample, the OLS specification finds positive and nontrivial impacts on retail employment attributable to Wal-Mart. Both estimates suggest that retail employment rises by 3.4% in rural counties and 1.4% in urban counties when a Wal-Mart is present. This translates into roughly 75 net new retail jobs in rural counties and 112 new jobs in urban counties. Within the model containing endogeneity corrections, the statistical power drops modestly in the rural county and drops below common levels of statistical significance within urban counties. The magnitude of the impact increases by roughly 25% in the rural counties, implying an increase of 106 jobs for each new Wal-Mart.

---

economic activity in adjacent counties. The matrix is row standardized to account for the differing number of contiguous counties to the 92 counties in the state, a common approach. This specification includes the time-autoregressive components Φ for one lag. The ε denotes the error term, assumed to be white noise. Another common representation of the fixed effects is as a representation of an error component where $e = m + v$, with m being the fixed effect and v the observation-varying component of the error term.

TABLE 4.4

The Effect of Wal-Mart on Indiana Retail Employment

	Rural		Urban	
Coefficient	OLS	2SLS	OLS	2SLS
Intercept	−0.09	−0.98	0.84***	−0.63
	(−0.69)	(−0.69)	(5.09)	(−0.35)
Wal-Mart presence	0.034***	0.048*	0.014**	0.012
	(3.85)	(1.73)	(2.11)	(1.22)
Adjacent Wal-Mart	−0.031**	−0.12	−0.003	−0.11
	(−2.14)	(−0.40)	(−0.23)	(−1.50)
Spatial lag	0.91***	1.03***	0.85***	1.06***
	(54.49)	(5.14)	(52.34)	(5.13)
Time autocorrelation ($t-1$)	0.84***	0.85***	0.95***	0.96***
	(19.3)	(18.55)	(38.17)	(37.68)
Adjusted R^2	0.99	0.99	0.99	0.99
D-W statistic (panel)	1.85	1.82	2.18	2.21

Note. The *t* statistics are presented in parentheses. County fixed effects are not reported. The D-W panel statistic reported is derived from Bhargava, Franzini, and Narendranathan (1982). I whitewashed the variance matrix using a version of White's (1980) heteroscedastic consistent variance–covariance matrix derived from Driscoll and Kraay (1998). As is common, to preserve space, I have not reported the values of the cross-sectional fixed-effects coefficients. OLS, ordinary least squares; 2SLS, two-stage least squares; D-W, Durbin-Watson.
*$p = 0.10$. **$p = 0.05$. ***$p = 0.01$. †$p = 0.15$.

Adjacent Wal-Marts affect employment in the OLS specification for rural counties and in the instrumental variable (endogeneity controlled) model in the urban counties, although the latter has very low statistical certainty. It is difficult to draw powerful inference from these estimates, especially because it is clear that the statistical (endogeneity) bias in the OLS estimates renders these values unreliable. One pattern that may emerge is that a more spatially unconcentrated distribution of retail Wal-Mart is playing a role in spreading retail employment out of urban centers and into more rural counties. This may induce more retail sales, because consumer search and travel costs decline. Also, coincident changes in Indiana's labor market may favor the retail sector.

In the end, these estimates find that Wal-Mart's impact on retail counties in which they locate ranges from zero to just over 100 new jobs. In this sample, the presence of a Wal-Mart in an adjacent county reduces retail employment in "own county" by an almost equal amount (although the statistical certainty is far smaller). These results point toward some retail clustering associated with Wal-Mart.

Importantly, retail agglomeration and diffusion of retail across the state are not mutually exclusive if pre-Wal-Mart retail was heavily concentrated in urban areas. The post-Wal-Mart entrance period could simply result in more counties with retail agglomeration. In this case, Wal-Mart could actually be reducing the size of the cluster at which agglomeration benefits accrue to firms.

In evaluating Wal-Mart's impact, it is also useful to evaluate the role of the retailer's distribution centers on wholesale employment in the counties in which they locate.

WAL-MART DISTRIBUTION CENTERS

As of 2006, Wal-Mart operated 86 distribution centers in 40 states. These distribution centers provide regional support to stores and are organized for special purposes to supply a wider area. These special purposes include grocery, Sam's brands, jewelry, optical, shoes, storage, import centers, return centers, fashion, tires, and pharmacy. See Figure 4.7.

The operations of these distribution centers and their contributions are subject to much review in the management literature, especially the logistics industry newsletters and other publications.[6] For the purposes of this book, the impact of the distribution centers on wholesale employment and earnings is of interest. The estimation of this relationship is far more straightforward, because the potential endogeneity of location decision is not of concern. Distribution centers are placed to support retail, and I am unconcerned with spatial dimensions as well,

---

[6] See Schonberger (2006) for an example.

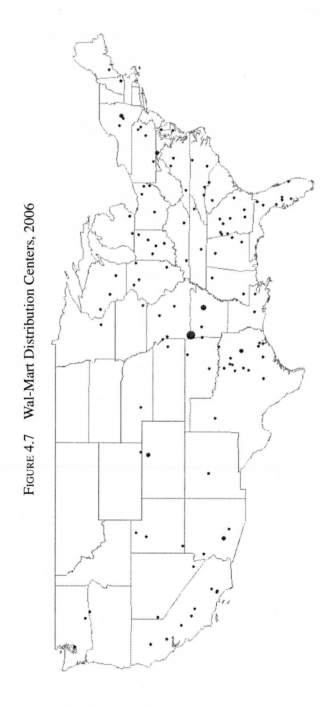

FIGURE 4.7   Wal-Mart Distribution Centers, 2006

because distribution centers are footloose. Thus, a straightforward model is appropriate. I propose the following relationship:

$$\Phi_{i,t} = \alpha + \alpha_i + \beta(WMDIST_{i,t}) + \delta\phi_{i,t-1} + e_{i,t} \tag{4.3}$$

in which wholesale employment and earnings Φ is a function of common and cross-sectional (county) fixed effects, the number of Wal-Mart distribution centers in a county, time autocorrelation, and a white noise error term. The variables are stationary, so I estimate them in levels for Maryland, which has three distribution centers. Results appear in Table 4.5.

This model estimates that wholesale employment resulting from the presence of a Wal-Mart distribution center increases by roughly 200 new full-time and part-time employees, which represents a roughly 4% increase in the average county. Total earnings increase by a relatively smaller 0.21% in the average county. The only existing studies

TABLE 4.5
Wal-Mart's Impact on Wholesale Employment and Earnings

	Employment	Earnings
Intercept	5198.686***	1276.755***
	(6.93)	(4.49)
Wal-Mart Distribution center	199.7603**	67.57331***
	(2.50)	(2.61)
Autoregression ($t-1$)	0.933594***	1.120330***
	(19.37)	(24.11)
Adjusted R^2	0.99	0.99
Durbin-Watson	1.17	1.31
Observations	229	229

Note. The Durbin-Watson panel statistic reported is derived from Bhargava, Franzini, and Narendranathan (1982). I whitewashed the variance matrix using a version of White's (1980) heteroscedastic consistent variance–covariance matrix derived from Driscoll and Kraay (1998). As is common, to preserve space, I have not reported the values of the cross-sectional fixed-effects coefficients.
**$p = 0.05$. ***$p = 0.01$. *$p = 0.10$. †$p = 0.15$.

of wholesale employment, performed by Basker (2005), estimate wholesale impacts caused by a Wal-Mart retail store, not a distribution center. The impacts reported here provide for net employment increases consistent with a new distribution center. This is probably not a surprising result. However, the total income increases suggest that workers in a Wal-Mart distribution center may be modestly lower paid than competing wholesale workers in Maryland.

SUMMARY

The early literature on Wal-Mart's impact on labor markets suffered from failure to control for endogeneity in the store's entrance decision. Although many of these studies contain useful insights to Wal-Mart's impact, this weakness renders the actual estimates uninformative. Subsequent research accounting, or testing, for endogeneity is more helpful. However, these results vary greatly by technique, location, and timing. Thus, it is more likely that the impacts may vary by the type of impact that occurs: the three theories of Wal-Mart's local impact. This is supported by the impacts of Wal-Mart in Indiana reported in this chapter.

This research and those findings reviewed previously carry a significant caveat regarding actual job estimates. We cannot determine from these data whether job growth or destruction occurs in full- or part-time employment. Further, we cannot tell whether Wal-Mart actually reduces (or increases) wages when we control for skill differences among employees. We cannot even deduce whether Wal-Mart workers are more skilled on average than other retail employees, although the job skills required at most Wal-Mart occupations are well below the national average for all industries. Thus, the estimates of employment and wage flows do not fully answer these job quality questions.

These labor market impacts are by no means the sum of the important impacts of Wal-Mart. The distribution and competitiveness of firms are also of interest. Thus, we next turn analytical attention to the impact of Wal-Mart on the markets for goods and services.

CHAPTER FIVE

THE IMPACT OF WAL-MART ON THE MARKET FOR GOODS AND SERVICES

In addition to the focus on the labor market impacts of Wal-Mart, Stone's (1989) economic research has focused on the effects of the retailer on competition and structure of local retail markets. The same concerns over method and testing and correction for endogeneity affect the early studies of Wal-Mart. Hence, a detailed review of the work of Stone and his contemporaries provides little useful information about Wal-Mart's impact on retail market structure. Instead I focus on the more recent studies that test or account for the possibility that Wal-Mart chooses its locations using factors that would bias estimates of its subsequent impact. Many of these studies also evaluated labor markets, as discussed in Chapter 4. There are also related studies that examine the role of big-box retailers on marketing matters and recommend strategies for incumbent firms following a Wal-Mart or other similar retailer's entrance. Although interesting, such studies do not advance an understanding of what happens to local economies when Wal-Mart comes to town.[1]

Franklin's 2001 study examined Wal-Mart supercenter impacts on the grocery store industry in large urban areas across the United States. Franklin found that Wal-Mart had no effect on the concentration of that industry, suggesting that competitive food markets would result. My study with Kristy Wilburn (Hicks and Wilburn, 2001) tested Wal-Mart discount store impact on competing retailers in West Virginia counties. We found that Wal-Mart's entrance increased the number of competing retailers by roughly five stores. We attributed this increase to growing retail clustering in the third of West Virginia counties that then had the store. Emek Basker found very modest changes to the retail structure (measured as retail stores per capita). She found a one- to two-store loss in small businesses (fewer than 100 employees) and concluded that Wal-Mart was not leading to local retail agglomeration.

Panle Jia (2005) estimates a structural model of retail competition. These types of models explicitly account for firm and regional characteristics. Her model accounts for firm competition using interaction of market size, population, and existing retail structure. She also controls for endogeneity in the entrance decision by simultaneously solving for entrance decisions by large and small retailers. This is an alternative to the methods used by Basker (2005a), Neumark, Zhang, and Ciccarella (2005), Dube, Eidlin, and Lester (2005), and Hicks (2006a). Jia's technique enjoys the benefit of eliminating much of the discussion incumbent on the choice of instrumental variables. One drawback to her approach is that it requires strong assumptions regarding firm behavior and interaction. Her work does result in an estimate that each new large big-box store (she uses data on Wal-Mart and Kmart) reduces the number of small retailers by roughly two.[2]

---

[1] See Brennan and Lundsten (2000) and Ryan, Filbert, Janke, and Brault (1998).

[2] Holmes (2006) has a preliminary model that estimates economies of density, but to date does not have direct competitive effects on the retail sector.

West Virginia University professor Russell Sobel and graduate student Andrea Dean in their 2006 study estimated the impact of Wal-Mart on small businesses (entrepreneurs and firms with fewer than 10 employees). In a statistical model that accounts for spatial interaction across regions in the United States, they found no changes to these firms attributable to Wal-Mart. In an interesting extension of typical economics, Mark Fox (2005) evaluates Wal-Mart's impact on record industry sales. His analysis, published in the journal *Popular Music and Society*, focused on suggestions that Wal-Mart has engaged in pricing music (CDs) below cost. Although he reports, without the benefit of empirics, that Wal-Mart does engage in below-cost pricing of music CDs, he argues that it does not meet the legal standard of predatory pricing since it is not designed for anticompetitive purposes. He also allows that no analysis of Wal-Mart's impact on music store sales has been performed.[3]

The limited numbers of studies are disparate in method, location, and time. As such, it is entirely possible that their findings, although seemingly different, are not inconsistent. Agglomeration effects in rural West Virginia may lead to net firm increases, as Kristy Wilburn and I found. This evidence of agglomeration may be entirely absent in a study of more urban and prosperous counties, such as the analysis performed by Emek Basker, although the latter has far broader relevance. Notably, Wilburn and I found a negative adjacent county effect of Wal-Mart that reduces the net impact of the retailer to almost zero. In addition, the modest negative impacts found by Basker and Jia may not capture adjacent county effects, which may net the state total to zero, as suggested by Sobel and Dean (2006) and Hicks and Wilburn (2001). In the end, the range of impacts found in these studies (from just under a five-firm increase in Wal-Mart counties to a loss of two firms) is so small that any policy intervention at the local level would have to be very low cost to yield net benefits. For a summary of these studies, see Table 5.1.

---

[3] Such a study is unlikely to be undertaken with this degree of specificity because the data on these firms are not readily available from the traditional sources as a result of data suppression at this level.

TABLE 5.1

Studies of Wal-Mart and Market Structure (Retail and Grocery)

Study	Region	Findings
Franklin (2001)	Grocery markets in U.S. MSAs 1993–1999	No impact of Wal-Mart on grocery store concentration
Hicks and Wilburn (2001)	County-level study of retail market in WV 1988–2000	Small positive impact on number of retail firms in Wal-Mart county attributable to agglomeration
Basker (2005a)	County-level study of retail sector in 1,700 U.S. counties 1972–1997	Small long-term reduction in retail firms attributed to Wal-Mart
Jia (2005)	County-level study of U.S. retail 1972–1997	Small reduction in number of firms attributable to Wal-Mart (or Kmart)
Sobel and Dean (2006)	State-level study of small businesses 1997–2003	No impact of Wal-Mart on growth or number of small firms.

Note. MSA, metropolitan statistical area.

However, this dissonance in results across methods compels additional research. As I have argued, the geographic and temporal variation in findings argues for repeated studies on smaller geographic areas. One way to do so is to reexamine the more famous research on the subject. I turn to Iowa, the state where Wal-Mart's impacts received their first serious study.

WAL-MART IN IOWA: A RIGOROUS EXAMINATION OF STONE'S CLASSIC WORK

Professor Ken Stone's research of the 1980s established the economic research on Wal-Mart's impact on local markets. Although the work has been correctly criticized for substantive methodological flaws, it remains a very useful source of the types of research questions that should guide inquiry into Wal-Mart's impacts.

In this chapter, I reexamine findings from two of Stone's reports, one an analysis of retail pull factors (Stone, 1989), which compared loss of retail sales across a number of firm categories from 1983 through 1993, and the second (Stone, 1997) a retrospective analysis of his earlier research (Stone, 1989) on Wal-Mart's impact on the number of retailers in cities with Wal-Mart.

The current analysis differs from Stone's in two ways. First, I use techniques that are more appropriate to estimating the incremental impact of Wal-Mart on retailers. These involve econometric modeling that accounts for the endogeneity of Wal-Mart's choices. Second, I focus my analysis at the county level, a point of departure from Stone's city-and-town level of analysis.

The first difference is clearly an improvement on Stone's work. The second simply provides for a different research question and is largely a necessity because of data constraints. Using subcounty data endangers my ability to perform a correction for endogeneity. I believe it is prudent to trade off geographic precision for a reduction in statistical bias. Further, there are data concerns at the subcounty level, particularly in the suppression of key data that trouble this type of research. This is why virtually all major studies are performed at the county level or higher. I test Wal-Mart's impact on county-level pull factors 1981 through 2003 and the number firms, by size category, in the retail sector from 1988 through 2003. These pull factors are simply the share of retail sales that occurs in a county that is greater than the population share in the state. This represents how much retail in a county is pulled from an adjoining county. The pull factor is calculated using the following share equation:

$$PF = \frac{RS_i / Pop_i}{\sum_{i=1}^{n} RS_i / Pop_i} \tag{5.1}$$

My general model of Wal-Mart's impact on Iowa's markets for goods and services takes the form

$$\Psi_{i,t} = \alpha + \alpha_i + \beta_1 T \times WM_{i,t} + \beta_2 T$$
$$\times WM_{j,t} + \gamma \tilde{W} \Psi_{j,t} + \delta \phi_{t-1} + e_t \tag{5.2}$$

where Ψ is the effect measured (e.g., pull factor, number of firms) in county i as a function of a common and county-specific fixed effect, a Wal-Mart presence / count dummy measured as years since opening, and the number of Wal-Marts in j adjacent counties. To this basic model specification I include a first-order spatial lag of the dependent variable (calculated using a row-normalized, first-order contiguity matrix $\tilde{W}$) and a time autocorrelation variable, with the white noise error term.

This specification suffers from the potential of endogeneity bias and thus requires an identification strategy. This strategy requires an instrumental variable, which is correlated with the independent variable of concern (here, Wal-Mart's entrance) but not the error term of the regression. Further, the use of a correction for spatial auto-correlation generates a second endogeneity bias concern since the value of the dependent variable in county i, time t, is unlikely to be uncorrelated with the same variable in county j in time t. This means simply that if the pull factor in my county grows, those in adjacent counties will probably decline. The most common correction to this endogeneity problem is to include the lagged value of all the regressors as instruments.

The identification strategy I use follows that used by Neumark, Zhang, and Ciccarella (2005) and Hicks (2006a). Neumark et al. use a very clever instrumentation of the equation, with distance from Bentonville, Arkansas, as their identifying equation, to which they add a distance / time product from the original opening of the store in Bentonville in 1962:

$$\Omega_{i,t} = \alpha + \sum \alpha_i + \delta_1 DIST_i + \delta_2 (DIST_i \cdot T) + e_{i,t} \qquad (5.3)$$

A very similar identification strategy has also been developed independently by Dube, Eidlin, and Lester (2005) and has subsequently been used also by Holmes (2006). Neumark et al. argue that the physical distance and time separation from the original store opening serve to place the timing and location decision of Wal-Mart independently from the variable they measure. As I mentioned earlier, this instrument was derived from a reading of Sam Walton's biography in which he discusses the Wal-Mart store location decisions.

The second instrument is similar to one I use in an earlier report (Hicks, forthcoming) and describe in Chapter 4, where market size was used to identify the county and timing of Wal-Mart's entrance. This estimate sums the total personal income in county i with the total personal income in j adjacent counties:

$$\Omega_{i,t} = \alpha + \sum \alpha_i + \delta_1 \left(\sum PI_{j,t} + PI_{i,t} \right) + e_{i,t} \qquad (5.4)$$

This instrument was developed following the revelation by a Wal-Mart spokesman that the size of the market area is a key determinant of location choices.

Both of these instruments are imperfect. Neumark et al. have been criticized in the popular press, but the adoption of the instrument by other researchers, myself included, is probably a better indication that researchers who understand these issues find it an attractive method. However, it is uncertain that the dependent variable (wages) is uncorrelated with distance from Bentonville, Arkansas. Clearly, wages on both coasts tend to be higher than in the center of the nation. One potential correction for this is through county fixed effects, but for my purposes this is not necessarily a problem since I am not examining wages. The second instrument also suffers one key drawback in that personal income in a county may not be uncorrelated with the dependent variables (pull factor or number of firms) since it will tend to be highly correlated with more densely populated areas with higher incomes. However, as Curs, Visser, and Stater (2005) argue, this is not necessarily where Wal-Mart will choose to locate because of relatively high land costs in urban areas (for which there is some tentative empirical support in Chapter 3). So, if total market area (in county i and j surrounding counties) is correlated with Wal-Mart's entrance in county i but not the preexisting pull factor or number of firms in county i, it will prove to be a useful instrument. This is intended to remove the endogeneity bias.

So, because my variables appear to be nonstationary, having no time trend, I perform my regressions in levels. Beginning with total retail pull factor, the results appear in Table 5.2.

These results are startling in their similarity. Both instruments yield impacts with nearly identical magnitudes and levels of statistical significance. Importantly, Neumark et al. express some concern that the usefulness of their instrument declined after 1995 as a result of Wal-Mart stores having fully reached each of the lower 48 conterminous states. This, they argue, weakens the usefulness of the instrument because the distance measurement from Bentonville is no longer a useful treatment of endogeneity. Recognizing this, I abbreviate my sample to account for the entrance patterns of Wal-Mart in Iowa. I tested the model on the

TABLE 5.2

Wal-Mart's Impact on Retail Pull Factor in Iowa

	Time / Distance	Market Size
Common intercept	−0.012806	−0.043726
	(−0.07)	(0.87)
Wal-Mart	0.004554***	0.004654***
(with time exposure)	(3.07)	(2.58)
Adjacent Wal-Mart	−0.003952***	−0.003782***
(with time exposure)	(−2.57)	(−2.58)
Spatial lag	1.013963***	1.053307***
	(4.86)	(2.99)
Autocorrelation ($t - 1$)	0.818503***	0.818624***
	(19.43)	(19.29)
Adjusted R^2	0.96	0.96
Durbin-Watson panel	2.18	2.18
Observations	2,178	2,178

Note. The Durbin-Watson panel statistic reported is derived from Bhargava, Franzini, and Narendranathan (1982). I whitewashed the variance matrix using a version of White's (1980) heteroscedastic consistent variance–covariance matrix derived from Driscoll and Kraay (1998). As is common, I have not reported the values of the cross-sectional fixed-effects coefficients to preserve space.

***p = 0.01.

period from 1981 through 1994, the last year of the big push of Wal-Mart stores. The estimated impact of the Wal-Marts was higher for both own county and adjacent counties by a total of 0.003. This is about a 75% increase in both cases. This suggests a fairly immediate impact of the retailer (at least consistent with Basker's, 2005a, estimates of the speed with which the impacts materialize). I believe the use of the longer time period is still appropriate because it allows for the estimation of a longer run impact while still accounting for the initial entrance.

The important elements of this estimate are the impacts of a same-county Wal-Mart on pull factors. In both estimates, the presence of a Wal-Mart in a county increases total retail pull factors by almost 0.5%. The presence of a Wal-Mart in an adjacent county reduces the county pull factor by almost 0.4%. This finding is very consistent with the direction of the impacts observed by Stone (1997), in which he describes retail flows moving toward a Wal-Mart in a subcounty region. However, the size of the impact at the county level is far different. He reports increases in Wal-Mart towns on the order of 50%, with non-Wal-Mart towns losing as much as 20% of their sales.

Tables 5.3 and 5.4 illustrate selected impacts from the remaining pull factor categories. (I do not report the coefficients of the remaining variables, but the adjusted R^2 ranges from 0.86 to 0.97 and there appear to by no other diagnostic concerns with these models.) I report these impacts as compared with those estimated by Stone at the city / town level for the same categories.

The own county effects illustrated are derived from the distance to Bentonville / time instrument. The impacts to the pull factors are rather modest everywhere, with general merchandise showing the largest impact at just under a 1% increase in the pull factor. Only eating and drinking establishments and total retail experience both positive and statistically significant impacts. The relative small magnitude of these, 0.4% for total retail and 0.2% for eating and drinking establishments, suggests a mild impact in any case. The interpretation of these impacts in terms of total retail sales is

Table 5.3

Effect of Wal-Mart on Own County

Pull factor category	Wal-Mart Entrance / Time	Normalized 3-year effect	Stone's (1995) 3-year change— normalized effect
General merchandise	0.009385*** (3.35)	2.8%	43.6%
Food	−0.001274 (0.52)	0	−4.0%
Apparel sales	−0.004396 (−0.56)	0	−12.9%
Building materials	−0.001233 (0.71)	0	−13.4%
Services sales	−0.001034 (−0.97)	0	N / A
Home furnishings	0.004290 (1.28)	0	32.0%
Eating and drinking	0.002444** (2.50)	1.2%	4.8%
Specialty stores	0.000198 (0.87)	0	−80%
Total pull factor (from prior regression)	0.004554*** (3.07)	1.3%	4.8%

Note. The Durbin-Watson panel statistic reported is derived from Bhargava, Franzini, and Narendranathan (1982). I whitewashed the variance matrix using a version of White's (1980) heteroscedastic consistent variance–covariance matrix derived from Driscoll and Kraay (1998). As is common, I have not reported the values of the cross-sectional fixed-effects coefficients to preserve space.
***p = 0.01. **p = 0.05.

somewhat more difficult because the Wal-Mart treatment variable is, in essence, a count of the number of stores open each year since the opening of the first Wal-Mart in each county. The average of this value is roughly 6, so evaluating the impact of Wal-Mart at the mean exposure value results in an increased pull factor for general merchandise of about 5%. Accordingly, the total retail sales and the eating and drinking impacts are thus 2.4% and 1.2%, respectively.

TABLE 5.4
Impact of Wal-Mart in Adjacent County

Pull Factor Category	Adjacent Wal-Mart	Normalized 3-year effect	Stone's (1995) 3-year change— normalized effect
General merchandise	−0.009461***	−2.8%	−9.2%
	(−2.90)		
Food	−0.001293	0	6.1%
	(0.77)		
Apparel sales	−0.002140	0	−10.0%
	(−0.40)		
Building materials	0.000987	0	−14.6%
	(0.89)		
Services sales	0.000381	0	N / A
	(0.28)		
Home furnishings	−0.002494	0	−13.1%
	(−0.58)		
Eating and drinking	−0.001202	0	−5.6%
	(−0.68)		
Specialty stores	0.000264	0	−14.0%
	(0.12)		
Total pull factor (from prior regression)	−0.003952***	−1.1%	−7.5%
	(−2.57)		

***$p = 0.01$.

In an effort to compare these results with Stone's work, I compare his 3-year impact, normalizing my estimates to a 3-year impact. The resulting changes are total changes in the pull factor in each category. My zero values are those that fail to rise to any acceptable level of statistical significance (I report any p value better than about 0.20). The very obvious conclusion from this estimate is that Stone's reported range is from five to 10 times greater than mine at their closest point. Before I discuss the potential reasons for these divergences, it is useful to look also at my estimates of Wal-Mart's influence on own county pull factors when a Wal-Mart is in an adjacent county.

The same concerns apply to these interpretations, and I note that the mean exposure to an adjacent Wal-Mart was over 6 years. The normalized 3-year effect is displayed in Tables 5.3 and 5.4. My estimates are once again far below the impacts reported by Stone (1997). This is a particularly useful improvement in Stone's method because, in addition to its statistical rigor, it permits me to account for the impact of Wal-Mart in an adjacent county, even when a county has one or more Wal-Marts itself. Stone's work only permitted comparison of counties with and without a Wal-Mart.

In comparing these estimates with Stone (1997), it is useful to bear in mind not only the difference in econometric estimate but also the geographic region. I do not believe time plays much of a factor in these estimates. First, my econometric methods account for the potential endogeneity of Wal-Mart's entrance decision using two different methods, which yield remarkably identical results. The use of this type of model also controls for other factors, notably all county-level differences that are fixed over the sample period and spatial and time autocorrelation. Further, my method simultaneously accounts for both own county and adjacent Wal-Marts. This is likely to explain some of the differences in the magnitudes. But it is likely that the geographic unit of measurement explains much of the impact difference.

Stone's analysis was centered on towns, the bulk of which had populations in the range of 20,000 to 50,000 residents. My analysis is of counties, and although the mean county population in 2003 and across all years is about 28,000, they are obviously much less densely populated than cities. The data Stone and I use account for trade rigidly at borders, be they city or county. So Stone's analysis of the retail sector finds that Wal-Mart accounts for considerable retail trade wherever it locates. His essential argument is that if Wal-Mart locates immediately outside a city, there is considerable reallocation of trade across these city or town borders. This may well be so, although his methodology cannot speak meaningfully to this point. However, if it is so and the impacts Stone measures are correct for towns, it is very likely, given my results, that the net impact of Wal-Mart's trade reallocation is nonexistent, the reason being that the impacts described by Stone (1997) dissipate rapidly within a county. My estimates are uniformly far smaller than his. This means either that almost all the reallocation of retail trade flows occurs within a county or that he was very wrong. It is, therefore, possible that small towns may lose retail trade as a consequence of Wal-Mart's decision to locate nearby. However, the net loss within a county is virtually nonexistent. Further, impact of retail trade pull factors resulting from the presence of a Wal-Mart within or outside a county is almost the entirely offsetting. Observe the impact of Wal-Mart and adjacent Wal-Marts on general merchandise (+2.8% and −2.8%, respectively) and the impact on total retail (+1.3% and −1.1%, respectively). Thus, these net impacts are both statistically and economically not different from zero.

This finding regarding pull factors does not fully inform the question regarding the impact of Wal-Mart on the local markets for goods. To do this, it is necessary to also test the impact of Wal-Mart on the structure of the industry, which I do, like Stone, by examining the number firms in these industries.

Constructing models similar to those discussed previously, I test the impact of Wal-Mart on the total number of firms and the disaggregated sectors analyzed by Stone in 1997. I further examine total number of firms, specialty store sales, and food store sales, which were not examined in Stone's work. Results for the total number of firms appear in Table 5.5.

These two models illustrate again the close proximity of the two methods. Notably, the dominant explanatory factor in determining the number of firms is the county fixed effects and the values in the previous years. Shortening the sample period from 1980 through 1994 does not materially alter the results (recall that I do this to account for Neumark et al.'s concern over the usefulness of the instrumental variable at the end of Wal-Mart's wave of market penetration).

However, Stone's focus was on the disaggregate sector of the economy, not merely the total number of firms. Again I stress that my comparisons are with counties, not small towns. I report here

TABLE 5.5

Impact of Wal-Mart on the Total Number of Firms in Iowa

	Instrument	
	Distance / Time From Bentonville	Market Size
Common intercept	1200.628	1100.529
	(1.13)	(0.80)
Wal-Mart	−10.7105	−10.8158
	(−0.47)	(−0.65)
Adjacent Wal-Mart	1.505729	2.390258
	(−0.06)	(0.14)
Spatial lag	−0.12298	−0.03029
	(−0.11)	(−0.02)
Autoregression (t − 1)	0.940471***	0.942159
	(59.46)	(34.64)
Adjusted R^2	0.99	0.99
Durbin-Watson panel	2.12	2.12
Observations	2,178	2,178

Note. The Durbin-Watson panel statistic reported is derived from Bhargava, Franzini, and Narendranathan (1982). I whitewashed the variance matrix using a version of White's (1980) heteroscedastic consistent variance–covariance matrix derived from Driscoll and Kraay (1998). As is common, I have not reported the values of the cross-sectional fixed-effects coefficients to preserve space.
***p = 0.01.

the coefficient estimates (and t statistics) for the own county Wal-Mart, with normalized impacts that can be compared to Stone's work. One caution is that my estimates, for econometric purposes, are total number of firms.[4] Stone (1997) reported percentage changes. To normalize the impacts, I estimate the percentage changes of my impacts comparing the total firm changes to the average county in the sample. I also translated Stone's impact to county-level changes (recognizing that his

---

[4] Estimating percentage differences (here bounded by 0 and 1) potentially requires limited dependent variable techniques to account for censoring of the data performed within a panel estimate, which presents additional problems.

estimates are for cities). I did this to give not merely percentage changes but some idea of the potential magnitude of the real economic consequences that arise in this discussion. The results appear in Table 5.6.

The first noticeable result of this estimate is that my model finds no statistically reliable impacts on the number of firms within a county that can be attributed to Wal-Mart. Three of my estimates (food, eating and drinking, and specialty stores) enjoy statistical significance between 10% and 20% and should be interpreted with caution because these do not enjoy a very high level of statistical reliability. The second and

TABLE 5.6
Impact of Wal-Mart's Entrance on Number of Firms in Retail
Subsectors in Iowa

Number of Firms	Wal-Mart	Normalized 10-year effect	Stone's (1997) 10-year change— normalized effect
General merchandise	−0.32 (−0.56)	0	25% (4.25 firms)
Food	−0.42†† (−1.25)	22%†† (4.2 firms)	N / A
Apparel sales	0.57 (0.52)	0	−28% (−7 firms)
Building materials	−0.029 (−0.73)	0	4 (1 firm)
Services sales	−2.58 (0.57)	0	N / A
Home furnishings	0.015 (0.20)	0	−1% (−0.28 firms)
Eating & and drinking	−0.37† (−1.44)	−5%† (−3.7 firms)	5% (3.6 firms)
Specialty stores	−0.42†† (1.11)	−2.08%†† (−4.2 firms)	−17% (−30 firms)
Total no. firms (from prior regression)	−10.7105 (−0.47)	0	N / A

†p = 0.15. ††p = 0.20.

more pronounced observation is the very large difference between the size of my estimates and those of Professor Stone. When comparing the percentages of my analysis, only the estimate of impact on eating and drinking establishments is similar to Stone's, but my estimates are very statistically uncertain and in the opposite direction.

The implications of my findings are fairly clear. First, when a properly specified model of Wal-Mart's impacts is estimated at the county level, there are no retail structure impacts that can be attributed to Wal-Mart. Second, even if the small town impacts reported by Stone (1997) are attributable to Wal-Mart (and his method simply cannot isolate the Wal-Mart effect), then the spatial reallocation of trade is confined to the county. No net changes to the number or composition of firms can be attributed to Wal-Mart's location within a county.

Stone also examined the changes in sales in non-Wal-Mart towns. It appears that his purpose in doing this was to create an ad hoc control group, but part of the implication was that towns without Wal-Marts would see an outmigration of retail sales and hence a loss of stores. I test this through estimating the impact of a Wal-Mart's presence in an adjoining county. Because my estimates of these effects are performed within the same model, I can isolate the incremental effects of a Wal-Mart that locates in an adjoining county, even if a Wal-Mart is present within the county in question. The coefficient estimates and my normalized comparisons appear in Table 5.7.

As with the estimates of the impacts of an own county Wal-Mart, my estimates here suggest that a Wal-Mart in an adjacent county plays no statistically meaningful role in the number of retail firms in a county. Also the magnitudes of the impacts are very small, especially when compared with Stone's very large estimates within towns.

Importantly, my estimates differ from Stone's in two ways. First, I estimate the incremental impact of a Wal-Mart in an adjoining county in an effort to infer the change in retail patterns associated with this type of spatial dispersion of stores. Stone reports retail changes in non-Wal-Mart towns as an ad hoc control group for his estimates of Wal-Mart's impact on counties in which it had located. He also suggests that there is outmigration of retail sales associated with nearby

TABLE 5.7

Impact of Adjacent Wal-Mart's on Number of Firms in Retail
Sub-sectors in Iowa

Number of Firms	Adjacent Wal-Mart	Normalized 10 year effect	Stone's (1997) 10 year change— normalized effect
General merchandise	0.38	0	−34%
	(0.76)		(−5.7 firms)
Food	−0.18	0	N / A
	(−0.25)		
Apparel sales	0.39	0	−28%
	(0.82)		(−7 firms)
Building materials	0.09	0	−25%
	(1.12)		(−6.7 firms)
Services sales	3.15	0	N / A
	(0.51)		
Home furnishings	0.55††	19%††	−31%
	(1.30)	(5.5 firms)	(−8.7 firms)
Eating and drinking	0.91	0	−9%
	(1.13)		(6.5 firms)
Specialty stores	0.32†	1.8%†	−28%
	(1.45)	(3.2 firms)	(−49 firms)
Total no. firms (from prior regression)	1.505729	0	N / A
	(−0.06)		

†p = 0.15. ††p = 0.20.

Wal-Mart stores. This will happen even in counties with a Wal-Mart, depending on the relative locations of stores within the county (e.g., I live in a county with three Wal-Marts, and my nearest store is in an adjacent county). Second, I examine counties as my unit of measure, whereas Stone focuses on towns. My purpose in evaluating counties was twofold. First, there are limitations on the subcounty data. Second, and more importantly, my estimates provide a mechanism of calibrating the net impact of the retail changes reported by Stone. In describing in some detail the loss of retail in small firms, Stone focuses on a very small geographic area. He is clearly correct in identifying the firm losses in these towns (these are public data), but what is not clear from the questions he asked is the area in which the spatial adjustment of retail trade occurs. My estimates strongly suggest that the net losses and declines described by Stone (1997) are isolated at the county level, and that the magnitude of cross-county trade flows is largely unaffected by Wal-Mart. This is fairly startling because even as of 2006 the majority of Iowa's 99 counties do not have a Wal-Mart store.

To be clear, what I present in this chapter is not an intended indictment of Stone's research or his findings. There is, of course, room for criticism, and as I have mentioned earlier, his method of analysis simply cannot assign causation to retail changes of any type. So, despite the titles of his reports, what he describes as a Wal-Mart effect cannot be attributed as such. This does not mean that his findings are wrong, simply that we cannot know from his method what Wal-Mart's impact was in Iowa. Importantly, the widespread interest in his publications was never due to their quality but rather to their resonance with many observers. However, if we are to ask what effect Wal-Mart has had in Iowa, it is useful to ask what has happened to retail, in aggregate, in the state. To do so, I illustrate the mean number of firms in total retail and in the disaggregate sectors. I begin with the smaller sectors and report the mean number of firms per county in Iowa's 99 counties. See Figure 5.1.

Figure 5.1   Mean Number of Firms Per County, Iowa

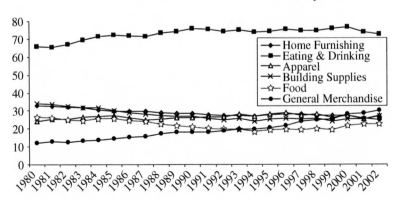

These data reveal that, consistent with the population declines of the 1970s through the 1990s, Iowa lost a number of firms in building supplies, food, and home furnishings. However, general merchandise stores and eating and drinking establishments saw modest increases in the mean number of firms per county. There clearly was not the type of dramatic loss in number of firms overall that Stone reported as occurring in the state's small towns. Figure 5.2 shows the mean number of firms for the aggregate and larger sectors of Iowa's retail industry.

As can be seen, the total number of retail firms and specialty and service sales firms actually experienced considerable growth from 1980 through 2002. Recognizing that the state's average county population declined from the 1960s through 1991 and only modestly recovered in the 1990s, this retail growth points to a strong, not weak, retail sector in Iowa.

Professor Stone's reports attributing loss of retail sales and number of firms in Iowa's small towns have engendered much criticism of Wal-Mart. His data are correct, and it is likely that small towns in Iowa and elsewhere have continued to lose retail sales and stores, as they likely did in the years before Wal-Mart coming to town. However, his analytical technique is wholly unable to support his conclusion that this effect was caused by Wal-Mart. In addition, even if he is

FIGURE 5.2   Mean Number of Retail Firms in Iowa's Counties

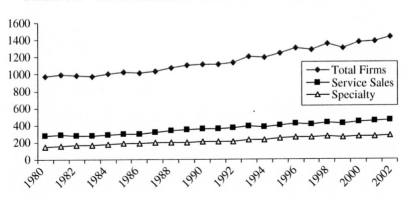

correct, it is very clear that, although there is some cross-county retail trade flow differences attributable to Wal-Mart, the impact on the number of retail stores in a county is unaffected by Wal-Mart. These results speak directly to Iowa, but the changes in retail nationwide frame the structure of the industry in which Wal-Mart operates.

THE STRUCTURE AND SPATIAL DISTRIBUTION OF THE RETAIL INDUSTRY

The retail sector in the United States has changed dramatically in the past century. Even the introduction of the cash-and-carry method did not uniformly replace the credit-and-delivery system until much after World War I, and barter was common until then.[5] The growth of retail since then is often characterized in the popular literature as a growing phenomenon, and there is a significant (in terms of volume) academic treatment of the culture of consumerism. Recall from the chapter on chain store history that retail and wholesale trade's share of personal income has been declining since the Great Depression. A snapshot of employment suggests that total employment has increased since the 1960s, albeit very slowly, and that the retail sector's share of total employment has also risen since the 1960s. These data include part-time work, and importantly there is a small decline in the latter years of the 20th century. The newer data (after 2000) differ dramatically because of the transformation from the Standard Industrial Classification to the North American Industrial Classification System. This break in the data series shows a plunge in retail employment as occupations within retail were reclassified to other sectors. However, the increasing trend in total employment continued after the data break. See Figure 5.3.

The U.S. consumer today certainly buys more consumer goods than their grandparents or great-grandparents in the 1930s. But the share

---

[5] Interestingly, writing in the *American Economic Review* in 1923, Lawrence Mann felt that the credit-and-delivery system would prove to be a source of continued competitive advantage by non-chain retailers.

FIGURE 5.3 Retail Employment and Retail's Share in the
United States

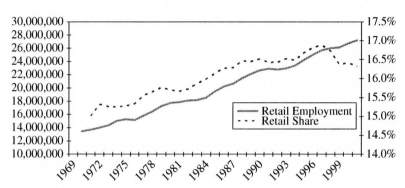

of the U.S. economy as measured by personal income dedicated to wholesale and retail trade is perhaps a third smaller than it was in the 1920s (recall Figure 1.3). However, there has been an increase in the total share of U.S. employees in retail trade (about 2% over the last 40 years). It is very likely that much of this growth has been in part-time or casual employment. However we examine these data, for those arguing that consumerism is a significant cultural force, these data provide daunting counter-evidence.

Throughout this book I offer evidence that retail trade is becoming more geographically available. The example of Moran's I for Indiana discussed in Chapter 4 is an example. Part of this may be due to a more spatially diffuse population or direct efforts by stores to locate more proximally to their customers. The geographic spread of Wal-Mart also illustrates the obvious location choice of retailers near their consumers. Recall the maps from Chapter 3. Some evidence of the distance retailers locate from customers is revealed on a contemporary study of big-box location strategies (Holmes, 2006). This study calculated mean distance to population blocks by population density using U.S. Census data and firm-specific locations drawn from a number of data sources. These data suggest that Wal-Mart and other retailers are fairly close to a large number of their consumers. See Figure 5.4.

FIGURE 5.4   Big-Box Distance to Residents by Population
Density Ranges

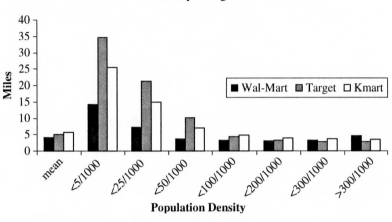

Source: Holmes, 2006.

The retail and wholesale trade industry is a significant portion of the United States economy. Wal-Mart enjoys considerable market share and may exercise impacts on the structure of the retail industry. This impact has been called the Wal-Mart effect within the popular literature (see Fishman, 2006) and in some sociology conference papers (Lichtenstein, 2005). Economists have been more reticent to eponymously label these "the Wal-Mart effect." One reason may be that the business journalists and noneconomic researchers do not ascribe the same benefits to the process of competition that economists have traditionally afforded it. I turn my discussion to this issue.

WHY VALUE COMPETITION?

Economists tell a pretty simple story about markets, and it is useful in the context of a book about Wal-Mart. However, the simplicity of the story masks the power of the interactions for improving society. Here's the story.

Businesses dislike competition. It makes work harder, reduces profitability, and requires firms to do things to please consumers. For all the workplace bravado about beating the competition, the goal of a business is to arrive at the point where they no longer have to compete. Business journalists often speak ill of competition, although in subtle ways, reflecting their trade in following the news of individual industries and businesses.

Consumers like competition. It lowers prices, ensures better products, and requires firms to do things to please consumers. Consumers understand this and observe that firms often differentiate themselves by these attributes of price, quality, and service.

The interaction of these businesses and consumers is the market. And the numbers of consumers and producers and their gift for seeking the optimal conditions are what make competitive markets attractive to economists.

Of course, when it comes to selling labor, this relationship is reversed, and workers (formerly known as consumers) now sell their services to employers (businesses). Workers like noncompetitive labor markets for all the same reasons firms like noncompetitive markets for goods. Workers in noncompetitive labor markets enjoy higher wages and don't have to work as hard at pleasing their employer. Employers like competitive markets because they don't have to pay these higher wages and their employees have to perform or employers will seek services elsewhere.

One way to simplify our understanding of the way firms and consumers behave is to ascribe to them simple behavioral formulas. One such formula is that all actors within these markets formulate their decisions based on a desire to maximize profits (for businesses) or what economists call *utility* (for consumers). It is easy to see that firms maximize profit, but this assumption about consumers seems to many much less obvious. So let me be clear: The desires of a utility-maximizing consumer can be very simple, involving only the choice of price or consumption of a couple of goods, or enormously complex, involving intertemporal maximization of a utility that incorporates, for example, a bequest to one's children or one's alma mater, financing basic research on HIV / AIDS, and buying a lakeside villa in Italy. The story is largely the same because it motivates the same types of behaviors.

Because actors in markets are making decisions in these ways, many of the forecasts of endlessly plummeting wages or firms growing beyond all bounds never materialize. Workers faced with very low wages prefer leisure, or change occupations, yielding higher wages for the remaining workers, who, importantly, are making themselves better off. Firms don't own all of a market because competitors, actual or imagined, lie in wait for a leisurely monopolist. Thus, they keep prices low and continue to innovate. This, by the way, is the real story of Wal-Mart. Unlike A&P, on the death of its founder, it didn't abandon the time-honored techniques that made it grow rapidly.

In the end, these processes are called *competition*. Competition, as described in the popular media, is a verb. To economists, it is an adjective describing a state of a market. And to economists, the benefits of competition are profound and preferable to any other market outcome, say monopoly or something like it.

In a competitive market, firms price their goods so that they are receiving a "normal" profit. This normal profit differs from accounting profit in that it includes some payment sufficient to bring together all the factors of production: land, labor, raw materials, machinery, and management talent. There's no easy way to calculate the magnitude of a normal profit like there is an accounting profit. But economists argue that the presence of a normal profit provides no incentive for a new firm to enter the market or an incumbent firm to exit. In short, this is the market in stasis or equilibrium. Of course, this equilibrium never occurs, so the adjustment of short-term profit rates around a long-term mean is completely understandable. High profits induce entrance by firms; low profits induce exits.

Firms that enjoy some capacity to keep prices above the competitive level enjoy profits that are greater than normal. This condition induces entrance by other firms, and for firms to retain this super-normal profit they must exercise some mechanism to keep other firms out. Many of these mechanisms are prohibited by antitrust laws, but businesses have found no shortage of methods to preserve monopoly profits through methods that are not outlawed. There is no shortage of these efforts where Wal-Mart is concerned. The local efforts to keep Wal-Mart out of communities have often been led by local incumbent retailers. Recent calls by Wal-Mart's CEO for increased minimum wage is a classic example of raising rivals' costs, since Wal-Mart rarely, if ever, pays a minimum wage. To be fair, though, Wal-Mart is far more the victim of these efforts than the victimizer (as I'll discuss later).

It should be clear from this discussion that economists have a very different feeling about high profits than business journalists. Business journalists often tout profits as a source of economic growth, an understandable response since it is the measure of a firm's success. Thus, higher profits are good. Economists will not necessarily agree but may want to know what causes the higher profits. (Is it monopoly or greater efficiency?)

Economists are so enamored with competitive markets because the presence of competition in a market results in the greatest overall good for society. This may or may not mean simply higher profits for an individual firm. In competition, markets simultaneously achieve two difficult and universally held social goals that cannot otherwise be achieved: allocative and productive efficiency (Figure 5.5).

This figure provides a very clear illustration of the gains to competition. Suppose a firm is pricing like a monopolist at *Pm*, with the associated level of output *Qm*. In practice, this need not be a monopoly but a firm with some market power. Juxtapose this outcome with the competitive market where a firm sells a good at *Pc* and sells quantity *Qc* (remember that the average cost includes the normal profit, so this firm is making an accounting profit).

Obviously, in competition, the consumer is better off, whereas the producer is not. Many business journalists see this as a zero sum transfer, and the only concern is equity (who gets the benefits of higher prices). However, this misses an important point. Society as a whole gains from competition, even if individual agents are not directly participating in the market.

The gains to society of competition occur through the allocation of inputs and outputs. The presence of any market power that allows

FIGURE 5.5   Productive and Allocative Efficiency
Gains of Competition

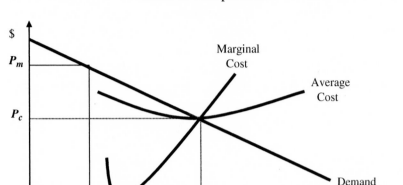

firms to increase price (and following the law of demand reduce the quantity sold) misallocates resources in two ways. At any price above Pc, the producer is operating at a point on the average cost curve that is above the minimum point. The firm is inefficiently using its inputs, which may be land, labor, raw material, or managerial talent or all of these. The point is that unless a good is produced at its most efficient level (where the average minimum cost curve is at its trough), then society suffers the misallocation of its resources. Economists refer to this as a deviation from productive efficiency. This could manifest itself in the continued presence of a small, inefficient mom-and-pop store or as an opportunity denied a young worker employed there. This inefficiency also means that we are not using our inputs in places that yield more desirable outcomes, which need not be limited to commercial markets. They could be used for environmental remediation, youth ministries, or malarial research. Of course, in this example, the individual impact is almost trivial, but, magnified across 3,500 county retail markets, the impact can be enormous. However, this is the small part of the inefficiency created by monopoly power. The misallocation of the outputs, as opposed to the inputs, is perhaps more costly.

Firms engaged in monopoly pricing do not produce the competitive quantity of goods. Because of the law of demand, they must produce less to price at the monopoly level. However, more units of the good or service could be produced at a marginal cost beneath the selling price. In essence, this means that more items could be produced at a cost beneath which consumers are willing and able to pay for them. The presence of market power then leaves consumers unable to buy goods that they are willing and able to pay for. When competitive markets occur, price is equal to the marginal cost of production (marginal cost intersects the average cost curve at its lowest point). Thus, competition yields the fortunate outcome of both productive and allocative efficiency. This result can be achieved through no other market outcome. Of course, we are speaking here of consumer goods, and there are many who view consumption as a vice. I ascribe no moral value to it, but if I did and I wanted to use my resources for other purpose I viewed as moral (e.g., giving to my church, supporting environmental causes, or donating to the local children's museum), then more resources for these purposes would be freed up by lower priced diapers, which happy circumstance forces me to purchase. Thus, virtually all economists argue that competition in markets yields better outcomes for society, even if you aren't participating in these markets. (Of course, some goods generate externalities, or negative effects on third persons, and so may require intervention, but this is a different matter altogether that I will touch on in later chapters).

The effect of Wal-Mart on its competitors could well be to move markets toward the competitive price and quantity. Economists would find relief in this outcome. So it is research in this area where some of the most fascinating findings lie.

WAL-MART'S EFFECT ON CONSUMER PRICES

The Bureau of Labor Statistics (BLS) estimates changes to the price of goods in an effort to measure inflation. Estimating the magnitude of inflation is important for monetary and fiscal policy, so getting the estimates right is critical. Professor Jerry Hausman of Massachusetts

Institute of Technology and Ephraim Leibtag, an economist at the U.S. Department of Agriculture, estimated the impact of Wal-Mart on consumer prices in the United States in an effort to motivate the BLS to modify some of their data collection methods (Hausman and Leibtag, 2004). The details of their critique of the BLS methods are not important for our purposes here, but Hausman and Leibtag's findings with respect to Wal-Mart are.

Hausman and Leibtag used a set of commercial data from ACNielson on a large (over 61,000) sample of consumers from 1998 through 2001, including detailed information on the price and location of food purchased in the households. They compared these prices for purchases of homogeneous items in supercenters (not exclusively Wal-Mart) and supermarkets. They found two interesting effects. First, the supercenter prices were lower, by 5% to 48%, than the supermarket prices. Second, the average regional price of these food items decreased through competitive effects.[6] In their examination of consumer items such as eggs, chicken, yogurt, and bananas, they found no consistent magnitude of the effect, but it was universally a lower price (and higher per unit quantities) because of the presence of a supercenter. I believe this is what I characterize as an income effect of Wal-Mart's entrance.

Later, Hausman and Leibtag (2005) calculated the magnitude of these effects on consumers. In this study, they measure the impact on consumer of changing shopping patterns and found an impact that translates into a roughly 25% reduction in food costs. This is further

---

[6] Hausman and Leibtag's estimates were not strictly price differences but *compensating variation*, a theoretical definition used by economists to measure benefits where markets cannot directly observe consumers behavior. What Hausman and Leibtag mean is this is how much consumers should, if they are rational, be willing to spend to shop at a Wal-Mart. It is the value of Wal-Mart to shoppers (although most of the impact is obviously in price). Interestingly, a survey of incumbent responses to a new Wal-Mart found that price reductions were the most effective strategy, with half engaging in innovative or aggressive pricing (McGee and Rubach, 1996).

concentrated in lower income families, because they are more likely to shop at the supercenters.[7]

Also in 2004, five researchers at Occidental College's Urban and Environmental Policy Institute published a report that compared food baskets at three major grocery chains in California: Wal-Mart's supercenters, Stater's, and Vons. This basket mix was probably the most extensive cross-section used. The authors examined a wide range of products, including meat, fish, and dairy (10 items); canned fruits and vegetables (11 items); fresh fruits and vegetables (25 items); sugars, fats, and oils (7 items); and breads, grains, and legumes (20 items). The results conclusively depict Wal-Mart as the low-cost retailer, with Stater's prices 19.7% higher and Von's 22.6% higher than Wal-Mart.[8]

Basker (2005b) attempted to measure a similar price effect using a data set on prices compiled by The Council for Community and Economic Research (formerly ACCRA). This data set is a cross-sectional basket of goods compiled by volunteers in locations around the country.[9] Using the raw data from 10 individual items in the basket, Basker calculated the impact of Wal-Mart's entrance on prices of several homogenous items (e.g., toothpaste, aspirin, Kleenex) in 165 cities. Like Hausman and Leibtag (2004), she found that price reductions varied but were uniformly (except for underwear, for which there was no price effect) lower in counties with Wal-Mart stores. She found the average short-term impact was a 1.5% to 3% reduction. Basker calculated long-term impacts at as much as four times the short-term impacts. She also estimated the effect of the entrance of

---

[7] In somewhat related research, Van Heerde, Gijsbrecht, and Pauwels (2005) examine price wars in retail markets, and Jensen and Webster (2005) find that market power in grocery stores is an important determinant of price.

[8] This report, quite surprisingly, went on to recommend anti-Wal-Mart policies in some detail. See Villianatos, Shaffer, Beery, Gottleib, and Wheatley (2004).

[9] The Center for Business and Economic Research at Marshall University participated in the voluntary survey while I was director of research (1999–2004). We collected the ACCRA Cost of Living Index for Huntington, West Virginia.

a second Wal-Mart, finding that the net effect of a second entrance was in the opposite direction (while the net effect was still a lower price). She also found that the price effect was larger in smaller cities, where conceivably there was less existing competition in the retail markets. Basker (2005b) also cites a UBS Warburg pricing study that confirms both her analysis and that of Hausman and Leibtag (2004).

A State University of New York–Oneonta study examined rural grocery store prices in four central New York towns (Thomas, Martin, and Dai, 2005). The researchers created a basket of 38 common goods and then tested the prices by comparing list price at 26 different stores. The authors carefully included a smart shopper strategy that permitted them to choose alternative or store brands to compare across comparable goods when name brands were unavailable. They collected all these prices during a single November week in 2004. In addition to finding some demographic differences in the communities, they found that two of the three least expensive baskets were from Wal-Mart (with a Hannaford's grocery ranking second, a penny less expensive than the third-place Oneonta supercenter). The most expensive store (a Marquis supermarket) was more than 25% more expensive than either Wal-Mart or the remaining 22 grocery stores, which included several of the big Northeast regional groceries along with the once dominant A&P.

Todd Sharkey and Kyle Stiegart, writing for the Food System Research Group at the University of Wisconsin, tested the impact of market power on grocery store prices. Using BLS data on grocery store prices in 23 metropolitan statistical areas from 1993 through 2003, they constructed a model in which prices could be affected by a number of existing local conditions and supercenter-type stores (Wal-Mart, Target, and Kmart) and existing competition in the markets. They found that the less competition that existed in a market, the higher were the prices. This is good evidence that their model is robust, because it is among the most replicated scientific findings in economics (right behind the law of demand). Also they did not find statistically significant evidence that supercenters were increasing competition and hence reducing prices. However, using a measure of the degree of supercenter presence, they did find that metropolitan statistical areas with higher presence of supercenters were experiencing lower prices. The authors went so far as to conclude that "this result may suggest that if the current rate of supercenter development continues, it would be advisable to retest the hypothesis that supercenters are causing downward pressure on prices in the U.S. food retailing industry" (Sharkey and Steigart, 2006, p. 62).

Beyond these studies there are few pricing studies available that are of sufficient value to make comparisons. Interestingly, in the early days of anti-Wal-Mart activism, there was considerable argument that Wal-Mart did not have lower prices (although apparently consumers did not read many of these studies). One example of these is a January 2005 market basket study by a local advocacy group in Potsdam, New York. This group collected data on 31 items in a Wal-Mart in another nearby city and comparative prices on 31 goods at other local retailers. They concluded that Wal-Mart actually had higher prices on the basket ($206.08–197.00) and that shopping at Wal-Mart would be 4.4% more costly. However, their study was flawed. Almost half of their products are items that are not directly comparable. Examples of these are girls' name-brand flare-leg five-pocket jeans. Although these items have some comparison (and are part of the methodological disagreement that spawned Hausman and Leibtag's 2004 study), for the purposes of comparing Wal-Mart, using directly comparable prices is far more appropriate. Interestingly, it is the comparison of these nonhomogeneous types of products that one might expect Wal-Mart to have lower prices. This is in part why Hausman and Leibtag performed their analysis. So, ignoring the potential for sample selection bias in the Potsdam data, I compare the reported price for exact brand-name comparisons. One note is that the authors adjusted the price to account for unit packaging differences, which is an appropriate method. These data appear in Table 5.8.

TABLE 5.8
Direct Comparison of Potsdam Study Data

Item	Wal-Mart	Other	Difference (%)
Pampers disposable diapers	$9.44	$9.99	5.8
Bounty paper towels (90/2 ply)	$3.02	$1.98	−34.4
Puffs tissues (108 tissues)	$1.06	$1.00	−5.7
Scott toilet paper (4 rolls)	$2.84	$3.09	8.8
Tide powder detergent	$12.83	$16.88	31.5
DAP all-purpose caulk (10.1 oz)	$1.72	$1.74	1.2
Purina Dog Chow	$7.94	$3.94	−50.4
Purina Friskies cat food (6.3 lbs)	$5.37	$6.83	27.2
Suave Naturals shampoo / conditioner	$0.96	$0.97	1.0
Crest toothpaste (8.2 oz)	$2.24	$2.50	11.6
Band-Aid bandages (60 pack 3/4" × 3")	$1.77	$3.44	94.1
Advil ibuprofen (200 mg, 165 tabs)	$10.93	$14.83	35.7
Generic ibuprofen (200 mg, 50 coated tabs)	$1.96	$2.99	52.6
Centrum Advanced Formula multivitamin (50 tabs)	$5.78	$4.03	−30.2
Flintstones chewable multivitamins (60 tabs)	$5.97	$7.49	25.5
Vicks Nyquil (10 oz)	$4.77	$5.99	25.6
Pepsi (2 L)	$1.08	$1.08	0.0
Total	$79.68	$88.77	11.4

Ironically, using data collected by the Potsdam group opposed to Wal-Mart and correcting for the specific brand-name products assembled in the survey, I find that the cost of purchasing the same goods at the local (non-Wal-Mart) retailers is roughly 11.4% higher. These findings are quite consistent with those of Basker (2005b) using a very similar product set.[10]

However, there is one state that has a lengthy history of collecting cost-of-living data at the county level. Florida State University's Bureau of Business and Economic Research has been collecting the Florida Cost of Living Index (FCLI) since the early 1970s. This index is similar to the ACCRA data in that it makes geographic, not temporal, analysis of relative prices of a basket of goods. These relative data can be used to compare the impact that Wal-Mart entrance and presence has had on overall cost of living.

These data, like those of the ACCRA sample, have some limitations. The county-specific survey measures very few food and consumer items, of the type Wal-Mart might sell, in the basket. There is a possibility that these specifically measure Wal-Mart prices, which evidence pretty clearly suggests are lower. Also the items even potentially affected by Wal-Mart account for only 30% of the weighted basket of goods, so variation in other items might account for much of the relative change. Also, although I find the evidence unlikely, it is possible that Wal-Mart focused their entrance into lower price counties. To account for that possibility, I use an instrument of a 2-year lagged-entrance dummy; I report both the ordinary least squares (OLS) and this estimate. The basic specification of my model is

$$FPLI = \alpha + \alpha_i + \beta WM_{i,t} + \delta\phi_{t-1} + e_t \qquad (5.5)$$

in which the county-level FCLI is estimated as a function of a common and fixed-effect intercept, a Wal-Mart presence / count dummy or, in alternative specification, the presence dummy times the number of

---

[10] My favorite anti-Wal-Mart "study" is from the group Co-op America, which reported price comparisons that included Wal-Mart jeans ($19.77) and jeans purchased at a yard sale ($5.00). I have both beat, since I have written much of this book in a pair of Wal-Mart jeans purchased at a yard sale for $0.50!

years the Wal-Mart has been open. The δ is the time-autoregressive element and e, a white noise error term. I count on the fixed effects capturing potential effects of persistent amenity differences (such as an oceanside view) that influence relative price differences across counties. To this I also include the instrument of lagged entrance. My data are for both Wal-Mart and supercenters from 1980 through 2004. See Table 5.9.

This model presents fairly strong evidence that Wal-Mart entrance reduces the relative cost of living in Florida counties, but the impact may not be as large overall as those suggested by Hausman and Leibtag (2004). I find that the presence of a Wal-Mart or supercenter reduced overall relative prices by just over one tenth of 1% from the state average price level. The magnitude of this impact is insensitive to the instrument I use, suggesting either an absence of endogeneity or a wholly inappropriate

TABLE 5.9
Wal-Mart's Impact on Florida Cost of Living Index (1980–2004)

	Presence		Exposure	
	OLS	2SLS	OLS	2SLS
Common intercept	95.81130***	95.83196***	95.77175***	95.76736***
	(974.00)	(911.64)	(1049.41)	(1025.69)
Wal-Mart presence	−0.126675***	−0.140604**	—	—
	(−2.59)	(−2.55)		
Wal-Mart persistence	—	—	−0.003680**	−0.003571**
			(−2.38)	(−2.20)
Autoregression ($t - 1$)	0.453328***	0.453302***	0.454434***	0.454448***
	(20.68)	(20.67)	(20.76)	(20.75)
Adjusted R^2	0.88	0.88	0.88	0.88
Durbin Watson panel	2.25	2.25	2.25	2.25

Note. The Durbin-Watson panel statistic reported is derived from Bhargava, Franzini, and Narendranathan (1982). I whitewashed the variance matrix using a version of White's (1980) heteroscedastic consistent variance–covariance matrix derived from Driscoll and Kraay (1998). As is common, I have not reported the values of the cross-sectional fixed-effects coefficients to preserve space.
***$p = 0.01$. **$p = 0.05$.

instrument.[11] The measurement of Wal-Mart's impact as a persistence (presence weighted by number of years since opening) yields smaller total results than the presence measurement when weighted across the mean number of years Wal-Mart has been open at the midpoint of the sample (roughly 4 years in 1992). This suggests that much of the change is likely to happen early following the opening of Wal-Mart.

The magnitude of total price-level changes is small compared with that found in the other studies noted previously (although not far off some of Basker's estimates). However, if I assume that the whole of the variation in the impact is captured in the relevant consumer goods and services part of the basket, then the impact of Wal-Mart results in a roughly one third lower total price for consumer goods in a county in which Wal-Mart is located. I must stress that these types of studies present considerable data concerns, and these series' greatest concern is the very few consumer items contained in the survey. However, the range of my findings is potentially within the range of impacts found by Hausman and Leibtag and by Basker.

Clearly, Wal-Mart charges less, sometimes far less, than the competing stores. A more important question is whether Wal-Mart affects the competitive equilibrium price within the markets in which it operates. The analysis provided previously clearly suggests that the overall price for goods drops when Wal-Mart locates within a county, very likely as a competitive response by incumbent firms.

This retail impact on prices is critical, and so too are local impacts on firms. This area has, as reviewed previously, seen considerable research of mixed quality and method. However, the potential that Wal-Mart's influence spreads beyond the retail sector has been subjected to some research. The following chapter examines that question and provides some additional empirical research on Wal-Mart's impact on the aggregate economy.

---

[11] This instrument is similar to Basker's (2005b) and those used by Hicks (2006c). Although I do not report it, an alternative specification that included the entrance dummy variable in the OLS specification did not change the magnitude or statistical certainty of the other coefficients.

CHAPTER SIX

THE IMPACT OF WAL-MART ON THE AGGREGATE ECONOMY

Wal-Mart's impact on retail labor markets and local markets for goods and services has received the bulk of research and policy attention. However, as a number of researchers have noted, any impact observed within the retail sector may simply be a realignment of employment across sectors of the economy. Thus, focusing solely on retail or wholesale sector employment fails to fully answer a question as to whether Wal-Mart is engaged in net job creation or destruction.

To better understand these two issues, it is important to understand the job accounting data used by the Bureau of Labor Statistics and Bureau of Economic Analysis and to better appreciate the magnitude of employment dynamics that occur within these employment categories.

For the first issue, Basker's (2005a) estimate that wholesale employment declined as a result of Wal-Mart's entrance into a county is a classic example. The resulting impact could be a simple employment accounting issue. As Basker explains, the more vertically integrated

Wal-Mart actually leads to less employment in wholesale employment. This may well be simply that workers performing the same tasks are now employed by a retail firm (Wal-Mart) instead of a wholesale firm. There may be no net change in jobs or even occupations. This may merely be because the data account for these workers in different sectors. Economists worry little about this transformation. However, the formal prose of economics does not rightly capture the difficulty to both workers and firms of this type of employment dynamics. However, in past decades, economists have come to understand that job turnover in retail and wholesale trade is far greater than previously thought.

Employment dynamics are a relatively new line of inquiry made possible by the matching of U.S. Census and employment security data (collected for unemployment insurance purposes). These new lines of data are appearing sporadically across the United States as funding from state employment agencies becomes available.[1] The new program, originally the Longitudinal Employer-Household Dynamic Program (now Local Employment Dynamics [LED]) at the U.S. Census Bureau offers considerable data insights and analytical extensions. Beginning with Davis, Haltiwanger, and Schuh (1996), analysts have developed much improved econometric techniques (Abowd, Creecy, and Kramarz, 2002) and have attempted to answer much more sophisticated questions than was previously possible (Lane, Burgess, and Theeuwes, 1998). Although these data continue to offer much for researchers, accessing the data in their fullest form (consistent with U.S. Census privacy constraints) makes some uses restrictively resource intensive. To bridge this gap, a publicly available set of data, the Quarterly Workforce Indicators (QWI), is available for several states from 2001 through early 2005.[2]

The QWI data offer gross, not net, job flows and calculated weekly wages for both existing and new workers. This data set also includes

---

[1] As of summer 2006, only 20 states were fully participating in the program now known as Local Employment Dynamics.

[2] Full resourcing of these data may not occur until closer to the end of the decade.

job turnover. The data are parsed by industry (1-2 digit North American Industrial Classification System or Standard Industrial Classification), age category, gender, firm type (private or all firms), and county, metropolitan statistical area (MSA), or state level. The resulting series, although more aggregated than other LED data, offer the potential to explain a number of workforce dynamics not addressed by other publicly available data sources. A more complete description is contained in Table 6.1.

Little work on Wal-Mart specifically has been undertaken using the LED data. I examined the Local Employment Dynamics in six Pennsylvania counties in which Wal-Mart entered in 2002 (Hicks, 2005b). In addition to a preliminary estimate of net job impacts, this report revealed the degree of employment dynamics in retail that occurred both before and after the entrance of Wal-Mart. Figure 6.1 illustrates the magnitude of the retail turnover rates for both pre- and

TABLE 6.1
Quarterly Workforce Indicators Definitions

QWI Series	Description
Average monthly earnings	Total quarterly earnings of all full-quarter employees divided by the number of full-quarter employees, divided by 3
Average new hire earnings	Total quarterly earnings of all full-quarter new hires divided by the number of full-quarter new hires, divided by 3
Job creation	The number of new jobs that are created by either new area businesses or the expansion of employment by existing firms
Net job flows	The difference between current and previous employment at each business
New hires	Total number of accessions that were also not employed by that employer during the previous four quarters
Separations	Total number of workers who were employed by a business in the current quarter but not in the subsequent quarter
Turnover	Turnover rate = (1/2) * (accessions + separations) / employment stable jobs
Total employment	Total number of workers who were employed by the same employer in both the current and previous quarter

FIGURE 6.1   Retail Employment Turnover Rates in Select
Pennsylvania Counties

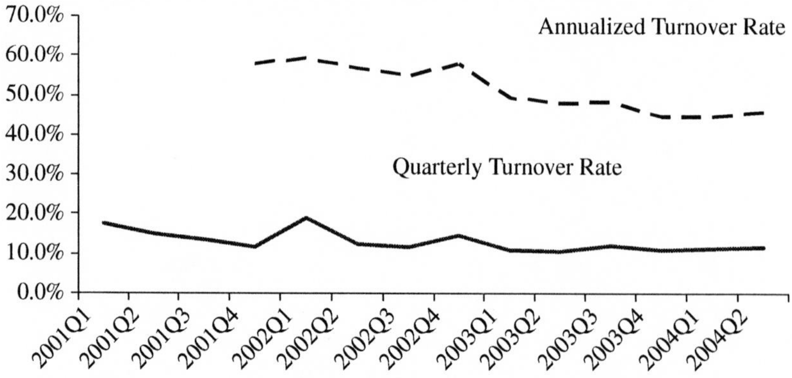

Source: Hicks, 2005b.

post-Wal-Mart periods. What is remarkable is the extreme magnitude of job flows during an annualized period from 2001 through 2004. Throughout this period, between 4.5 and 6 of every 10 jobs changed hands. This magnitude of employment flows is an important piece of data because it better demonstrates the role that the normal job-change pace plays in local economies.

At about the same time I published this report, the Wal-Mart Alliance for Reform Now (WARN) published a study of Wal-Mart turnover in Florida (WARN, 2005). They report a quarterly turnover in Florida's Wal-Mart's of 17.3% for the first quarter of 2005. The U.S. Census reported in the Local Employment Dynamics a turnover rate of 13.8% statewide in retail for the same quarter and 14.4% per quarter for the preceding three quarters. These data suggest that turnover in Wal-Mart is higher than for retail in general (as might be expected) but not dramatically so.

The aggregate local impact of Wal-Mart is embodied in the adjustment to overall employment and wages, not simply those in retail. Thus, to examine whether or not Wal-Mart is engaged in net job creation or destruction and job quality, as reflected in compensation, devolves on estimating its impact on the aggregate labor market.

THE AGGREGATE LABOR MARKET

To date, only three studies have examined the role of Wal-Mart in overall local employment. Their estimates range from no discernible impact to a small positive impact of Wal-Mart on aggregate employment. Using the basic framework described earlier, Neumark, Zhang, and Ciccarella (2005) estimate that aggregate local employment increases by roughly 2% following Wal-Mart's entrance. However, they find that average wages decline by roughly 5%, and that duration of exposure to Wal-Mart (especially in the southeastern United States) is correlated with higher wage reductions.

Using the same model described in the local retail impact section, Global Insight's 2005 study found that Wal-Mart was responsible for employment growth across all the counties it entered of roughly 0.15%. Focusing on local employment markets (in the Dallas–Fort Worth area), they found similar net employment gains (mostly concentrated in the retail sector) associated with the presence of Wal-Mart.

Both studies have been criticized. Neumark et al. have been challenged on their choice of instrument in the popular media, but their instrument is receiving considerable attention by economic researchers. The Global Insight study has also received considerable criticism from Bernstein, Bivens, and Dube (2006), who, in an extensive sensitivity analysis of its findings, found that it is sensitive to differing specifications. Importantly, the specification of the Global Insight model was overseen by senior economists across the political spectrum. This oversight committee required that the model be constructed before data collection. So it may be fairly concluded that if Bernstein, Bivens, and Dube are correct, the sensitivity of the model is clearly not the result of intentional manipulation by Global Insight's well-regarded researchers. However, their findings could still be incorrect, and the Bernstein, Bivens, and Dube argument is quite strong.

The most recent distinct study of Wal-Mart's aggregate impact evaluates the role of the retailer on entrepreneurial activity and small business. Professor Russell Sobel and Andrea Dean (2006) estimate Wal-Mart's impact using a model that accounts for geographic interactions (a spatial autoregressive model) and controls for variables that earlier research has indicated influences entrepreneurship. This nationwide model specifies the following relationship:

$$Y = f(\% \ urban, \text{age, poverty, income, } \% \text{ non-white,}$$
$$\text{land area, college, } \% \text{ male}) \qquad (6.1)$$

to which they add the spatial components to account for cross-border effects and spatial autocorrelation, which are not depicted in the equation. This procedure provides a correction for spatially related bias, which has not been treated as extensively in the Wal-Mart literature as is common in most regional economic studies. They test the impact of Wal-Mart through two variables: a count of stores in states and a store growth rate at the state level. Testing this model on three different treatment areas—entrepreneurs (firms with no employees), firms with one to four workers, and firms with five to nine workers—they find no long-run impact of Wal-Mart on employment in these firm size ranges.

This study performs a cross-sectional analysis using more recent data (1995–2003) to provide growth rate estimates. Further, these authors detail the process of Joseph Schumpeter's "creative destruction," in which new innovations lead to economic growth. Perhaps most interestingly, they extend previous studies' estimates of Wal-Mart–induced job losses to the aggregate economy (only Neumark, Zhang, and Ciccarella, 2005, and the Global Insight study had previously reported economy-wide impacts). Sobel and Dean provide an especially strong empirical critique of Stone's 1997 and earlier studies on Wal-Mart in Iowa. By using the reported firm losses from Stone's studies, Sobel and Dean report that the extrapolated total impact of Wal-Mart on Iowa would be a reduction of 11.3% of all businesses. Further, they calculate Stone's estimated impact of Wal-Mart on small business to be almost one third that of small business (those with one to four employees) in the state. Reporting actual firm data from the County Business Patterns data set, they indicate that, in contrast to Stone's estimate, Iowa's growth rate of small business was about 1.62% during the period that Stone examined Wal-Mart. This is a healthy growth rate, quite at odds with Stone's analysis and very close to my estimates presented in an earlier chapter.

Clearly, the estimates of Wal-Mart aggregate effect locally vary considerably across these studies. One possible explanation for these divergent findings is that the studies are performed at the national level at very different time periods. Neumark et al. ended their sample in 1995, Global Insight's examination continued through 2004, whereas Sobel and Dean reviewed more recent years only. All of these choices were made for good technical reasons; they are not simply arbitrary periods selected to lend confusion to the question. Further, these studies make very different assumptions about endogeneity and spatial dependence. Neumark et al. provide a relatively brief treatment of spatial interdependence (and illustrate that this approach has little overall effect on their estimates) but spend considerable effort treating entrance endogeneity. This latter process also leads the authors to eliminate from their data counties that did not experience a Wal-Mart entrance in a portion of their modeling. Global Insight tested for endogeneity in the entrance decision (as did Franklin, 2001, and Hicks and Wilburn, 2001) and did not model spatial interdependence. Sobel and Dean use the evidence from the earlier studies on entrance endogeneity but extensively model spatial interdependence. None of the foregoing comments should be viewed as criticism of these studies. This is simply how research is performed, with careful attention to details and methodology.

In the end, the level of analysis does not fully answer the question of a nationwide Wal-Mart effect. As I argued for the retail sector, I believe the evidence more strongly suggests that the impact varies locally in ways that argue against nationwide estimates. To further that argument, I will revisit Iowa and the impact Wal-Mart has had on its aggregate employment.

Using data from the Regional Economic Information System on employment and wages combined with data on retail pull factors (retail market size) from Iowa State University's Office of Social and Economic Trend Analysis, I construct a basic model of Wal-Mart's impact on aggregate employment and wages. The model tests both total county

employment and the average wage per job as reported in the Regional
Economic Information System. I use the standard Wal-Mart count data
from the data releases discussed earlier. To this, I add data on the pull
factor for retail trade as an instrument to account for the endogeneity of
Wal-Mart's entrance decision. The pull factor for retail trade is calculated as

$$PF = \frac{RS_i / Pop_i}{\sum_{i=1}^{n} RS_i / Pop_i} \tag{6.2}$$

which is the ratio of per capita retail sales compared with the average
per capita retail sales across the state. Thus, if residents from each
county bought all their retail goods from within a county and spent
the same amount on retail goods, the pull factor would be 1 for all
counties. As Figure 6.2 illustrates, the retail pull factor has exhibited
some decline, on average, but there has been, at least during Wal-Mart's
initial period of entrance (in the 1980s), an increased concentration
of retail sales as shown by the increasing maximum and declining
mean and minimum pull factors.

I instrument the entrance of Wal-Mart, positing that the retail pull
factor suggested location decisions for Wal-Mart in Iowa. This choice

FIGURE 6.2   Iowa's Retail Pull Factor

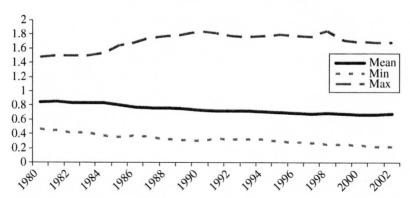

of instrument was motivated by a December 6, 2005, WUNC (North Carolina public radio) broadcast of "The State of Things," featuring Glen Wilkins, community affairs manager for the southeast region of Wal-Mart. In this broadcast, Wilkins identified market size as a location choice consideration (see Hicks, 2006c, for the full description). Similarly, Graff (1998) suggests that location decisions for supercenters are expressly linked to mid-sized towns in less densely populated areas proximal to other Wal-Mart stores (where the firm is already known). This is clearly linked to the retail pull factors and has appeared as an instrument choice in an earlier section (and supported by empirics in my brief analysis of Wal-Mart's entrance decision). Thus, the identification strategy I use is a straightforward element of what is likely to have been Wal-Mart's strategy for choosing locations within Iowa. This is one other method of getting at the elusive concern over the way Wal-Mart's location patterns influence any subsequent statistical estimate of its impact.

The basic structure of the model is then a simple estimate of the effect Wal-Mart has on employment and average wage per job in Iowa. Unfortunately, both the average wage per job and the total employment in Iowa from 1980 through 2002 (corresponding to the available pull factor data) appear to be nonstationary.[3] This necessitates estimating these impacts on annual changes, not in levels. I thus have

$$\Delta Y = \beta^0 + \beta^1(WM_{i,t}) + \delta\phi_{t-1} + e_{i,t} \qquad (6.3)$$

where the change in the variable under consideration (employment or average wage per job) is a function of a common intercept, a Wal-Mart presence / count variable, and a one-period autoregressive value. The error term, e, is assumed iid $\longrightarrow N(0,\sigma)$, a white noise term. In a second

---

[3] Nonstationarity means that these variables are nonmean reverting, or exhibiting a trend. Using them directly in the estimation will lead to a spurious regression. I determined that they were nonstationary by using both the augmented Dickey-Fuller and alternative tests in a common sample. The variables are strongly stationary in their first difference (year-to-year change) and base the estimates on these data.

specification, I use a presence / persistence measurement, which takes the value 0 when no Wal-Mart is present and is a count of years since opening when there is a presence of a Wal-Mart. This presence / persistence measure is similar to that used by Neumark et al. (2005). I adjusted the nominal real wage per job using the national consumer price index, all urban consumers. Both dependent variables were also expressed in natural logarithm form for ease of interpretation.[4] Results appear in Table 6.2.

TABLE 6.2
Wal-Mart's Impact on Iowa's Aggregate Labor Markets

	Employment		Average Wage per Job	
	Presence	Presence / Persistence	Presence	Presence / Persistence
Intercept	0.001208	0.002***	0.004012***	0.006012***
	(1.34)	(2.84)	(5.16)	(9.38)
Wal-Mart	0.009094***	0.000185**	0.015087***	0.00022***
	(4.32)	(2.52)	(8.10)	(4.65)
Autoregression	0.193133***	0.19***	0.042970***	0.070***
$(t-1)$	(7.98)	(8.15)	(7.98)	(2.76)
Adjusted R^2	0.13	0.12	0.05	0.01
Durbin-Watson (panel)	1.85	1.85	1.99	1.98
Observations	2277	2277	2277	2277

Note. The Durbin-Watson panel statistic reported is derived from Bhargava, Franzini, and Narendranathan (1982). I whitewashed the variance matrix using a version of White's (1980) heteroscedastic consistent variance–covariance matrix derived from Driscoll and Kraay (1998). As is common, I have not reported the values of the cross-sectional fixed-effects coefficients to preserve space.

***$p = 0.01$. **$p = 0.05$.

---

[4] The natural logarithm of the dependent variables translates the interpretation of the coefficient into percent changes. The magnitude and direction of the estimated impact are roughly the same for tests in actual changes and in the natural logs of the changes. Also I tested a fixed-effects model on these data, which results in roughly comparable impacts assuming that even with first differenced dependent variables there are some county-specific factors that do not vary.

These results strongly suggest that Wal-Mart played a role in the aggregate economies in the counties in which they located. The presence of each Wal-Mart in a county increased total employment by just under 1%, or roughly 255 jobs per county. This is about half of the impact estimates by Neumark, Zhang, and Ciccarella (2005), who found that total employment in Wal-Mart counties rose by roughly 2%. These estimates show an increase in the average wage per job of roughly 1.5% for each new Wal-Mart. This differs from both the Neumark et al. results and those from Global Insight's analysis of wage impacts, both of which found small reductions in wages in their national samples.

Importantly, both estimates are sensitive to the method of counting Wal-Mart presence. When I use the presence / persistence measure, the statistical reliability of the estimate is preserved but the magnitude of the effect on both wages and employment becomes economically irrelevant at roughly five jobs per county.[5]

In summary, there remains some disagreement over the size of Wal-Mart's impact on the aggregate local economy but not the direction. No estimates of employment impacts find a net decline in jobs. The studies reviewed previously find that the impacts range from very small (or with weak statistical reliability) to modest, but non-trivial, increases of as much as 2%. That perhaps five major studies (including the results presented previously) suggest Wal-Mart is associated with net employment increases rises to the level of a robust conclusion that Wal-Mart is creating, not destroying, jobs in the aggregate local economy. This is not, however, the whole story on aggregate employment.

The issue of job quality is not so clear. The results of earlier studies provide mixed findings of small positive and small negative impacts on wages (measured in various ways). Given these findings, it seems that an appropriately cautious interpretation of the evidence would be that Wal-Mart is having no substantive effect on wages in local

---

[5] Interestingly, Goetz and Swaminathan (2006) report a roughly similarly small impact on county-level poverty rates because of Wal-Mart presence.

communities in which they locate. Further, the way we measure jobs in the aggregate data does not clearly distinguish between full-and part-time employment. In addition, if we knew with certainty these distinctions, it still would not be clear whether any resulting impact was good or bad from a policy perspective. Although there are undoubtedly many workers in part-time jobs who would like full-time jobs, the vast majority do not, and the growth of part-time employment may well indicate more flexible labor markets. I discuss this more in the chapter on social impacts.

Again, it is clear that Wal-Mart is associated with net employment growth in the counties it enters, but less clear is by how much and what type of job. Further, the mechanism by which this empirically observed job growth occurs has not been clearly described. In the end, though, much of the concern about Wal-Mart surrounds its impact on nonlocal employment because of its sourcing of manufacturing goods from lower cost suppliers.

WAL-MART AND MANUFACTURING

Much popular interest has developed regarding Wal-Mart's role in altering the level of global trade. Conference publications such as Professor Nelson Lichtenstein's collection of essays *Wal-Mart: The Face of 21st Century Capitalism* and popular books such as Charles Fishman's (2006) *The Wal-Mart Effect* describe a purported shift in labor and goods markets attributable to this retailer. There is also a strong argument that Wal-Mart is leading overall productivity growth through their practices. Hoopes (2006) is a particularly good example (cited in Lichtenstein, 2006). Although evaluating these critiques and accomplishments of Wal-Mart is well outside the scope of this work, it is useful to consider some of the broad characterizations of the role the retailer has played in sectors beyond retail in the United States.

The economic research on the role of retail in manufacturing is limited to a very fine study by Basker and Van (2005), which provides a theoretical model of Wal-Mart's role in fostering import growth.[6] The authors provide a model in which a retail firm enjoys two types of economies of scale: firm level and import level. In this model, the commonly understood economies of scale for the firm interact with reduced per unit costs associated with increasing experience importing goods to create, in essence, a cost advantage for a firm. Along with a description of some of the general media descriptions of this process, Basker and Van outline how the mechanism has worked through a case study of Wal-Mart. They argue that it is this combination that motivated Wal-Mart to shift focus from domestic suppliers to imports in the mid-1990s.[7]

Unlike the work in sociology offered in Lichtenstein (2006) or the popular media (Fishman, 2006), Basker and Van do not suggest that this process involves long-term negative consequences, nor do they suggest that it is Wal-Mart specifically that generates this phenomenon. They are careful to identify supplier techniques (such as RFID technology) that stimulate productivity. This distinction regarding the net benefit of trade is important, but explaining it requires a divergence into the political economy of international trade.

Although the popular debate regarding free trade is outside the scope of this book, it is useful to appreciate the dimensions of the argument. Virtually all economists hold that free trade is almost universally beneficial to economies. This belief is embodied in theoretical literature dating to the late 18th century to the present. It is also embodied in literally thousands of empirical studies. It is perhaps worth noting that economists across the political spectrum, from Milton Friedman to Paul Krugman, are advocates of free trade. Further, it is likely that no occupation is as subject to the competitive forces of free trade as

---

[6] Basker (2005a) estimated Wal-Mart's impact on local manufacturing as a calibration tool for her endogeneity model, assuming that local Wal-Marts and local manufacturing are unrelated. She reported no relationship between local manufacturing and Wal-Mart as expected.

[7] This report was unfairly criticized in the popular media as presenting only the possibility that Wal-Mart stimulated imports from China. Basker and Van's paper is an important mechanism for understanding how trade and economies of scale interact to promote international trade.

academia. These economists who are proponents of free trade are far more likely to have their employment challenged by imports (professors from other countries) than are manufacturing workers in the United States.

Much of the debate over trade is also played out in media circles. Although there are free trade advocates in the media, the bulk of popular publications have treated imports as a persistent threat through much of the history of the republic. The persistence of this critique is likely linked to the fact that the inevitable loss of local firms through the dynamics of trade appears to illustrate the negative effects of trade on a local economy. The benefits, although much greater on the whole, are far less obvious to participants in a local economy. It is the local effects of major firm relocations that capture attention, not the subtle, persistent, and much larger beneficial effects of trade.

In the end, this work is not the place for an extensive political economy discourse on trade. Rather it is a book about Wal-Mart's local impact. Among the potential impacts of Wal-Mart are the losses of manufacturing employment in sectors that supply the retailer. These would most likely be the nondurable goods manufacturers (although some durable goods are also sold at Wal-Mart stores). Wal-Mart reports its sales by categories that may be loosely linked to the manufacturing sector, and from these data it is clear much is manufactured. See Table 6.3.

Happily there are robust statistics on manufacturing that can enlighten the debate. To evaluate fairly criticism of Wal-Mart's effect on manufacturing, it is useful to understand what has actually happened to domestic manufacturing in recent years. Fortunately, these data are available for both durable and nondurable goods manufacturers who produce the types of goods Wal-Mart sells. The following graph illustrates the monthly sales in both consumer durable and nondurable goods, with inflation adjusted to 2005 constant dollars. See Figure 6.3.

These data clearly show that monthly shipments of consumer non-durables experienced only seasonal declines, with a very pronounced growth through the first half of 2006 in what will almost certainly prove a record year. Consumer durables shipments peaked on the eve of the last recession but have not experienced a broad decline, as

TABLE 6.3

Wal-Mart Sales by Categories

Category	Percent of Sales
Grocery, candy, and tobacco products	28
Hard goods	19
Soft goods and domestics	16
Pharmaceuticals	9
Electronics	9
Health and beauty aids	7
Sporting goods	6
Stationery and books	3
Others (photo, jewelry, and shoes)	3

Source: Wal-Mart form 10-K as reported by Brenner, Eidlin, and Candaele (2006).

FIGURE 6.3   U.S. Shipments of Consumer Goods, 1992–2006

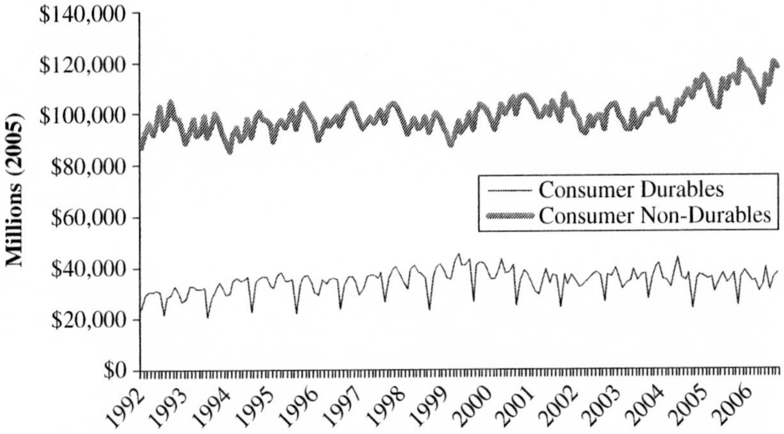

suggested by the popular media. Even accounting for potential data errors (erroneously counting foreign manufacturing as domestic production), these data provide no evidence that the domestic manufacturing industry is in decline, much less that Wal-Mart is to blame. However, there is an underlying reason why so many commentators

FIGURE 6.4   Manufacturing Employment in the United States (in thousands)

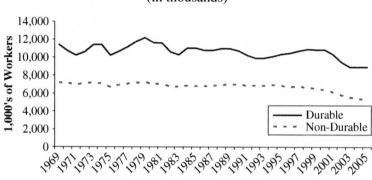

Source: Bureau of Labor Statistics.

in the popular media worry about domestic manufacturing, and that is the static or declining employment the industry has experienced. See Figure 6.4.

From these data, it is clear that no stark employment declines are occurring in the manufacturing sectors, although there is obviously a declining trend. From these data, it is also clear that the share of manufacturing employment in the United States is declining and has been since the 1960s as the total workforce grew. Furthermore, although there have been recent declines in employment that are modestly below the 50-year range, actual production of goods in the United States remains near record levels (and will almost certainly set a new record in 2006 or 2007).

The manufacturing employment declines apparent in these data and very obvious in anecdote demand attention from researchers. In addition to Basker and Van's analysis, the dominant explanations for the decline in manufacturing employment in recent years are summarized by the Congressional Budget Office (CBO; Brauer, 2004). The CBO argues, and I believe most economists agree, that the dominant affect on domestic manufacturing is productivity growth. Simply, through technological and process improvement (and perhaps an aging, more effective workforce) U.S. firms can do more with fewer workers. Far from being an unfortunate predicate of joblessness, productivity growth is the sole source of economic growth that improves individual standards of living. Second, the decline in manufacturing is a statistical anomaly. When we measure employment in an industry in these data, the Bureau of Labor Statistics counts all workers (e.g., production, health and safety, transport) within the classification of the firm that employs them. Thus, if firms are outsourcing nonproduction workers to other firms (e.g., contract health and safety, maintenance, human resources), this is counted as a decline in the manufacturing industry, even if more jobs overall are created.

The CBO study also suggests that the manufacturing industry may be less inclined to hire new workers as demand increases, and that demand for some types of manufactured goods might be declining as consumers' tastes shift toward other items (e.g., yoga lessons and downloadable music). Finally, the CBO discusses the issue of foreign trade, most especially with China. They provide data on the trade deficit with China (which is today equal to about a month's worth of nondurable manufacturing in the United States). Here the authors note that the majority of the trade balance changes between the United States and China are due to a shifting of U.S. purchases from other Asian countries to China. Josh Bivens, an economist at the Economic Policy Institute (EPI), disagreed with this CBO report and attributes a little more than a third of domestic job losses in manufacturing to rising imports (Bivens, 2004).[8] He argues that U.S. demand has not shifted away from manufacturing goods, and that the level of productivity growth is insufficient to account for the total job loss.

Both reports, which are really just policy briefs, omit some explanation of the problems as space requires. Nevertheless, I am not as sanguine as the CBO report nor as alarmed by the EPI author. However, faced with record high levels of production and declining employment

---

[8] This is the same author who, with Bernstein and Dube, provided a strong critique of the Global Insight report.

in manufacturing, both authors admit (albeit implicitly for one) that the productivity to cost ratio of much of the U.S. manufacturing industry pushed production elsewhere. This effect is particularly hard felt by low-skilled U.S. workers (e.g., in textile manufacturing). Bivens recommends an activist devaluation of the U.S. dollar, which in the end seems an odd mechanism by which to aid low-skilled workers, who will face higher prices for consumer goods. The CBO is silent on policy recommendations. Bivens' work provides a good decomposition of employment flows (although his extrapolated employment figures are based on assumptions that would tend to inflate them, albeit very modestly). Bivens' greatest flaw is in his failure to even acknowledge the very real statistical artifact that the earlier CBO study suggests is a primary culprit of manufacturing job losses.

In the end, Wal-Mart cannot be held to task for the decline in U.S. manufacturing for the simple reason that U.S. manufacturing is not really in decline. While anecdotal characterizations of Wal-Mart's role in closing U.S. manufacturing plants are entertaining, any extrapolation to the aggregate economy faces daunting counterfactual data.[9]

If casting doubt on the criticism of Wal-Mart's impact on U.S. manufacturing is as simple as illustrating actual employment, is it as easy to discount those who claim Wal-Mart's practices are responsible for aggregate growth through efficiencies in the supply chain? The short answer here is that the evidence in support of those claiming Wal-Mart is responsible for the productivity explosion in recent years is far more compelling. At first, the simple data on productivity in manufacturing speak strongly to those who argue that productivity is growing at an increasing rate. See Figure 6.5.

---

[9] My favorite stories from Fishman's book are Levi's, which I discuss later, and Huffy Bicycle Company. The purported supplier squeeze is characterized by Fishman as the cause of Huffy's recent bankruptcy. Bankruptcy courts and the Security and Exchange Commission are not quite so cavalier with the facts, and both attribute Huffy's bankruptcy to a corporate financial scandal. This revelation wouldn't have made them quite as innocent a victim of Wal-Mart as he preferred, so the book made no mention of this despite the fact that the bankruptcy happened long before the book was published.

FIGURE 6.5   Output Per Hour Index and Compensation Index,
U.S. Manufacturing

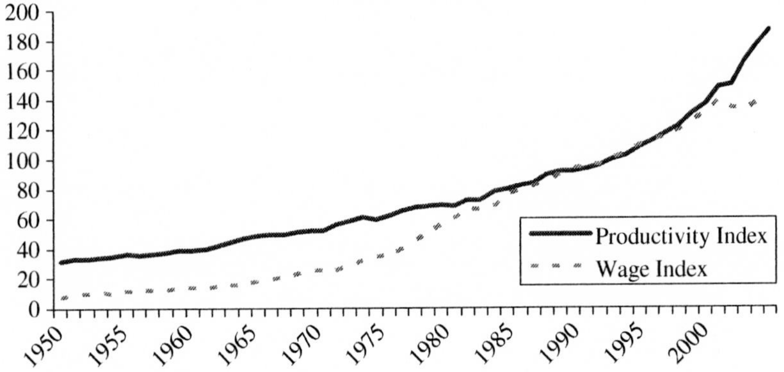

Source: Bureau of Labor Statistics.

These data present evidence that the output per hour worked by U.S. manufacturing employees has seen a fairly sharp increase in its rate of growth in the recent decade. The compensation index, which counts wages and some other fringe benefits, has grown also, though having stagnated somewhat during the recent recession. It is thus far more difficult to discount the popular argument in favor of Wal-Mart's contribution to productivity growth.

In addition to these data, at least two research teams have found some significant contribution of retail chains (implicitly Wal-Mart) to overall retail and wholesale productivity through the use of information technology (Klimek, Jarmin, and Doms, 2002; McKinsey Global Institute, 2002). The latter study attributes a quarter of U.S. total productivity growth to that in the retail sector, which was clearly influenced by Wal-Mart.

There are many other links between Wal-Mart and the manufacturing sector. These include not only the supply chain to consumers but also the role of Wal-Mart as an end consumer of information technology, transportation goods, warehousing, and other facilities. However, I find the argument that Wal-Mart is responsible for significant aggregate impacts on manufacturing less than persuasive. And despite characterizations in books that herald and criticize Wal-Mart, the linkage between local manufacturing jobs and wages and the presence of a local Wal-Mart lacks a transmission mechanism worthy of a statistical test.[10]

However, the anecdotal reports in the popular media and many books (especially Fishman, 2006) provide stories of Wal-Mart's high-stakes bargaining with suppliers. I have even heard them second-hand. A colleague, Dr. Mark Burton, now at the University of Tennessee, while on a domestic airline flight struck up a conversation with a fellow passenger, a representative of a well-known candy company who had just returned from a sales trip to Bentonville. Mark related the story to me that, after a midflight cocktail or two, the man began to weep as he shared with him the financial pain of his lost commission on the new sales. It is indeed hard not to feel uncomfortable about Wal-Mart when you hear stories such as this, but then how many of us would be equally moved if competition required our realtor to reduce her commission a point or two on the sale of our house?

WAL-MART'S PROFITS: A SUPPLIER COMPARISON

Wal-Mart is a profitable company, and its size offers profit figures that are large, even to economists used to seeing weapons systems cost data. For example, per store profits in 2005 were over $9.2 million. However, it is not total profits that ultimately matter but the profit rate of a business. Other factors matter in securing investment dollars for expansion (such as return on assets), but profit rates are the signal for capital investment. Profit rates vary across industries and markets, and two factors—risk and competition—provide the bulk of explanation for why this variation occurs. Higher risk demands higher rates of profit, and less competition results in higher profit rates. Risk is usually attributed to variation in the rate of return to assets,

---

[10] In fact, Emek Basker (2005) used the absence of the local manufacturing / Wal-Mart linkage to test her model for a spurious correlation. She found no impacts between local manufacturing and Wal-Mart.

whereas competition is the presence (or threatened presence) of firms actually competing for customers in local markets. For Wal-Mart, competition occurs at the local retail market, and it's the presence (or threat) of local competition that influences Wal-Mart's pricing decisions and ultimately its profit rate. Data on profits are available for public firms and reported by Wal-Mart through their annual reports to shareholders and the Security and Exchange Commission. From these I calculated their profit rate. See Figure 6.6.

These data are remarkably similar to data on chain stores available from the 1930s. As a representative example, I adapt a chart from Nichols' (1940) history of chain stores (Figure 6.7).

Although this analysis from the 1930s is dated in some respects, most particularly in the proportion of state and federal taxes out of total income, it is interesting that the reported profit rate is in line with Wal-Mart's historical 3% to 4.3% since 1968.

Existing analysis of the supplier impact of Wal-Mart operations is limited to private consulting reports, the popular media, and one article from *Journal of Retailing* (Bloom and Perry, 2001). The consulting reports, which are largely unavailable for review, and the popular media report that suppliers face annual requirements from Wal-Mart

FIGURE 6.6   Wal-Mart's Profit Rate, 1968–2005

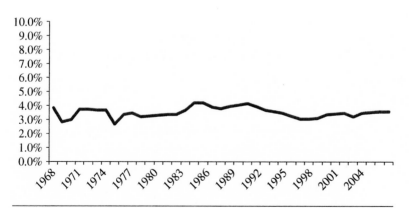

Source: Wal-Mart annual reports, various years.

FIGURE 6.7   Chain Store Expenses

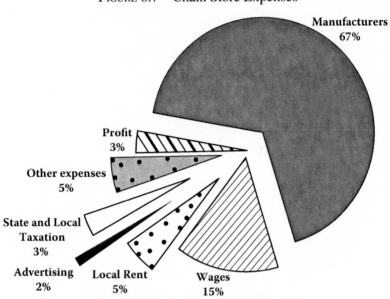

Source: Nichols, 1940, p. 48.

to either reduce price or increase quality. This is the famous "plus one" rule.[11]

Although the descriptions of the process are fairly similar across the media and popular work, the interpretations of the benefits of this process are not uniform. For example, Fishman (2006) centers his criticism of Wal-Mart on the reduced profits of suppliers and the incipient harm that this generates for the aggregate economy. Petrovic and Hamilton (2006) describe the issue well in a collection of articles that span both academic and popular writing:

> Partnering with Wal-Mart holds both the promise of reaching major global markets with minimal advertising and promotional outlays, and the danger of adapting

---

[11] Descriptions of this appear in both Fishman (2006) and Petrovic and Hamilton (2006).

one's business model to the retailer's strict demands
only to find out that the resulting lowered profit margins
and the efficiency pressure are more than one's organizational capacities can bear ... The fact that more than
five hundred large vendors have established permanent
sales offices near Wal-Mart's Bentonville headquarters,
and that tens of thousands of global suppliers attend
its global purchase fairs, shows that many manufacturers consider the prospect of becoming a Wal-Mart
partner worth the gamble. (Petrovic and Hamilton,
2006, p. 131, in Lichtenstein, 2006)

Fishman (2006) details the history of several companies whose
dealings with Wal-Mart purportedly led to their demise. His analysis
is difficult to evaluate because most of the companies on which he
reports are private or were acquired by other firms (e.g., Lovable Apparel
and Vlasic). For these firms the data are simply unavailable. Huffy
Bicycle Company, which Fishman described in some length, stopped
manufacturing in the United States in the 1990s but suffered bankruptcy
because of financial irregularities.[12] Throughout this period, it continued to sell bikes through Wal-Mart and Kmart.

Fishman's story of Levi Strauss & Company's challenges in supplying
Wal-Mart provides a good comparison because Levi Strauss provides
financial data through filings with the Securities and Exchange Commission. Reporting on 2005's profits compared with recent years labeled
"disappointing," the textile manufacturer reported profits of 6.1% in
2002 and 14.3% in 2005. Thus, in Levi Strauss' bad year, it enjoyed
profit rates almost twice that of Wal-Mart for the same year. And in
2005 Levi Strauss reported a profit rate more than fourfold higher
than Wal-Mart. See Figure 6.8.

Fishman (2006) develops this point to argue that Wal-Mart's effect
on markets results in both lower profit rates for suppliers, and thus

---

[12] The irregularities in reporting continue to plague the company, as evidenced in
"Huffy Faces 2 Class Action Lawsuits," *Dayton Business Journal,* January 25,
2005.

FIGURE 6.8   Profit Rates for Wal-Mart and Levi Strauss

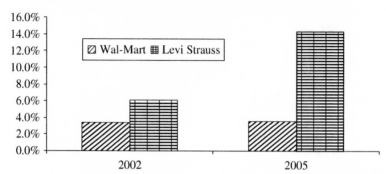

their quest to seek lower production costs, in part through displacement of domestic manufacturing. Both Fishman and a 2005 study from the AFL-CIO report job losses among manufacturing firms. The AFL-CIO report is particularly interesting in that it targets one state (Ohio) and traces the movement of factories out of the state. The real causal linkage to Wal-Mart is meaningless, but the report is an interesting description of the gross job flows in manufacturing, even if it intentionally misses any net impacts.

There can be little doubt that firms suffering declining profits experience incentives to cut costs. However, both the aggregate manufacturing data (employment and output) offer no evidence that U.S. manufacturing is in decline, much less that Wal-Mart is a contributor. Further, the relative profit rate of Wal-Mart and Levi Strauss illustrates the folly of lamenting the influence of the profit motives impact on the U.S. economy. Throughout the narrative period described by Fishman, Levi Strauss enjoyed greater profit rates than did Wal-Mart. More directly, assuming that Wal-Mart's profits are distributed evenly across their product lines, more of the sales price of Levi's signature jeans purchased at Wal-Mart finally ends up as profit with the owners of Levi Strauss than the stockholders of Wal-Mart.

This comparison is not an isolated case. Bloom and Perry (2001) perform a very detailed and useful comparison of supplier profitability. They examine dominant Wal-Mart suppliers, firms that are affiliated with other retail firms, and firms that don't have a dominant supply chain relationship with a single firm, including, respectively, 78, 2,835, and 3,745 firms in each category. They construct models, which are specified as

$$Z(P) = f(WM, \text{MarketShare, Interaction, Scale})   \tag{6.4}$$

where the deviation of a firm's profit from the industry average (the firms z score of profits) is a function of their supplier relationship, their market share, a variable that interacts these (their multiplicative product), and a logarithmic measure of the firms size to account for scale economies.

Bloom and Perry carefully test this model on total profits on data from each category and compare the size of the impact of Wal-Mart. Although they thoroughly describe the potential for data inaccuracies that may cloud their results, they do find that, when controlling for other factors in their model, total profits may be lower for Wal-Mart's suppliers. Fishman reports this study and these findings in his book. Among the findings that Fishman does not report, however, is that Bloom and Perry also compared suppliers with a Wal-Mart relationship with firms that have a relationship to other retailers. They find that "Wal-Mart may offer a better relationship [to suppliers] than its smaller retail competitors. The market share and the interaction market share coefficients are superior for the comparison of suppliers to *other* retailers to unaffiliated suppliers" (Bloom and Perry, 2001, p. 390). In addition, despite the authors' very cautious explanation of the potential data anomalies in their work, they go on to say

> It may also be the case that Wal-Mart simply does a better job of forging relationships that permit its suppliers to be more efficient when they get large. Or, larger-share suppliers that distribute primarily through retailers other than Wal-Mart may be at a disadvantage and perform poorly when forced to compete with larger-share rivals that have strong Wal-Mart connections. (Bloom and Perry, 2001, p. 390)

This is hardly the story that Fishman tells.

The excellent work by Bloom and Perry also yields another insight. Although they directly analyzed the impact of supply relationships, market size, and scale economies on profit deviations from the industry norm, they also report profit rates. Again, it is profit rates that provide a comparison of the average markup above costs for each unit sold. Importantly, profit rates vary by industry for a variety of factors (including risk), so deviation of profit rates across industries (as with my previous comparison of Wal-Mart and Levi Strauss) neglects some important issues. However, it does clearly illustrate how much of each dollar spent by the consumer finally rests with the firm's owners. Direct comparison of Bloom and Perry's data across the three supply relationships clearly shows that Wal-Mart's suppliers enjoy greater profit rates than do firms with supply relationships with competing retailers and unaffiliated suppliers. They also have higher market shares. And, perhaps more importantly from the standpoint of the popular literature, the profit rate and market share of Wal-Mart were considerably lower than those of its suppliers in 1994. See Table 6.4.

Further, Fishman (2006) characterizes Bloom and Perry's excellent study as a condemnation of Wal-Mart's supplier relationships. It is not. Indeed, the conclusion is considerably more sanguine. They end with

> Further, our data suggest that developing a relationship with Wal-Mart could lead to a boom rather than a bust for the astute manufacturer, once a certain market share is reached. Large-share suppliers to Wal-Mart extract more profits from their market share than do their counterparts without such a relationship. This raises another question of interest. Could Wal-Mart leave this money on the table deliberately in order to attract better suppliers? (Bloom and Perry, 2001, p. 391)

There can be little doubt that that the preference of a sufficient number of suppliers is to engage in business with Wal-Mart. There is also anecdotal evidence, reported selectively by Fishman and others (e.g., Bianco, 2006), to suggest that engaging in a supply relationship with

TABLE 6.4

Wal-Mart Supplier Relationship and Wal-Mart Stores Comparison (1994)

	Supply Relationship			Wal-Mart Stores
	Wal-Mart	Other Retail	Unaffiliated	
Income (millions)	366.93	419.79	884.15	67,344
Net income (millions)	42.14	34.12	95.24	2,333
Profit rate	11.48%	8.13%	10.77%	3.5%
Market share	14%	10%	13%	7%
No. firms	78	2,853	3,745	1

Source: Bloom and Perry, 2001; Wal-Mart 2004 Annual Report.

Wal-Mart is demanding. It is also profitable, and the evidence reported here strongly suggests that supplying Wal-Mart yields a profit rate greater than actually being Wal-Mart. This debate is informed by a very good study by Perry and Bloom (2001), whose work is not, as characterized by Fishman, an inconclusive piece of analysis. It is, rather, a detailed, clever, and highly useful treatment of the supplier–retailer relationship. When objectively examined, its results clarify the role of Wal-Mart (at least during its period of greatest growth) in satisfying supplier relationships. The work is especially helpful to local policymakers concerned with the impact of Wal-Mart on firms that produce the goods Wal-Mart sells.

A very interesting theoretical economics study by Zhiqi Chen uses a game theoretic approach to assess the relationship between retailers and their suppliers. This report evaluates the countervailing power hypothesis argued by the well-known economist John Kenneth Galbraith. The countervailing power hypothesis was developed in the 1950s and was used to describe the rise in power of A&P, Sears, and other larger retail firms. The author concludes that the rise in "countervailing power" by retailers because of their size can result in lower consumer prices but only if there is a competitive fringe of smaller retailers (Chen, 2003). Consumers should view this as a happy circumstance. In addition, the reduction in supplier profits generated by

Wal-Mart (and other large retailers) is essentially a wealth transfer from stockholders of these manufacturing firms to the families who shop at Wal-Mart.

The effect noted by observers of Wal-Mart suppliers is not a new phenomenon, as many suggest. The difficulty that such firms as Levi Strauss has experienced is not a Wal-Mart effect but instead has an older pedigree. It is likely that the experiences with suppliers chronicled in the popular media are a lament. What these firms are experiencing is the loss of what Nobel Laureate John Hicks observes as the best of all monopoly profits: a quiet life.

WAL-MART AND LAND VALUE

There are many studies on the retail property values, including at least one that noted the increased attractiveness of retail property, even in the face of increasing big-box competition (Wheaton and Torto, 1995). Also, in two working papers providing theoretical depictions of Wal-Mart's effects and choices of location with respect to prices, Bradley Curs, Mark Stater, and Michael Visser (2004; 2005) make some very tentative predictions concerning Wal-Mart's impact on land prices and their optimal choice of locations. As with studies by Panle Jia (2006) and Thomas Holmes (2006), the results of their work are not yet finalized as of this writing.

In a paper in the *Atlantic Economic Journal* (Hicks, 2007), which is a derivative of a paper I presented at the 2005 Global Insight Wal-Mart conference, I estimate Wal-Mart's impact on commercial property values in Ohio. I find that Wal-Mart has a significant impact on commercial property values—by as much as 10% in a rural county— most likely simply because of the increased value of the retailer and its tenant stores. My intent in this report was to estimate property tax increases, not valuation adjustments, and this finding was simply a step toward that end.

A direct analysis of Wal-Mart's impact on home values was performed in 2006 by Melvin Corlija, Emilian Siman, and Michael Finke, three researchers at the University of Missouri–Columbia.

They used a well-known method for nonmarket valuation. The hedonic pricing model they use estimates the sale price of a house based on known house and lot characteristics, zoning and tax characteristics, and proximity to a Wal-Mart. The model takes the form

$$\text{House Price} = f(\text{L,H,}WM) \tag{6.5}$$

with such measures as lot size, square footage of house, presence of a pool, and the distance and square distance to Wal-Mart, the latter to account for a nonlinearity in the impact. They find that Wal-Mart influences home prices through an inverted U-shaped curve as distance from the store increases. Homes that are close to Wal-Mart increase in value, all else being equal, as their distance from Wal-Mart increases. However, at some point, this effect reverses and being farther away from a Wal-Mart actually reduces home values, holding other characteristics unchanged. This type of finding is very consistent with other hedonic pricing studies of community amenities such as parks. Their model performed well, and given its broad acceptance in such arenas as environmental economics and real estate research, these authors present an important finding that is sure to see additional analysis (Corlija, Siman, and Finke, 2006).

AN EXAMINATION OF WASHINGTON AND ECONOMIC STABILITY

Another element of Wal-Mart's role in the aggregate economy is the potential impact of the firm in regional economic stability. This issue has received some attention but not in the more recent analysis, which treats the endogeneity problem. For example, Barnes, Connell, Hermenegildo, and Mattson (1996) note that the unemployment rate in counties with Wal-Mart were lower than in those without Wal-Mart. More recently, Hicks (2005c) found that Wal-Mart reduced both separations and job turnover in counties where they located. Both studies have flaws; Barnes et al. is not structured to decisively account for the impact of Wal-Mart, whereas my study has been criticized for not effectively treating endogeneity (see Dube, Eidlin, and Lester, 2005).

Therefore, evaluating the stability impact of Wal-Mart with new data may shed some light on the aggregate impact of Wal-Mart.

To evaluate the impact of Wal-Mart on aggregate stability, I examine Washington State's experience with Wal-Mart. The first entrance of Wal-Mart in Washington occurred in 1993, and, as is typical, entrance increased rapidly in subsequent years. As of 2004, more than half of Washington's counties had no Wal-Mart, with the greatest number in a single county being four (Wal-Mart's and supercenters). See Figure 6.9.

To test the impact of Wal-Mart on stability of the market, I construct two measures of economic variability. The first is the log of the 3-year variability in per capita personal income. This takes the form

$$V1 = \log \Delta \left[\left(\frac{PI_{t-1}/pop_{t-1} + PI_{t}/pop_{t} + PI_{t+1}/pop_{t+1}}{3} \right)^2 \right]^{1/2} \quad (6.6)$$

The second is the mean average variance from the state average. It is calculated as

$$V2 = \left[\left(\frac{PI}{pop} - \frac{\sum (PI/pop)}{n} \right)^2 \right]^{1/2} \quad (6.7)$$

As with all measures of economic stability, this broad measure of stability has limitations. In this case, using personal income includes regional transfer payments (e.g., unemployment compensation), which may dampen the measurement of a potential increase in regional variability. The first measurement, $V1$, is a measure of variability over time, while the second, $V2$, measures the relative variability of a county from the state average. Higher levels of $V1$ imply

FIGURE 6.9   Total Wal-Marts and Supercenters in Washington State

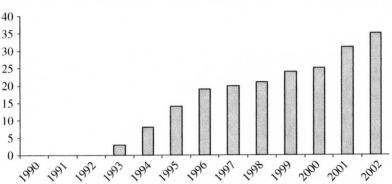

a less stable county, whereas higher levels of $V2$ imply increasing regional inequality. To test these measures on Washington State, I construct the familiar model of Wal-Mart's impact:

$$V(N) = \alpha + \alpha_i + \beta_1 WM_{i,t} + \delta\phi_{t-1} + e_t \qquad (6.8)$$

where the variability measures ($V1$ or $V2$) are a function of a common intercept, county fixed effects (county specific intercepts), a presence / count measure of Wal-Mart, and a one-period time-autoregressive component. In keeping with the endogeneity concern, I include a market size correction for endogeneity spelled out in Hicks' (forthcoming) comparative study of instruments on Maryland. This is the sum of real personal income in county i and j adjoining counties. Because of the unresolved endogeneity issue, I report both the ordinary least squares and two-stage least squares (instrumental variable) estimates. The use of spatial data in the identifying equation also necessitates using lagged explanatory variables as instruments in this model. The results of the tests appear in Table 6.5.

These estimates present mixed findings concerning Wal-Mart's influence on regional economic stability. For $V1$, the time variable, both estimates suggest that the presence of Wal-Mart reduces instability

TABLE 6.5

Wal-Mart's Impact on Temporal and Spatial Economic Stability
(Washington State, 1990–2004)

| | V1 | | V1 | |
	OLS	2SLS	OLS	2SLS
Common intercept	4.639762***	4.636632***	122309.4**	171065.1
	(12277.01)	(1136.76)	(2.16)	(1.45)
Wal-Mart	−0.008030*	−0.001308	−101.8701	−514.0687*
	(−1.65)	(−0.20)	(−1.33)	(−1.84)
Autoregression	0.412802***	0.404989***	0.992235***	0.994589***
$(t-1)$	(8.83)	(8.63)	(232.03)	(237.45)
Adjusted R^2	0.99	0.99	0.98	0.99
Durbin-Watson (panel)	1.68	2.25	2.35	2.36
Observations	585	585	585	585

Note. The Durbin-Watson panel statistic reported is derived from Bhargava, Franzini, and Narendranathan (1982). I whitewashed the variance matrix using a version of White's (1980) heteroscedastic consistent variance–covariance matrix derived from Driscoll and Kraay (1998). As is common, I have not reported the values of the cross-sectional fixed-effects coefficients to preserve space. OLS, ordinary least squares; 2SLS, two-stage least squares.
***$p = 0.01$. **$p = 0.05$. *$p = 0.10$.

in county-level incomes. However, the impact enjoys common levels of statistical significance in only the model that does not account for potential endogeneity in Wal-Mart's entrance decision. In the two-stage least squares estimate that accounts for the possibility that Wal-Mart is using market size as a guide for locating stores, the results differ. Here Wal-Mart has no impact on temporal stability/ instability in incomes.

In V2, our measure of relative income differentiation, we find that the presence of Wal-Mart reduces the level of income difference in the counties in which it locates. This finding is very similar to Hicks (2006b), who found that Wal-Mart reduced the spatial inequality in retail in Indiana counties. Here the level of statistical significance is at 10% in the model, which accounts for Wal-Mart's entrance decision, and drops to just under 20% in the ordinary least squares estimate.

My estimates point to the possibility that Wal-Mart makes local county economies more stable over time. Also I find that Wal-Mart makes county economies look more like the state average, in essence a reduction in spatial inequality across Washington's counties that can be attributed to Wal-Mart. However, both of these interpretations should be conditioned on the fact that statistical reliability in the models is sensitive to the possibility that Wal-Mart is choosing locations for their stores in a way that is influenced by the existing level of instability and regional differences.

SUMMARY

Wal-Mart's role on the aggregate local economy has received some conclusive economic analysis but nothing like that which characterizes the popular media and press. It seems likely that Wal-Mart is increasing overall local employment, but the effect on wages and job quality is mixed or weak. Wal-Mart's impact on the manufacturing industry, either through enabling international trade or squeezing suppliers, simply is not of a magnitude to generate worry. Indeed, the weight of evidence is that this process is necessary for economic growth. However, the commercial impacts reviewed in this and the previous two chapters represent only a small portion of the overall impacts on a local economy.

SECTION III

THE FISCAL IMPACTS OF WAL-MART

The role of Wal-Mart is not confined to commercial economic activity but extends to impacts on state, local, and potentially federal governments. As with most commercial economic activities, these impacts are largely explained as impacts on the fiscal health of governments: their tax collections and expenditures.

In Chapters 7 and 8, I review and provide additional estimates of Wal-Mart's impact on tax collections and expenditures. Here I focus on state and local fiscal conditions, as this is a book about local impacts. In Chapter 9, I extend the analysis to Wal-Mart's impact on antipoverty programs, primarily Medicaid. Although Medicaid has significant state impact, the federal component of financing represents its largest share. I have decided to include this issue since health care issues surrounding Wal-Mart have come to be an important part of the debate over its efficacy.

CHAPTER SEVEN

WAL-MART AND LOCAL TAX REVENUES

Local policy considerations regarding any commerce often focus on the tax revenue implications. Thus, economists who study state and local tax policy have analyzed taxation with focus on two issues: the role of tax policy in motivating firm location decisions and the impact of changing economic structure on tax collections. Because economists study markets, Wal-Mart–specific analysis is dominated by types of studies called microsimulations and relies on very strict assumptions regarding the overall economic consequences of Wal-Mart's entrance.

Even a modest treatment of the extensive study of state and local tax instruments is far outside the scope of this book. More importantly, with perhaps 25,000 tax-collecting bodies (from local park districts to the federal government), only broad descriptions will do. Fortunately, a few stylized facts will suffice in effectively characterizing the tax revenue implications of a Wal-Mart. I'll approach this from the top down, beginning with federal tax policy. I do this to provide a better example of how a progressive tax system is likely to make the problem of estimating the tax implication of Wal-Mart among the easiest of the empirical challenges described in this book.

The federal corporate income tax is a progressive tax, meaning the higher the net taxable income, the higher the proportion of this that is taxed. Let me provide an example using approximate federal tax rates and a representative firm income and profit rates for a small firm. Suppose two retailers each sell $1,000,000 in merchandise. If Firm A makes no profit (net income before taxes), it will not be subject to income taxes. If Firm B makes a profit of 5% ($50,000 in pretax net income), it will be taxed at a 15% rate, for an income tax liability of $7,500.

Now, suppose, as many studies do, that a single large store (Wal-Mart) with $10,000,000 in sales comes to town and replaces the sales of 10 Firm Bs (whose total federal tax liability is $75,000), and each of the incumbent firms exit the market. (Note: As I have detailed in the previous chapters, this is a very strong, and unrealistic, assumption but illustrative here.) The Wal-Mart will then have $10,000,000 in sales. Now suppose that this big firm actually makes a smaller profit rate (e.g., 3.5%), so its net income before taxes is $350,000. However, because of the progressive income taxes, the federal tax liability on this firm will be 35%, for a total federal tax of $122,500. So, from a purely corporate income tax perspective, replacing 10 small firms with a Wal-Mart generates a 63% increase in tax collections.

Of course, for total federal tax liability, there are other adjustments. Personal income tax rates for employees may vary, and there may be differences in the number of workers employed by the total number of small retailers and Wal-Mart. Examining this also is instructive. Suppose Wal-Mart reduces total wages by 10% (more than twice the largest estimated impact), and wages are one third the operating cost. If the effective tax rate of the average Wal-Mart employee is 10% (which is probably 4–8% too high), then the tax loss would be $34,000. This still results in a net increase in federal revenues.

Using these very unrealistic assumptions (all decreasing the tax levels for Wal-Mart), I still find a net tax increase due to the retailer. In the end, no legitimate study will find that federal tax collections

FIGURE 7.1 Wal-Mart's Federal Corporate Effective Tax Rate

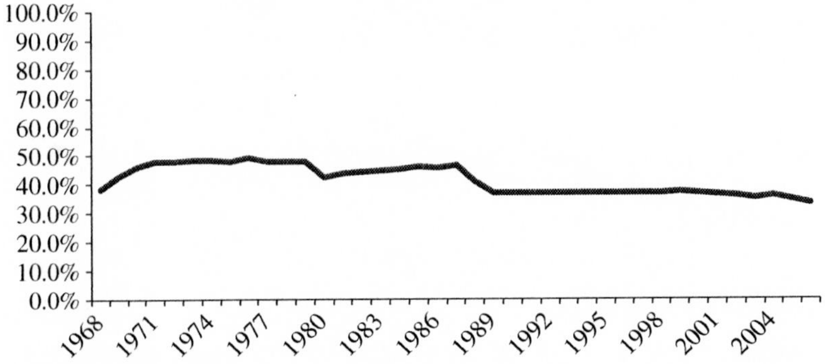

Source: Wal-Mart annual reports, various years.

are negatively affected by Wal-Mart (or other large firms). This is true, of course, unless the firms are particularly effective at tax avoidance. Wal-Mart's federal corporate income tax liability has been between 30% and 50% since the firm went public. This suggests the firm is not effectively avoiding taxes. See Figure 7.1.

These findings are broadly applicable to state corporate income taxes. Here the degree of progressivity varies considerably. One mechanism available for relative tax comparison purposes is a micro-simulation of Wal-Mart versus alternative business forms. A major weakness in microsimulation analysis is the use of broad assumptions regarding business structure. This is especially problematic with property taxes, in which mixes of real and personal property are quite variable. Further, data on such things as the relative property value of firms, compensation, income ranges, and profit rates are speculative. What is presented here is a fairly high-level estimate of total state and local property taxes with a focus on just a few tax instruments. Beginning this analysis are assumptions of some key business characteristics for my four representative firms. See Table 7.1.

For this analysis, I used values close to the 2005 Wal-Mart national numbers on profit rates, number of employees, and revenues per store. I preserve these profit rates across stores, although it is likely

TABLE 7.1
Firm Characteristics for Microsimulation

	Revenues	% Food	Net profit before federal tax	No. employees	Property value	Hourly wages
Wal-Mart	$75,000,000	15%	$4,500,000	250	$15,000,000	$9.38
Medium-size retailer	$15,000,000	10%	$900,000	55	$1,400,000	$10.49
Grocery	$15,000,000	85%	$900,000	55	$1,400,000	$10.49
Small retailer	$1,500,000	10%	$90,000	6	$250,000	$9.62

that groceries and smaller stores have higher profit rates. I thus understate their tax contributions. I assume a lower hourly rate for Wal-Mart workers, which could be interpreted as simply more part-time employment. I make Wal-Mart slightly more productive and give it a higher capital stock, which translates into higher property values (both real and personal). My choices of food–nonfood ratios are highly speculative, and if these matter it is in states that do not tax food.

I use tax rate data from 2005 values reported by the Federation of Tax Administrators. I apply the high rates of local sales taxes as representative, although there may be much substate variation (however, in several states, notably Virginia, there is not). Given the hourly wage rates, I use the lower income tax brackets for each state in my estimate of individual income taxes. For corporate taxes, I use the appropriate highest bracket for all but four states, where the smaller net incomes of the small retailer necessitated using lower tax rates. I treat these as average, not marginal, tax rates on net income. For property tax rates, I use 35 mils as the rate on total property (personal and real) with full valuation. There is far too much intrastate variation to do otherwise. I do not include many other taxes, such as user and city fees and business franchise taxes. However, with few exceptions, these are a small component of overall taxes. My tax data appear in Table 7.2.

TABLE 7.2
State and Local Tax Data, 2006

State	Corporate		Food taxed	Sales		Personal Income	
	Low	High		State	Local	Low	High
Alabama	6.5	6.5	Yes	4	7	2	5
Alaska	1	9.4	Yes	0	7	0	-
Arizona	6.968	6.968	No	5.6	4.5	2.87	5.04
Arkansas	1	6.5	Yes	6	5.5	1	7
California	8.84	8.84	No	6.25	2.65	1	9.3
Colorado	4.63	4.63	No	2.9	7	4.63	-
Connecticut	7.5	7.5	No	6	0	3	5
Delaware	8.7	8.7	No	5.75	0	2.2	5.95
Florida	5.5	5.5	No	6	1.5	0	-
Georgia	6	6	No	4	3	1	6
Hawaii	4.4	6.4	Yes	4	0	1.4	8.25
Idaho	7.6	7.6	Yes	6	3	1.6	7.8
Illinois	7.3	7.3	Yes	6.25	3	3	-
Indiana	8.5	8.5	No	6	0	3.4	-
Iowa	6	12	No	5	2	0.36	8.98
Kansas	4	4	Yes	5.3	3	3.5	6.45
Kentucky	4	7	No	6	0	2	6

(Continued)

TABLE 7.2 (Continued)

State	Corporate		Food taxed	Sales		Personal Income	
	Low	High		State	Local	Low	High
Louisiana	4	8	No	4	6.25	2	6
Maine	3.5	8.93	No	5	0	2	8.5
Maryland	7	7	No	5	0	2	4.75
Massachusetts	9.5	9.5	No	5	0	5.3	-
Michigan	9.8	9.8	No	6	0	3.9	-
Minnesota	3	5	No	6.5	1	5.35	7.85
Mississippi	6.25	6.25	Yes	7	0.25	3	5
Missouri	6.75	6.75	Yes	4.23	4.5	1.5	6
Montana	6.75	6.75	No	0	0	1	6.9
Nebraska	5.58	7.81	No	5.5	1.5	2.56	6.84
Nevada	0	0	No	6.5	1.5	0	-
New Hampshire	8.5	8.5	No	0	0	0	-
New Jersey[a]	9	9	No	6	0	1.4	8.97
New Mexico	4.8	7.6	Yes	5	2.25	1.7	5.3
New York	7.5	7.5	No	4.25	4.5	4	6.85
North Carolina[a]	6.9	6.9	No	4.5	3	6	8.25
North Dakota[a]	2.6	7	No	5	2.5	2.1	5.54
Ohio	5.1	8.5	No	6	2	0.712	7.185
Oklahoma	6	6	Yes	4.5	6	0.5	6.25

Oregon	6.6	6.6	No	0	0	5	9
Pennsylvania	9.99	9.99	No	6	1	3.07	-
Rhode Island	9	9	No	7	0	0	8.75
South Carolina	5	5	Yes	5	2	2.5	7
South Dakota	0	0	Yes	4	2	0	-
Tennessee	6.5	6.5	Yes	7	2.75	0	-
Texas	0	0	No	6.25	2	0	-
Utah	5	5	Yes	4.75	2.25	2.3	7
Vermont	7	8.9	No	6	1	3.6	9.5
Virginia	6	6	Yes	4	1	2	5.75
Washington	0	0	No	6.5	2.4	0	-
West Virginia	9	9	Yes	6	0	3	6.5
Wisconsin	7.9	7.9	No	5	0.6	4.6	6.75
Wyoming	0	0	Yes	4	2	0	-

Source: Federation of Tax Administrators, March 2006.

[a]Tax rates for income taxes used were less than maximum for the small retailer.

From these data and representative firms, I calculate total tax collections for each firm by state, which is then translated into tax burden per dollar of revenues. See Table 7.3.

TABLE 7.3
State and Local Taxes per Dollar Revenue

State	Wal-Mart	Medium-Sized Retailer	Grocery Store	Small Retailer
Alabama	$0.1208	$0.1174	$0.1114	$0.1141
Alaska	$0.0774	$0.0737	$0.0737	$0.0704
Arizona	$0.1126	$0.1093	$0.0533	$0.1060
Arkansas	$0.1230	$0.1195	$0.1105	$0.1162
California	$0.1001	$0.0965	$0.0340	$0.0932
Colorado	$0.1108	$0.1078	$0.0788	$0.1045
Connecticut	$0.0719	$0.0686	$0.0086	$0.0653
Delaware	$0.0693	$0.0659	$0.0084	$0.0627
Florida	$0.0841	$0.0804	$0.0204	$0.0771
Georgia	$0.0800	$0.0764	$0.0364	$0.0731
Hawaii	$0.0496	$0.0461	$0.0401	$0.0428
Idaho	$0.1010	$0.0975	$0.0885	$0.0942
Illinois	$0.1043	$0.1010	$0.0916	$0.0977
Indiana	$0.0725	$0.0693	$0.0093	$0.0660
Iowa	$0.0796	$0.0759	$0.0259	$0.0726
Kansas	$0.0938	$0.0906	$0.0827	$0.0874
Kentucky	$0.0699	$0.0664	$0.0064	$0.0632
Louisiana	$0.1124	$0.1089	$0.0689	$0.1057
Maine	$0.0597	$0.0562	$0.0062	$0.0530
Maryland	$0.0610	$0.0576	$0.0076	$0.0543
Massachusetts	$0.0642	$0.0612	$0.0112	$0.0579
Michigan	$0.0734	$0.0702	$0.0102	$0.0669
Minnesota	$0.0866	$0.0837	$0.0187	$0.0805
Mississippi	$0.0839	$0.0806	$0.0701	$0.0773
Missouri	$0.0979	$0.0943	$0.0880	$0.0911
Montana	$0.0103	$0.0067	$0.0067	$0.0034
Nebraska	$0.0808	$0.0775	$0.0225	$0.0742
Nevada	$0.0870	$0.0833	$0.0183	$0.0800
New Hampshire	$0.0103	$0.0066	$0.0066	$0.0033

(Continued)

TABLE 7.3   (*Continued*)

State	Wal-Mart	Medium-Sized Retailer	Grocery Store	Small Retailer
New Jersey	$0.0714	$0.0679	$0.0079	$0.0646
New Mexico	$0.0825	$0.0790	$0.0715	$0.0757
New York	$0.1000	$0.0969	$0.0544	$0.0936
North Carolina	$0.0886	$0.0858	$0.0408	$0.0825
North Dakota	$0.0844	$0.0810	$0.0310	$0.0777
Ohio	$0.0895	$0.0858	$0.0258	$0.0826
Oklahoma	$0.1147	$0.1110	$0.1043	$0.1077
Oregon	$0.0128	$0.0098	$0.0098	$0.0066
Pennsylvania	$0.0829	$0.0796	$0.0196	$0.0764
Rhode Island	$0.0805	$0.0768	$0.0068	$0.0735
South Carolina	$0.0806	$0.0772	$0.0697	$0.0740
South Dakota	$0.0670	$0.0633	$0.0573	$0.0600
Tennessee	$0.1070	$0.1033	$0.0928	$0.1000
Texas	$0.0895	$0.0858	$0.0233	$0.0825
Utah	$0.0804	$0.0771	$0.0699	$0.0738
Vermont	$0.0821	$0.0789	$0.0189	$0.0756
Virginia	$0.0606	$0.0572	$0.0512	$0.0539
Washington	$0.0960	$0.0923	$0.0273	$0.0890
West Virginia	$0.0725	$0.0692	$0.0602	$0.0659
Wisconsin	$0.0691	$0.0660	$0.0160	$0.0628
Wyoming	$0.0670	$0.0633	$0.0573	$0.0600

These data are a close approximation of the effective tax rates on these stores, except that they include, as a small proportion of their total, income taxes on employees. As is evident, the largest variability in the data is due to state tax differences on food. In many instances, Wal-Mart's tax rate is modestly larger than that on the medium and small retailer and will often be larger than the grocery store (always where food is not subject to sales tax).

The bulk of my assumptions are conservative in that they understate Wal-Mart's tax burden relative to the other firms in the microsimulation. However, two potential factors may mean that I have understated Wal-Mart's tax burden. First, if Wal-Mart locates in places that have lower property values than the existing firms, and no adjustment on value is made, then their per-dollar burden may be less. Second, in states with high fixed taxes (e.g., minimum user or license fees), then the relative burden for small businesses would rise. However, my estimates are in line with other estimates of state-level corporate tax rates; see Kentucky Long-Term Policy Research Center [KLTPRC], 2004. Nonetheless, it is fully in keeping with a progressive tax system that Wal-Mart would be more likely to pay a higher percentage of its total sales in taxes.

It is useful also to compare my estimates with other analyses of state and local tax burdens. One such study of the central states provides one of the few examples I have uncovered of effective corporate tax rates across a large number of states using similar methodologies. This study, by KLTPRC, analyzes the effective corporate tax rates for Kentucky and surrounding states. These are compared with my estimates of the corporate share of taxes reported previously. See Table 7.4.

TABLE 7.4

A Comparison of Corporate Effective Tax Rates (State and Local)

State	All Corporations	Wal-Mart
Alabama	8.68	11.95
Arkansas	11.06	12.24
Georgia	10.69	7.93
Illinois	9.87	10.23
Indiana	12.97	7.03
Kentucky	10.62	6.86
Michigan	13.11	7.08
Mississippi	15.34	8.19
Missouri	13.73	9.69
North Carolina	10.89	8.47
Ohio	14.44	8.90
South Carolina	10.35	7.90
Tennessee	12.34	10.70
Virginia	10.03	5.93
West Virginia	9.50	7.05

Source: Kentucky's Long-Term Policy Research Center and author's calculations.

The comparison of Wal-Mart's effective tax rate compared with other firms is interesting but should be viewed with caution. Regional differences in industrial composition influence these results profoundly. In one state with which I am familiar, West Virginia, corporate taxes are disproportionately shared by manufacturing, transportation, and mining firms, easing the burden on other industries.[1]

Overall, these findings suggest that the entrance of a Wal-Mart into a county will likely lead to higher gross tax receipts for state and local governments, even if there is no increase in retail sales. However, this relatively straightforward conclusion masks many of the real issues surrounding Wal-Mart and local tax rates.

THE RESEARCH ON LOCAL TAXES AND WAL-MART

Researchers have long been interested in how state and local tax rates influence firm location decisions. The effect of local taxes on big-box development is, therefore, a compelling issue. Wassmer (2004) examined the impact of public finance structure on retail location choice in 61 metropolitan statistical areas in the western United States. He constructed a model of retail location choice with 13 variables where

$$\text{Retail Sale} = f(\text{income, demographics, growth, local tax share, urban, price of land}) \tag{7.1}$$

Wassmer found that, when controlling for the other variables, with a higher reliance on locally sourced taxes (here municipal), there was a shift toward higher rates of retail sales away from the central city. These were clustered in big-box types of retail sales. According to this important study, big-box retail firms may find that communities with a higher reliance on locally sourced taxes look more favorably on their entrance. This suggests that tax structure, not just local commercial economic conditions (such as growth), may influence Wal-Mart's location decisions.

---

[1] See Burton, Kent, and Hicks (1999).

Hadsell (2002) examined Wal-Mart's impact on local taxes in New York State. He tested tax rates on a model that accounted for Wal-Mart using two equations:

$$\text{Tax Rate} = f(WM)$$
$$\text{Tax Rate} = f(WM \cdot T) \qquad (7.2)$$

one that treated Wal-Mart as either a presence dummy or one that included the duration of Wal-Mart's presence in a city or municipality. He found that the presence of a Wal-Mart leads to increased local property taxes. This affect is attributed to greater demand for public services induced by Wal-Mart's entrance. He notes further that these tax increases may be offset by adjustments to other tax instruments, which he could not test, and that the increased tax rates may result in better local services offsetting some of the obviously unpleasant aspects of increased local taxes on residents.

In Hicks (2007), I examine the fiscal effects of Wal-Mart's entrance into Ohio from 1988 to 2003. I first note the broad geographic distribution of Wal-Mart within the state. See Figure 7.2.

Ohio's local taxes are highly variable with city income taxes (of which internal township residents are exempt) and highly variable property tax rates; thus, I was compelled to use collections and countywide rate-adjusted collections from previous research. To calculate the impact of Wal-Mart discount stores and supercenters on Ohio's county tax collections, I specified the model:

$$T = f(WM_i, \text{WMSUP}_i, WM_j, \text{WMSUP}_j,$$
$$\text{INC, POP, Recession}) \qquad (7.3)$$

in which tax collections were modeled as the presence of a Wal-Mart or supercenter in a county and the presence of these stores in adjacent counties j, along with income, population and recession variables, and corrections for time and spatial autocorrelation and county fixed effects. To account for potential endogeneity, I used a lagged entrance dummy as an instrumental variable.

FIGURE 7.2   Wal-Mart in Ohio, 1988–2003

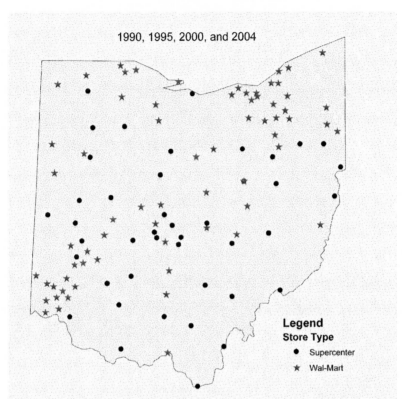

1990, 1995, 2000, and 2004

Legend
Store Type
● Supercenter
★ Wal-Mart

My results indicate that a Wal-Mart discount store in a county exerted a large, but statistically weak, increase in sales tax collections in the county (roughly $9 million per store). However, the presence of a Wal-Mart in an adjacent county reduced own county sales tax collections by more than $42 million, or roughly 10%. The impact of supercenters, both within and in adjacent counties, on sales tax collections was not statistically meaningful, most likely because Ohio does not tax the majority of food items in these stores.

Commercial property tax assessments rose dramatically for Wal-Mart stores within a county but were unsurprisingly not affected by either Wal-Marts or supercenters in adjoining counties. Own county supercenters also led to increased property tax assessments, but the impact was very statistically uncertain. I attribute the lack of statistical certainty regarding the property tax effects of supercenters to their possible location outside of higher priced areas, which would result in more modest impacts.

THE DYNAMICS OF LOCAL SALES TAX COLLECTIONS: EVIDENCE FROM MAINE

Maine experience with Wal-Mart has been chronicled by many of the early researchers, including Stone, Deller, and McConnon (1992); Ketchum and Hughes (1997); Barnes, Connell, Hermenegildo, and Mattson (1996); Artz (1999); and Artz and McConnon (2001). Only Ketchum and Hughes offered empirical analysis beyond nonstatistical comparisons of pre–post Wal-Mart entrance impacts. Ketchum and Hughes found no negative impact on the regional economy when comparing levels across counties that had experienced a Wal-Mart entrance between 1990 and 1994.

Maine is an especially useful geographic region to study since the state collects detailed tax records on specific retail market areas each month. These data consist of sales tax collections across firms of several different types and in market areas that consist of a central city and surrounding communities. I use the monthly data from 1987 through 2004. See Figure 7.3.

The most obvious characteristic is the very clear seasonality apparent in this and all retail data. Beyond this, these data offer several analytical options. The first is a straightforward estimate of Wal-Mart's impact on local consumer goods, restaurants, and general merchandise tax receipts. Using the model

$$T_{i,t} = \alpha + \alpha_i + \beta WM_{i,t} + \delta_1 \phi_{t-1} + \delta_2 \phi_{t-12} + e_{i,t} \tag{7.4}$$

where tax collections, T, are estimated on common and cross-sectional specific intercepts, a Wal-Mart presence / count variable, and first- and 12th-order time-autoregressive elements, which account for highly seasonal monthly sales volatility, with a white noise error term.

FIGURE 7.3   Selected Sales Tax Collections (2000 Constant Dollars)

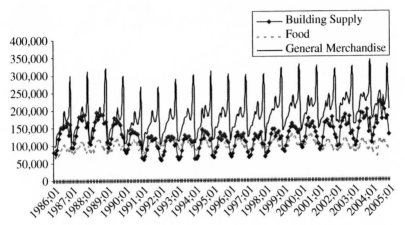

To identify the equation, we explore two mechanisms to account for endogeneity: the simplified version of Basker's (2005a) lagged entrance (18 months) and total consumer tax receipts as a measure of market size (lagged 18 months). Because of the specificity of the market area, I do not include spatial adjustments in this model specification. Results appear in Table 7.5.

These results suggest that the presence of a Wal-Mart increases sales tax receipts in both consumer goods and general merchandise by $16,000 and $9,000/month, respectively. These are very small effects. For general merchandise, this impact translates into less than one half of 1% of the median county's total receipts in these areas. For small counties, this represents roughly one third of total tax receipts in these categories. The impact on consumer goods is even smaller; indeed, with the exception of the potential impacts in small counties (in which Wal-Mart did enter), these are too small to be economically meaningful. The estimate also reveals that Wal-Mart does not affect restaurant sales tax receipts. This finding is heartening because it points to appropriate specification of the model to include the instrumentation choice that accounts for endogeneity. Interestingly, in all three models, the choice of instrument does not meaningfully affect the estimates.

Table 7.5

Wal-Mart's Impact on Maine's Sales Tax Receipts

	Consumer Goods	Restaurants	General Merchandise
Common intercept	31825.12***	5231.593***	9001.944***
	(17.65)	(28.80)	(6.56)
Wal-Mart	16.99133***	0.878191	9.161648***
	(3.58)	(0.76)	(4.98)
Autoregression ($t-1$)	0.070318***	0.129883***	0.059580***
	(8.8)	(8.45)	(8.14)
Autoregression ($t-12$)	0.883678***	0.765725***	0.912260***
	(108.41)	(48.10)	(122.40)
Adjusted R^2	0.99	0.98	0.98
Durbin-Watson (panel)	1.68	2.35	1.27

Note. The Durbin-Watson panel statistic reported is derived from Bhargava, Franzini, and Narendranathan (1982). I whitewashed the variance matrix using a version of White's (1980) heteroscedastic consistent variance–covariance matrix derived from Driscoll and Kraay (1998). As is common, I have not reported the values of the cross-sectional fixed-effects coefficients to preserve space.
***$p = 0.01$.

A second method of evaluating the impacts of Wal-Mart is through the use of a panel vector autoregression (VAR). This is a flexible estimation technique in which the causal relationship is not directly stated or specified; instead, variables interact on each other over time to yield estimation results. These estimation results are of less interest than the rate or level of response of one variable to another. This is called the *impulse response function.*

The VAR model also permits estimation across two variables that are cointegrated. Cointegration is a condition in which two variables share a single relationship, which may be interpreted as an equilibrium condition between the two variables. For purposes of this estimate, this condition is of interest when two or more variables have a trend (referred to as *nonstationary*). In this case, both the real sales taxes and the entrance of Wal-Marts are stationary, or have no trend. Further, we can reject a shared cointegrating equation and thus estimate the impacts using the levels of both variables, not their first differences as is frequently done.[2] The model is then the system of equations:

$$CONSUM_t = \alpha_1 + \alpha_n^t WMENT_{t-n} + \beta_n^t CONSUM_{t-n} + e_t$$
$$WMENT_t = \alpha_1 + \alpha_n^t WMENT_{t-n} + \beta_n^t CONSUM_{t-n} + e_t$$

(7.5)

where consumer sales tax (expressed in constant 2000 dollars) is a function of an intercept, lagged Wal-Mart entrance and lagged values of itself, and a white noise error term. Selecting the appropriate number of lagged variables is usually performed by optimizing a statistical measure of the smallness, or parsimony, of the model. The most common method is minimization of the Akaike information criterion (AIC), which in this case occurred at 12 lags.[3]

The impulse response function accounts for a shock to one of the variables (often referred to as *time series innovations*) and is transmitted across the values of both variables. Here we are interested in the impact of consumer sales taxes caused by the entrance of a Wal-Mart.[4] The results of both the shock and its cumulative effect appear in Figure 7.4.

Interpretation of this graph is straightforward and reinforces the estimates from the earlier panel regression. Although Wal-Mart does

---

[2] The augmented Dickey-Fuller test strongly rejects nonstationarity in the reported series (auto sales is an exception but not important for our purposes). This leads to, and was confirmed with, a MacKinnon test of cointegration, which finds that the variables are not cointegrated. If the variables were nonstationary and cointegrated, the variables are typically demeaned to make stationary, and the cointegrating equation is used in the estimation, which is termed an *error correction model*.

[3] Deviations from parsimony in a model result in an increasing risk of type II statistical error. Thus, smallness, or brevity, in a model is a very desired aspect of econometric analysis. The AIC is a measure of deviations of parsimony (like the adjusted R^2), which penalizes variance growth more than simply adding additional variables.

[4] This entrance is the shock; the resulting impacts can be expressed in many units (often standard deviations). I choose actual values for ease of interpretation.

FIGURE 7.4   Response of Consumer Goods Sales Tax Collections to
Entrance of a Wal-Mart

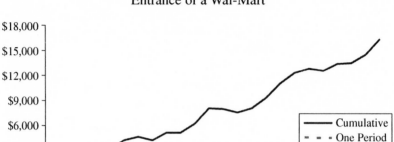

increase sales tax collections in consumer goods, the impact in Maine is small, with a cumulative 2-year effect of less than one half of 1% of average total monthly tax revenues.

These findings, both new and in the existing literature, are uniform in the assessment that Wal-Mart increases local sales tax collections when it enters a market. The tax estimates range from very large (almost $10 million per store) to nearly economically insignificant (a few ten thousands of dollars per store).[5]

However, tax revenues are only one part of the story of fiscal impacts. Local expenditures, such as infrastructure costs and increased local services related to Wal-Mart, will certainly offset some of the revenue increases. Chapter 8 addresses some of these issues related to local expenditures.

---

[5] This finding supports the belief that Wal-Mart does induce an income effect that is positive, since its lower prices still lead to higher levels of consumption of retail goods.

CHAPTER EIGHT

WAL-MART AND LOCAL EXPENDITURES

Local costs associated with Wal-Mart's impact on state and local governmental expenditures have received little scholarly attention. However, a number of advocacy group reports focus on Wal-Mart's fiscal impacts. Few of these exhibit any real value. For example, one anti-Wal-Mart group collected crime reports from a Wal-Mart shopping center and subsequently issued press releases arguing that Wal-Mart was responsible for the increased crime and the associated policing costs.[1]

Many local governments have assessed the local expenditure impacts of Wal-Mart (or similar stores) through a microsimulation of expenditures. Among the more balanced of these studies was a report on the fiscal impacts prepared for Barnstable, Massachusetts.[2]

---

[1] Wal-Mart Watch, May 1, 2006.
[2] Tischler and Associates, 2002, now TischlerBisch, LLC.

This study examined land use options, of which big-box retail was one component. In addition to evaluating revenues and expenditures for business types and households, they compared expenditures (including loss of revenue sources as a result of rezoning). These were then adjusted to a per capita basis and reported. See Table 8.1.

These types of studies can provide a useful understanding of the fiscal impact. They are, however, very sensitive to the underlying assumptions (most particularly regarding economic growth), and the impacts estimated for such things as police services are often average, not marginal, costs. The latter should provide the decision rules in a cost–benefit analysis (although even performing a cost–benefit analysis as part of considering private development is perhaps dubious). The Barnstable study is useful in that it appears to conscientiously evaluate several types of commerce and provide comparisons. Their results suggest that the service and infrastructure costs of big-box retail are fairly consistent with other types of development.

TABLE 8.1

Estimates of Per Capita Local Expenditures by Business Type

Expenditure	Business Park	Shopping Center	Big-Box Retail	Specialty Retail	Fast Food Restaurant	Office
Town council and manager	$7	$5	$4	$4	$11	$9
Community services	91	72	56	52	143	116
Administrative services	0	0	0	0	0	0
Police	331	769	629	486	4,496	460
Public works	152	322	265	200	2,031	206
Regulatory services	21	21	16	15	34	27
Schools	−140	−111	−87	−81	−222	−179
Other	69	80	65	54	336	90
Totals	$531	$1,158	$948	$730	$6,829	$729

Source: Tischler and Associates, 2002, p. 13.

For the purposes of this book, it is useful to consider the potential causes of expenditure changes as part of their estimation. There are really two types of cost—services and infrastructure—that account for the bulk of state and local expenditures that might be attributable to a new retail firm. I treat these in turn and follow them with a review of estimates of infrastructure costs directly attributable to Wal-Mart.

Any new commercial economic activity is likely to impose some costs on the governmental provision of local services. Many government services are provided as a fee for service, so such things as costs for construction permit applications enjoy a linkage between revenues and expenditures. These are typically a small part of total governmental expenditures and really are not a policy concern. Other services such as on-site help with new job applicants provided by the regional Workforce Investment Board may include costs that are directly related to the firm. However, these are not inadvertent costs but rather the provision of services intended to provide assistance to employees (and potentially employers). The costs may not all be borne locally. For example, most Workforce Investment Board funding is federal. Other types of services include police and fire protection, which may increase as a result of the expansion of commercial areas. These are usually funded through state and local property taxes, although there are great interstate differences in these mechanisms of payment.

Most infrastructure costs associated with new commercial economic activity is borne by the private sector. So, the extension of electricity, gas, and some water and sewer lines by the private sector are investments in local infrastructure, which are benefits. However, the government also provides part of this infrastructure to include roads (extensions, exits, or access), road safety (signage, traffic lights, or lane extensions), and often water and sewer extensions. The level of public provisioning of infrastructure tends to be highly variable relative to service provision. A Wal-Mart locating to an existing store or near existing water and sewer lines may generate almost no incremental infrastructure costs on a local government, whereas a new store located distant from water or sewer lines off a two-lane road may require considerable local infrastructure investment.

It is undeniable that local and state governments bear some additional burden related to commercial economic development. However, the relevant question for this book is not whether the location decision of new commercial economic activity is associated with higher costs to government services or higher infrastructure costs but whether Wal-Mart itself affects these costs.

Economic studies of this question are limited to my (Hicks, 2005d) unpublished paper on sprawl in Colorado. In this paper, I test proxies of urban sprawl on the presence of Wal-Mart. The questions of interest are whether or not Wal-Mart affects the level and the variability of service and infrastructure costs. As a point of departure, I will be more detailed in the modeling approach taken here so as to clarify the findings for readers. I begin with the estimate of the level of infrastructure costs associated with Wal-Mart. This model takes the form

$$\Upsilon_{i,t} = \alpha + \alpha_i + \beta WM_{i,t} + \delta \phi_{i,t-1} + e_t \qquad (8.1)$$

where the impact of Wal-Mart (and supercenter) entrance is estimated based on the level of expenditures in county i in year t from 1987 through 2002. The entrance decision is viewed as exogenous to infrastructure expenditures, so these models are estimated using ordinary least squares (without correction for endogeneity). A very bare model, including only the Wal-Mart presence / count specification and an autoregressive element, is used. I use data on infrastructure and local government services expenditures from the Colorado Economic and Demographic Information System. My Wal-Mart data are from the 2003 data release. I test these data on several administrative series of local expenditures. Select results appear in Table 8.2.

As with the other (unreported) expenditures, Wal-Mart's impact on expenditure levels is not statistically different from zero. The other estimates include water and sewage services and miscellaneous expenditures, both of which yield no impacts of Wal-Mart's presence. However, as

TABLE 8.2

Wal-Mart's Impact on Local Government Expenditures

	General Government	Roads and Highways	Public Safety
Intercept	−3626435	4017143***	895133.1
	(−0.09)	(33.24)	(0.05)
Wal-Mart	−0.320826	−149949.5	−28.86921
	(−0.10)	(−0.58)	(−0.18)
Autoregression (t −1)	1.026031***	0.536341**	1.038156***
	(10.12)	(2.12)	(13.2)
Adjusted R^2	0.98	0.92	0.99
Durbin-Watson (panel)	2.49	1.07	1.93
Observations	1008	1008	1008

Note. The Durbin-Watson panel statistic reported is derived from Bhargava, Franzini, and Narendranathan (1982). I whitewashed the variance matrix using a version of White's (1980) heteroscedastic consistent variance–covariance matrix derived from Driscoll and Kraay (1998). As is common, I have not reported the values of the cross-sectional fixed-effects coefficients to preserve space.

***p = 0.01. **p = 0.05.

posited previously, the entrance of a Wal-Mart (or any other large commercial activity) could affect either levels or the year-to-year variability of expenditures. Clearly, most budgeted expenditure items don't experience a great degree of variability because of random shocks. However, it is not uncommon for midfiscal year adjustments to budgets to occur across different types of local expenditures. Further, the entrance of a large facility could lead to adjustments in one type of activity (e.g., road construction) that is transient. To test this, I model the impact of Wal-Mart on the squared change in expenditures. This is a measurement of the magnitude of variability. See Equation 8.2.

$$\frac{d\Upsilon^2}{dt} = \alpha + \alpha_i + \beta WM_{i,t} + \delta\phi_{i,t-1} + e_t \qquad (8.2)$$

Table 8.3 provide results.

TABLE 8.3

Wal-Mart's Impact on the Variability of Local Expenditures

	Solid Waste	General Government	Roads and Highways	Public Safety	Misc. Expenses
Intercept	3.69E+11	9.06E+11	2.32E+12	2.74E+12***	3.69E+11
	(1.16)	(424.92)	(0.11)	(5.93)	(1.16)
Wal-Mart	−479620.1	−4260.477	−2458262	610781.7	−479620.1
	(−0.99)	(−0.53)	(−1.12)	(0.65)	(−0.98)
Autoregression	−0.025714	0.029956	−0.057206	−0.082677	−0.025714
$(t-1)$	(−1.03)	(1.30)	(−0.02)	(−0.51)	(−1.03)
Adjusted R^2	0.08	0.04	0.09	0.55	0.08
Durbin-Watson (panel)	2.06	1.92	1.96	2.25	2.06
Observations	945	945	945	945	930

Note. The Durbin-Watson panel statistic reported is derived from Bhargava, Franzini, and Narendranathan (1982). I whitewashed the variance matrix using a version of White's (1980) heteroscedastic consistent variance–covariance matrix derived from Driscoll and Kraay (1998). As is common, I have not reported the values of the cross-sectional fixed-effects coefficients to preserve space.

***$p = 0.01$.

These results provide no evidence that Wal-Mart affects the variability of local expenditures and are consistent with the relative paucity of analysis in this area. Simply, there seems to be little compelling evidence that Wal-Mart either increases or decreases local expenditures in a statistically meaningful way. This is perhaps why economists have not widely reported analysis of this issue.[3] However, one area of local expenditures that has seen considerable research is the role of tax incentives in firm location decisions. This is a major focus of study because the subsidization of firms by local governments is usually argued to enhance local economic performance. If it does, then the magnitude

[3] It is widely believed that papers that find no impact are less likely to get published in journals and so are less often reported in the academic literature.

of the effect should be considered in evaluating whether or not tax incentives generate net benefits to a local community.

TAX INCENTIVES AND CORPORATE WELFARE

Wal-Mart's receipt of state and local tax incentives is an area of ongoing criticism, both of the company and the local communities that offer the incentives. Among the studies that have broached the specific receipt of tax incentives and subsidies by Wal-Mart is the report by Shils (1997), then an emeritus professor of entrepreneurial studies at the Wharton School of Business. Although this work is plagued with a number of weaknesses and factual errors, it provides a fairly good record of some of the concerns about Wal-Mart, including an extensive criticism of "retail corporate welfare," to which an entire chapter is devoted.

Shils (1997) is particularly critical of California's experience with regional development areas (RDAs), which provided a number of incentives to firms, including Wal-Mart. Shils notes the cause of the increase in RDA use of tax incentives (Proposition 13, which limited property tax increases), outlines the potential tax affect, and highlights testimony by a number of individuals regarding the efficacy of tax incentives in California. Notably, the impacts of some of the RDA incentives were evaluated by legislative analysts. Shils summarizes testimony from one of the critics of the tax incentives:

> Rabousky then explained to the senators that there are four factors that temper the Legislative Analyst's estimate: (1) there is already some underlying growth in assessed value in project areas; (2) some projects capture growth that would have occurred anyway; (3) redevelopment affects the location but not the level of retail activity; and (4) some redevelopment spending is not always directed against blight. (Shils, 1997, Chapter VIII)

Interestingly, these first two critics of the legislative analysts are exactly the types of criticisms placed before much of the early research of

Wal-Mart. More recently, Mattera and Purinton (2004) compiled a very long list of examples of Wal-Mart using local tax incentives to support growth. The authors begin their report with an example from Napa, California, in which a Wal-Mart commercial features the city's mayor outlining the fiscal benefits of the local Wal-Mart. Mattera and Purinton describe the California experience in some detail. Perhaps most interesting about California is that it is one of the few states to heavily subsidize Wal-Mart's retail facilities as opposed to wholesale subsidies, which are more common.

Mattera and Purinton's work is especially useful in that it provides great details on subsidies to Wal-Mart and categorizes the subsidization. However, as the authors note, only those items that attracted local media attention made it into the report. Interestingly, Shils (1997) made a similar list of subsidized stores in California, and there is broad agreement across the two reports (although Mattera and Purinton compiled their data independently of Shils' efforts). The magnitude of the tax incentives offered Wal-Mart is significant, approaching $900 million. See Table 8.4.

Zach Schiller (2002), a writer with Policy Matters Ohio, offered a detailed outline of the types of incentives provided to three Wal-Marts in Ohio, among them state-level fixed-asset investment, job creation tax credit, local enterprise zone assistance, and several types of property tax exemptions. His study, although clearly an attack on Wal-Mart in particular, does provide a good treatment of the types of incentives that combine to generate considerable public investment in many types of new establishments.

Any concern over magnitude of these impacts should be tempered with two points. First, these values are not adjusted for the timing of their occurrence. For example, property tax abatements in the future are worth less in net present value than those accounted for here. Also many of these magnitudes may represent estimated, not market, value, which will typically inflate the values of these incentives. Second, the magnitudes of these impacts are not necessarily large in comparison to payments to other firms. For example, the Mattera and Purinton report details West Virginia's subsidization of four Wal-Mart stores (one discount and three

TABLE 8.4

Wal-Mart's Receipt of State and Local Tax Incentives

Incentive	Description	Expenditures (in millions)[a]
Free or reduced price land	Sale or grant of publicly owned property (often owned by government through property tax default)	$62.67
Infrastructure assistance	Subsidized infrastructure assistance (typically water, sewer, and road/highway construction)	$258.91
Tax increment financing	Use of increased property taxes (because of increased value of new construction) to finance infrastructure needs (typically water, sewer, and road/highway construction)	
Property tax breaks	Typically reduced or delayed application of property tax rates for an established period (usually linked to infrastructure costs)	$293.41
State corporate income tax credits	Typically reduced or delayed corporate income tax payments for a set period	$77.75
Sales tax rebates	Repayment of sales taxes for a set period, typically designed to pay for capital	$22.15
Enterprise zone	Very localized areas, typically enjoying lower taxes designed to spur development	$32.47
Job training and worker recruitment funds	Specific services for recruitment, screening, and training of potential employees	$7.24
Tax exempt bond financing	Creation of bonds that are not subject to local (and often state and federal) taxes; this is usually to offset of the cost of private infrastructure	$40
General grants	Direct payment by government to businesses	$33.02
Total		$827.62

Source: Mattera and Purinton (2004), author's calculations, and descriptions of Mattera and Purinton's categories.
[a]The Mattera and Purinton report has since corrected at least one estimate, and I include the correction here.

supercenters) totaling $9.7 million. As a comparison, the state provided Cabela's, a sporting goods retailer in Wheeling, perhaps as much as $120 million in direct subsidies and infrastructure assistance.[4] This is

---

[4] The true value of the state's subsidization of Cabela's will probably never be known because it occurred across several agencies, which did not separate the expenditures.

more than twice the single largest reported subsidy to a Wal-Mart site (in Sharon Springs, New York) and about 25 times the single largest subsidization of Wal-Mart by the state of West Virginia. Also, in one decade, beginning in the mid-1990s, the Michigan Economic Growth Administration (MEGA) provided $1.7 billion in grants (almost twice the total national grants to Wal-Mart), and 71 of these were greater than $5 million each, which is just about the mean expenditure of $5.17 million calculated from the 160 stores in Mattera and Purinton's estimate.

As Shils (1997) and Mattera and Purinton (2004) report, Wal-Mart is the recipient of considerable state and local subsidies. However, these types of subsidies are not extreme in comparison with expenditures to other firms. This does not mean that tax incentives are an efficacious public policy choice. Indeed, there is considerable analysis to suggest that the types of subsidies so excellently reported by Mattera and Purinton have little effect on firm location decision or, more importantly, the local economy where the firm locates.

THE EFFECTIVENESS OF TAX INCENTIVES TO WAL-MART

Tax incentives and subsidies to firms have seen considerable research. For example, Wasylenko (1997) reviewed research findings of over 90 studies that evaluated the role of fiscal policy in economic growth in the United States. A subset of these studies evaluated the effect of individual targeted tax policies on economic growth and found little evidence of any influence. Studies of subsidies and incentives include those by Gabe and Kraybill (2002), who evaluate firm-level tax incentives in Ohio; Hicks (2007), who examines specific firm incentives to a large retailer; and LaFaive and Hicks (2005), who estimate the impact of Michigan's MEGA program.

Gabe and Kraybill (2002) analyzed firms in Ohio from 1993 through 1995 that received targeted tax incentives. Using a treatment and control pool of over 350 firms, these authors found no positive, and in some instances a negative, influence of credit on job growth. Hicks (2007) found that extensive grants to a single large firm across many U.S. jurisdictions failed to generate net employment growth despite what was in several instances more than $50 million invested in a single firm. LaFaive and Hicks (2005) estimated the impact of the MEGA grants on local economic conditions in Michigan. They found that none of the expenditures affected the targeted industries. In addition, the subsidies resulted in a net increase in construction employment, although transient (under 2 years), at a subsidy cost of roughly $120,000 per construction job.

These empirical studies are a sample of the types of findings reported by economists over the past two decades. In truth, there is virtually no support within the economic research of the efficacy of tax incentives and subsidies. Many studies, perhaps a majority, find no impacts. Those that do (e.g., LaFaive and Hicks, 2005) find that the programs do not meet even minimal standards of efficacy. This question prompts further evaluation in this book.

WAL-MART AND SUBSIDIES IN CALIFORNIA

Both Shils (1997) and Mattera and Purinton (2004) single out California for criticism of their approach to subsidizing Wal-Mart. One argument both reports implicitly make is that subsidies for retailers are poor public policy choices, because these firms must locate near population centers and are far less footloose than manufacturing or warehousing firms. Pointedly, the economic research does not suggest that tax incentives to footloose firms play a significant role in local economic performance, but it is clear that the argument for supporting retail growth is weaker, at least from a political economy perspective. The subsidies reported by Mattera and Purinton (2004) were exclusively to Wal-Mart discount stores. See Table 8.5.

To assess the efficacy of this estimate, I test the subsidization effect on the entrance behavior of Wal-Mart as well as its impact on total retail employment. My first model is a very simple estimate of the marginal contribution of a dollar of subsidy on the number of Wal-Marts stores that enter a county in any given year. I limit the period from 1990 through 2000 in all of California's 58 counties. In any given year, the number of Wal-Mart stores that entered a county ranged from the obvious zero through six for Los Angeles County. This specification is

TABLE 8.5
California Subsidies to Wal-Mart

Location	Year	Subsidy
Colton	1991	$2.6 million reduced priced land
Corona	1994	$2 million sales tax rebate / parking lease
Corvina	1997	$5.3 million reduced-price land
Duarte	1995	$1.8 million reduced-price land
Gilroy	1993	$408,000 infrastructure
Hemet	1992	$1.8 million sales tax rebate, waived fees
Lake Elsinore	1994	$2.2 million infrastructure
Manteca	1992	$1.7 million site preparation
Perris	1992	$2.7 million infrastructure (via TIF)
Redlands	1991	$1.3 million sales tax rebate / parking lease
Rialto	1992	$2.6 million reduced-price land
Riverside	1993	> $2.2 million sales tax rebate / parking lease
San Diego	2000	$6.1 million infrastructure, parking lease

Source: Mattera and Purinton (2004).
Note. TIF, Tax Increment Financing.

similar to those tested by Franklin (2001) and Hicks and Wilburn (2001). The model takes the form

$$WM_i = \alpha + \beta(Subsidy)_i + e_i \qquad (8.3)$$

where the number of Wal-Marts that enter in county i in each year is a function of the dollar amount of the subsidy. This model is the well-known Poisson count model.[5] I test these data on cross-sectional data for each year from 1990 through 2000 in each of California's counties. The simple specification of the model suggests that the model should not be interpreted as a true representation of the entrance decision but rather as an estimate of the tax incentive's influence on entrance. Results appear in Table 8.6.

---

[5] See Cameron and Pravedi (1998) for a detailed description. The distribution of the dependent variable is assumed to be $f(y_i \mid x_i, \beta) = e^{-m(x\beta)} m(x\beta)^{y_i} / y_i$.

TABLE 8.6

The Impact of Subsidies on Wal-Mart Entrance ($N = 638$)

Variable	Coefficient
Intercept	−1.839552***
	(−18.46)
Subsidy (dollars)	4.58E-07***
	(7.63)
LR index (pseudo-R^2)	0.04

Note. These data were whitewashed using White's (1980) heteroscedasticity-invariant variance–covariance matrix LR, Likelihood Ratio.
*** $p = 0.01$.

The interpretation of these results is straightforward. Subsidies do affect the number of Wal-Marts in a county. The subsidy required to lead to a single Wal-Mart entering the market is roughly $2.1 million. However, this explains little of Wal-Mart's entrance decision—only about 4%—and, importantly, does not address the economic consequences of Wal-Mart's entrance. To do this we turn to our second model, which tests the impact of tax incentives on retail employment in each county. The model takes the form

$$R_{i,t} = \alpha + \alpha_i + \beta(Subsidy)_{i,t} + \delta\phi_{i,t} + e_{i,t} \qquad (8.4)$$

where retail employment in county i in year t is a function of common and county fixed intercepts, the dollar value of subsidies reported by Mattera and Purinton, a time-autoregressive component, and a white noise error term. This model imposes a new endogeneity problem, specifically that retail employment rates are contemporaneously correlated with the letting of subsidies to Wal-Mart. To correct for this concern, I estimate the following identifying equation:

$$R_{i,t} = \alpha + \beta_1(EZ)_i + \beta_2\left(\frac{R_{i,t}}{T_{i,t}}\right) + \beta_3(EZ_{i,t})\left(\frac{R_{i,t}}{T_{i,t}}\right) + e_{i,t} \qquad (8.5)$$

where retail employment in time t, county i, is identified as a function of a common intercept, whether or not the county was identified as an enterprise zone before its subsidy and the retail share of total employment, and the product of the enterprise zone and retail employment share. The purpose of this strategy and its efficacy are fairly straightforward. First, it seems unlikely that enterprise zone designation is influenced by total retail employment in a county. Further, the retail share of employment is unlikely to be influenced by the total retail employment, but it is very likely to affect the decision to provide tax subsidies to a retail firm. However, although there is some exogenous variation in the establishment of an enterprise zone, it will be highly correlated with the county fixed effects from the basic estimation (primarily poverty-related conditions). So, to provide the necessary identifying relationship, I must permit some exogenous variation within that variable. I do this by including the product of the retail share and enterprise zone designation. This also established an instrument that captures policy-inducing variation of retail employment share, which may explain the decision to provide retail subsidies. These are estimated in an instrumental variable setting using two-stage least squares (2SLS). I also report the ordinary least squares (OLS) results for comparison. See Table 8.7.

Both the 2SLS and OLS estimates yield results that strongly reject the statistical certainty of the subsidies on retail employment within the counties in which they are promulgated. Although this is likely of some surprise to economic developers, this finding is consistent with the overwhelming majority of economic analysis designed to identify the impact of tax incentives and subsidies to economic performance. One cautionary note is warranted. These estimates do not suggest that Wal-Mart plays no role in employment changes, since I am only testing the retail subsidization here. What these findings mean is that the subsidization of Wal-Mart in California has had no effect on local retail employment.

On balance, Wal-Mart's relationship with local public tax expenditures seems relatively benign. Although it is certain that individual Wal-Mart stores receive local infrastructure assistance and services, there is no evidence that Wal-Mart is receiving these benefits in a systematic

TABLE 8.7

The Impact of California's Wal-Mart Subsidies on Retail Employment

	OLS	2SLS
Intercept	54943.33***	52040.98***
	(3.13)	(7.99)
Subsidy	8.83E-05	−0.094488
	(0.25)	(−0.81)
Autoregression (t −1)	0.932347***	−0.096102
	(6.87)	(−0.79)
Adjusted R^2	0.99	0.83
Durbin-Watson (panel)	1.25	1.90
Observations	638	638

Note. The Durbin-Watson panel statistic reported is derived from Bhargava, Franzini, and Narendranathan (1982). I whitewashed the variance matrix using a version of White's (1980) heteroscedastic-consistent variance–covariance matrix derived from Driscoll and Kraay (1998). As is common, I have not reported the values of the cross-sectional fixed-effects coefficients to preserve space. OLS, ordinary least squares; 2SLS, two-stage least squares.
***$p = 0.01$.

way that is different from other types of commerce. The statistical analysis reported previously supports this contention. Further, although Wal-Mart is a nationwide recipient of government subsidies, the magnitude of the individual grants and the nationwide totals probably place Wal-Mart among the least exorbitant recipients of such incentives, although this is still a great deal of local revenue.

These findings simply suggest two things. From a local public expenditures framework, there is scant evidence that Wal-Mart imposes atypical costs on a community. Clearly, this experience will vary across communities. The effective treatment of this is a local issue. Also, although Wal-Mart often receives tax incentives or other forms of subsidies, these appear to be modest compared with those to other firms. Further, although Shils (1997) and Mattera and Purinton (2004) both single out Wal-Mart for receipt of these subsidies, most economists view the use of targeted tax incentives as a failure of state and local tax policy in general. It is the result of public policy failure at the local level, not commercial economic activity.

CHAPTER NINE

WAL-MART AND ANTIPOVERTY PROGRAMS

Among the more recent criticisms of Wal-Mart is that many of its employees have been reported to receive Medicaid, Temporary Assistance to Needy Families (TANF), Earned Income Tax Credit (EITC), and other transfer payments designed to mitigate poverty. Before assessing these impacts and evaluating the resulting policy implications, it is important to understand the role of antipoverty transfer payments in the United States.

A DISCUSSION OF ANTIPOVERTY PROGRAMS

The three major antipoverty programs I discuss in this chapter are Aid to Families With Dependent Children / Temporary Assistance for Needy Families (AFDC / TANF), food stamps, and Medicaid. Other programs may matter (e.g., low-income energy assistance), but these comprise a relatively trivial public expenditure compared with the big three just mentioned. Understanding the potential role of Wal-Mart in each of these is important in evaluating existing policy or formulating effective policy response in light of changing retail structure. I discuss them in turn in increasing complexity in their relationship to Wal-Mart.

The 1935 Social Security Act created Aid to Dependent Children, which was renamed AFDC in 1962 and then TANF as part of the 1996 Personal Responsibility and Work Opportunity Reconciliation Act (PRWORA). These programs have always supported children in poor, nonworking families and those not receiving other support. Following a peak enrollment in the early 1980s, program participation dropped throughout the 1990s and experienced only modest growth in the most recent recession (although this was accompanied by much alarm in the popular press). The issue that can be evaluated is whether Wal-Mart contributed to AFDC / TANF expenditures at the state level. I note that Wal-Mart's expansive growth occurred mostly during a period of rapid decline in caseloads of AFDC and TANF, with increases in the labor force participation rate of the most likely category of recipients (women in their 20s and 30s with children). One concern arises in that state and federal governments jointly establish payment rates for families. Thus, total expenditures imperfectly reflect the number of cases across states.

The Food Stamp Program, created in 1964 and later modified, provides supplementary income through the purchase of vouchers by poor families. As with AFDC / TANF, states control some eligibility guidelines, so expenditures do not translate directly into comparisons of caseloads across states. Again, the issue is clearly whether or not Wal-Mart's influence on the retail sector changes poverty expenditures. Food stamp eligibility begins with those receiving AFDC / TANF and extends to the working poor on an income-adjusted scale. Thus, even if Wal-Mart were to hire recent welfare leavers, these workers may still be eligible for food stamps depending on family income and size. Thus, evaluating the role of Wal-Mart in AFDC / TANF and food stamp expenditures is relatively straightforward. Medicaid, the focus of most of the criticism of Wal-Mart, presents a greater analytical challenge.

A central component of the war on poverty was health care for the poor and aged (in the 1967 Social Security Amendments). The Medicaid program today provides assistance to a variety of recipients: the poor, the disabled, and the aged. The primary role of Medicaid from its inception through the mid-1990s was as the health care component of welfare (then known as AFDC) and Supplemental Security Income. Medicaid experienced its greatest transformation as part of the 1996 PRWORA, in which the traditional linkage between welfare and Medicaid was severed, permitting the working poor to participate in Medicaid. The preservation of Medicaid for the working poor was a necessary concession to liberal lawmakers and was part of a reworked bill that had twice been vetoed by President Clinton.[1]

The arguments in favor of extending Medicaid support to the working poor are fourfold: Federal matching funds make state payments less onerous, PRWORA would likely lead to increases in the number of working poor, coverage promotes work as it is a benefits bridge to private sector employment, and it would provide the same level of access to poor working families as is available to those receiving traditional welfare payments (Guyer and Mann, 1998).

Today Medicaid is administered by states, with a variety of implementation plans, all of which are required to meet minimum established guidelines. Federal matching rates vary by state depending on per capita income. From 1996 through 1999, a dramatic decline in welfare rolls associated with both the economic expansion and PROWRA accompanied modest growth in Medicaid expenditures by federal and state governments (Hicks and Boyer, 1999). However, from 2000 through 2003 Medicaid experienced unprecedented growth at almost 11% per year. This growth was primarily caused by the increase in low-wage workers and the reversal in the decline of welfare caseloads, which accompanied the economic downturn. This expansion in costs came at a particularly bad time for states, the majority of which suffered from very elastic tax revenue sources.

---

[1] See Jencks (2002).

Thus, the economic downturn of 2001 reduced revenues while increasing expenditures, a very predictable combination of events.

During this time, considerable scrutiny of business practices prompted a number of organizations to examine more closely firms that employed large numbers of low-wage workers. The giant retailer Wal-Mart, among others, as well as the construction industry came under fire for employing workers who were either not eligible for employer-based health insurance or chose not to take advantage of plans (see Waddoups, 2004).

Another concern over the expansion of Medicaid eligibility involved Medicaid's role in crowding out employer-based health insurance for low-income workers. Shore-Sheppard, Buchmuller, and Jensen (2000) effectively isolated the impact of Medicaid on firm and employee behavior. While confirming earlier research (see Cutler and Gruber, 1996) showing that firms hiring large numbers of low-wage workers were less likely to offer insurance, they found no increase in the probability that these firms would offer insurance because of Medicaid eligibility changes affecting their workforce. However, the authors do not rule out the possibility that firms might make eligibility more difficult to motivate workers to drop coverage. The authors did find a small drop in the probability that firms would offer family coverage as the proportion of Medicaid-eligible workers increased. These authors also estimated employee response to Medicaid eligibility, finding that the take rate for employee-based health insurance dropped as the proportion of Medicaid-eligible workers increased. This is a similar argument offered by Becker and Posner (2005) as a counterargument to the critiques of Wal-Mart. They argue simply that Medicaid-eligible workers experience a real income increase by choosing Medicaid in lieu of standard employer-based health insurance for which premiums and copays are required. It is thus a utility-maximizing decision by workers under the current law.

In the end, the reduction of private health insurance because of increased Medicaid availability is likely. Importantly, it may be due either to employers adjusting coverage schemes to propel eligible workers into Medicaid or to individual workers trying to save money. The fiscal impacts, and probably the policy remedies, are likely the same.

University of Tennessee researchers Brad Kiser and Professor Bill Fox surveyed Tennessee firms, finding that only 52% of retailers and 53% of wholesale firms offered employee-based health insurance (Kiser and Fox, 2005). This study reports that roughly 65% of large firms (with more than 100 employees) offered health insurance to all their employees, whereas 30% offered insurance to only a portion of their employees. Firms surveyed in this study also report that cost and the share of part-time employees accounted for roughly 60% of those firms not providing insurance. Not surprisingly, the average salary of the firm's workforce played a large role in the firm's decision to offer insurance. With average incomes below $25,000, over 60% of firms offered no health insurance (at lower income levels, this proportion rises to over 90%). At all income levels over $25,000, the majority of firms surveyed offered some employees insurance, but even at income levels averaging over $55,000 one in five firms offered no health insurance. Kiser and Fox (2005) offer an interesting insight into the employer-based health insurance rates in Tennessee, a state that is probably facing the most daunting of the Medicaid-related problems (with its partially eponymous TennCare program).

In a very interesting study, Yale University and Brookings Institution researcher Nicole Kazee (2006) analyzes business response to public sector health care options through an evaluation of seven broad business surveys over a decade. She poses several hypotheses regarding the potential for strategic behavior by businesses regarding Medicaid expansion. Interestingly, she found compelling survey evidence that businesses support the expansion of public sector health care (Medicaid), presumably because it will lower their firm's costs.

Importantly, I have been unable to locate a study that evaluates at the macroeconomic level the relationship between changes in the structure of low-wage work, especially as it relates to the strong criticism of Wal-Mart, and Medicaid expenditures.

WAL-MART'S AFFECT ON ANTIPOVERTY TRANSFERS

The first important study to raise the point of Wal-Mart employees' reliance on Medicaid was by Dube and Jacobs (2004). These authors describe the potential for Wal-Mart workers to rely on government assistance by simulating individual worker use of such programs. This simulation model provides much-needed evidence of public finance concerns but does not provide unassailable evidence that Wal-Mart practices differ systematically from those of similar firms. These authors use data from a court case in which Wal-Mart was compelled to release wage data. From these data, the authors apply California take-up rates for a variety of public assistance instruments to estimate the difference between Wal-Mart and other retail firms in the state.[2]

Carlson (2005) offers a similar analysis of the government subsidization of Wal-Mart through a variety of transfer instruments in Oregon. This extensive analysis provides estimates of total subsidization of Wal-Mart using representative firm models on 2001 data (a simulation). As with any study of its type, it fails to provide controls for other factors. However, this study is as comprehensive an analysis of the state-level fiscal considerations surrounding the Wal-Mart debate as is available. Miller's (2004) congressional study offers a very partisan critique of the retailer. This analysis provides estimates of the expenditures for the working poor that would occur using a report on Wal-Mart's wage distribution released as part of litigation (Drogin, 2003). The report also criticizes Wal-Mart for labor practices and makes other allegations regarding the retailer.

A comparison of the findings of these three studies helps place into context the magnitude of the purported impact Wal-Mart has on antipoverty program expenditures.

Two factors inhibit the usefulness of these studies. The first is whether or not Wal-Mart workers use programs such as TANF and Medicaid at rates that differ from the retail industry in general. Second, as noted by Hicks (2005a) and Furman (2005), most of these programs

---

[2] See *Dukes et al. v Wal-Mart, Inc.* and Drogin (2003).

TABLE 9.1
Comparison of Expenditure Studies

	Dube and Jacobs (2004)	Carlson (2005)	Miller (2004) per 50 qualifying families (roughly one store)
Location	California	Oregon	United States
Medicaid	$730[a] per worker annually	$2.4 million annually	
TANF		$53,000 annually	
EITC		$1.08 million annually	$125,000 annually[b]
Food stamps		$550,000 annually	
School lunch programs		$750,000 annually	$36,000 annually
Title I expenses			$100,000 annually
SCHIP		$43,000 annually	$108,000 annually
LIEAP		$72,000 annually	$9,750 annually
Section 8 housing assistance		$41,000 annually	$42,000 annually[c]
Other / noncategorized	$1,222 per worker annually		

Note. TANF, Temporary Assistance to Needy Families; EITC, Earned Income Tax Credit; SCHIP, State Children's Health Insurance Program; LIEAP, Low Income Energy Assistance Program.
[a]All health care items.
[b]Includes all tax credits for low-income families, not just EITC.
[c]Assumes 3% of employees qualifying at common levels of reimbursement.

were designed to aid the working poor. In particular, EITC can only be paid to those working, while arguably the most important part of the 1996 suite of welfare reforms, and certainly one pursued by congressional Democrats and President Clinton, was the extension of Medicaid to the working poor. Discovering that these programs are working as designed is important and worthy of analysis, but breathless surprise at this result is silly and represents a real triumph of politics over policy.

A detailed comparison of other findings is also useful. The AFL-CIO compiled a list of states in which Wal-Mart has been named as having employees receiving Medicaid (or similar state programs). This list does not provide percentages, but it does offer basic data showing that, in the 10 states where actual numbers of take rates are known, Wal-Mart employees use Medicaid at rates ranging from 2.3% in Washington State to 24.9% in Tennessee's struggling TennCare program. See Table 9.2.

TABLE 9.2
Estimates of Wal-Mart Employees and Medicaid Expenditures

State	Wal-Mart Employees Receiving Medicaid	Medicaid Costs (per worker)	Source
Arizona	9.6%		*Arizona Daily Star* (confirmed by author calculations)
Arkansas	8.8%		AFL-CIO (reporting data from Arkansas Human Services Department)
Connecticut	8.9% (Huskey A-B)	$586[a]	AFL-CIO reporting data from state
Florida	13.25%		*Orlando Business Journal*, April 2005
Iowa	4.78%		Associated Press, August 2005
Massachusetts	6.9%	$246[a]	AFL-CIO reporting data from state
Ohio		$651[b]	Hicks (2005d)
Oregon		$311[b]	Carlson (2005)
Tennessee	24.9% (TennCare)		Memphis Commercial Appeal and author calculations
Washington	2.3%		AFL-CIO reporting data from Washington Health Care Authority
West Virginia	3.6%		AFL-CIO reporting data from state
Wisconsin	4.31 (BadgerCare)	$174[a]	AFL-CIO reporting data from state

[a]Data reported from direct expenditures.
[b]Data estimated from study.

The only industrywide average I have found for the trade sector (both retail and wholesale) is 11.8% in Nevada (Waddoups, 2004). Shore-Sheppard, Buchmuller, and Jensen (2000), in a microdata study, note high levels of low-income workers receiving Medicaid.

To date, two econometric studies have been undertaken that estimate the antipoverty impacts of Wal-Mart. Hicks (2005a, 2007) offers estimates of Wal-Mart's impact on Medicaid, food stamps, and TANF at the state level and provides a county study of these and other fiscal instruments in Ohio. The national study examined Wal-Mart from 1978 to 2003 in the 48 conterminous states. The model used in this study was as follows:

$$Y_i = f(\text{Wal-Mart, PCI, PROWRA, EITC,}$$
$$\text{\%Retail, LocalGov't / TotalGov't, recession} \qquad (9.1)$$

where specific impacts on Medicaid and other programs were a function of Wal-Mart's presence, state per capita income, post-1996 Welfare Reform (PRWORA), 1991 changes to the EITC, the retail share of employment, the local government share of total government employment, and a recession dummy. The study also included a common and a state fixed-effects intercept, a control for the North American Industry Classification System changeover in 2000 that affects data fidelity, and time- and spatial autoregressive variables. The original report assumed exogenous state-level entrance by Wal-Mart, but later versions incorporating instruments like those used by Basker (2005) and Neumark et al. (2005) also report similar results.

According to the study, Medicaid is heavily influenced by Wal-Mart's presence, with Medicaid rising roughly $900 for each Wal-Mart employee in a state. This finding is well within the simulation estimates offered in Table 9.2. I concluded that Wal-Mart actually reduced food stamps expenditures in states (but by less than $100 per employee) and that there was no impact on AFDC / TANF rolls.

In the second study (Hicks, 2007), I estimated these and other fiscal instruments (including revenues). The model was similar, excluding the variables designed to account for state-level tax collection variables and correcting explicitly for endogeneity using the lagged entrance variable from Basker (2005a). One important distinction was that I separated the Wal-Marts from the supercenters in this estimate.

I found that neither Wal-Mart stores nor supercenters influence welfare expenditures within the county in which it is located, unlike supercenters in adjacent counties, which do reduce Welfare costs within a county; however, the impact is quite small at only $43,000. The presence of a Wal-Mart or supercenter reduces countywide expenditures on food stamps, but the impacts are again small, representing the movement of between five and seven families out of the program (or a concomitant decrease in eligibility by a larger number of families). An adjacent Wal-Mart increases food stamp expenditures, offsetting roughly two thirds of the impact of a single Wal-Mart within a county. By comparison, the 1996 welfare reform (PRWORA) changes to eligibility, which affected most food stamp recipients, had an almost equal effect.

In contrast, Medicaid expenditures rose in counties with both Wal-Mart stores and supercenters and for adjacent county entrance. However, these impacts are quite small relative to countywide expenditures, accounting for between one half and three quarters of 1% of annual expenditures in the most recent years. With Medicaid expenditures averaging $13,660 per recipient in 2004 (Social Security Administration, 2005), new Wal-Mart–associated Medicaid expenditures in a county would account for roughly 16 additional individual recipients per county, translating into Medicaid costs of roughly $651 per Wal-Mart worker. This point estimate is higher but not inconsistent with estimates of per worker cost of $586 in Connecticut, $246 in Massachusetts, and $174 in Wisconsin. Nor does it differ dramatically from Carlson's (2005) estimate of $311 in Oregon.[3] It is somewhat lower than the national average estimated by Hicks (2005a) at roughly $900 per worker.

The final transfer payment I have analyzed is the EITC. This payment is especially helpful in that, since participation levels are scaled to

---

[3] See Hicks (2005a) for Medicaid review in the context of Wal-Mart.

income, it may better account for marginal changes in family economic well-being. A criticism of the EITC data is that participation rates are small relative to those who are eligible. However, these data may provide a better measure of incremental changes to poverty levels than do regional poverty rates or participation in other transfer payment programs.

The impact of a single Wal-Mart on EITC payments and cases are again mixed. A Wal-Mart was associated with an increase of family receipts of $119, or roughly 7% of the average state payments. Further, the number of cases rose between 16% and 43% depending on specification of the model (either fixed or random effects). However, in both cases, the statistical significance was not at the commonly reported levels, so definitive conclusions regarding Wal-Mart's impact on EITC are elusive. Explaining the opposing effects on EITC, food stamps, and Medicaid is an ongoing area of research, which suggests that changes in eligibility caused by increases in EITC will reduce food stamp and Medicaid expenditures. However, the dominant research in this area only suggests, but does not fully conclude, that this is occurring (see CBO, 2005; Mikelson and Lerman, 2004).

Again, the impact of Wal-Mart and its supercenters differed, with supercenters reducing the increase of EITC payments per family. These are sensitive to the data definition, and combining Wal-Mart with supercenters eliminated any impacts on EITC. The overall conclusion surrounding these results is that additional analysis is warranted.

WAL-MART AND MEDICAID ENROLLMENT IN MARYLAND

The concern over the role of Wal-Mart and Medicaid generated the greatest policy response in Maryland in 2005 and 2006. In December 2005, the Assembly passed legislation known as the Fair Health Care Act. Since only Wal-Mart was subject to its rules because of several carefully crafted exceptions (e.g., Johns Hopkins University among others), it is better known as the "Wal-Mart tax." This is also the name its proponents at several anti-Wal-Mart organizations gave it. Maryland

Governor Ehrlich vetoed the bill, and his veto was overturned by the Assembly. The legislation, which was to have taken effect in 2007, has subsequently been invalidated by the Maryland courts as a violation of Employee Retirement Income Security Act, which prevents states from imposing different rules on interstate firms regarding employee benefits. This is designed to enhance interstate commerce. However moot this legislation may be, the impact that Wal-Mart has had on Medicaid enrollment in Maryland is of interest. To test this, I use data from Maryland's Department of Health and Human Services on actual county-level enrollment in Medicaid. I test the model on the years 1998 through 2005.[4] With one point of departure from most other examples presented in this book, these data show evidence of nonstationarity. That is, even under this very short time period, these variables possess a trend. This means that I must make some modifications to my regression. The most common technique is to use their annual changes (or first differences) in the model. Since the first differences do appear to be stationary, I proceed with the annual changes. I construct the by now familiar model of Wal-Mart impacts:

$$\Delta M_{i,t} = \alpha + \alpha_i + \beta_1(WM_{i,t}) + \beta_2 \tilde{W}(\Delta M_{j,t})$$
$$+ \beta_3 R_t + \delta \phi_{t-n} + e_{i,t} \qquad (9.2)$$

where Medicaid enrollment, M, in county i in year t is a function of common and cross-sectional specific intercepts, the number of Wal-Marts in a county in each year (WM), and spatial lag (Medicaid enrollment in j contiguous counties in year t, which is estimated by the row-normalized first-order contiguity matrix $\tilde{w}$). I also include a recession dummy, using the National Bureau of Economic Research

---

[4] Maryland officials are loath to part with these data and, despite repeated requests, inform me that the data are absolutely unavailable before 1998. One employee even told me that computers were not used before this date. This is, of course, absurd, except perhaps when viewed through the prism of the state's other public policy misadventures, when it becomes eerily plausible.

designated dates, the most common approach. To this I add the time-autoregression variable with one lag and a white noise error term. An astute reader will note that I preserve the fixed effects, even with the first-differenced dependent variable. This is done because there is still widespread variation in total county-level Medicaid enrollment; thus, preserving a fixed-effects specification is appropriate.

Also I am concerned about endogeneity affecting my results. Although Wal-Mart's entrance decision is clearly not focused on existing Medicaid enrollment, it might seek to systematically enter markets focusing on a variable that is itself correlated with Medicaid enrollment. I use two instruments I have already discussed. The first is the time / distance from Bentonville instrument used by Neumark, Zhang, and Ciccarella (2005):

$$\Omega_{i,t} = \alpha + \sum \alpha_i + \delta_1 DIST_i + \delta_2 (DIST_i \cdot T) + e_{i,t} \tag{9.3}$$

The second is my instrument, in which market size identifies the impact equation:

$$\Omega_{i,t} = \alpha + \sum \alpha_i + \delta_1 \left(\sum PI_{j,t} + PI_{i,t} \right) + e_{i,t} \tag{9.4}$$

I also report ordinary least squares (OLS) estimates. Results appear in Table 9.3.

My estimates of Wal-Mart's impact on Medicaid enrollment in Maryland reveal no impacts that can be attributed to Wal-Mart. What matters most in a county is its size (as revealed by the unreported county-specific intercepts), followed by the number of enrollees in adjacent counties, and under the OLS specification a recession. It appears that, although Wal-Mart employs many workers on Medicaid in Maryland, the store does not contribute to overall Medicaid rolls; hence, the targeting of Wal-Mart is a prime example of a policy solution in quest of a problem.

TABLE 9.3

Wal-Mart's Impact on Medicaid Enrollment in Maryland

	OLS	Time / Distance	Market Size
Common intercept	−127.6055	108.2916	−683.9574
	(−0.25)	(0.15)	(−0.51)
Wal-Mart	416.1752	−15.51931	755.1339
	(1.266)	(−0.02)	(0.64)
Spatial lag	0.459110***	0.901558**	0.707869*
	(3.12)	(2.23)	(1.88)
Recession	337.4337**	54.75067	42.94852
	(2.40)	(0.07)	(0.08)
Autoregression ($t-1$)	−0.454700***	−0.466876***	−0.466920***
	(−9.12)	(−8.19)	(−7.24)
Adjusted R^2	0.84	0.81	0.85
Durbin-Watson	2.70	2.71	2.20
Observations	115	115	115

Note. The Durbin-Watson panel statistic reported is derived from Bhargava, Franzini, and Narendranathan (1982). I whitewashed the variance matrix using a version of White's (1980) heteroscedastic-consistent variance–covariance matrix derived from Driscoll and Kraay (1998). As is common, I have not reported the values of the cross-sectional fixed-effects coefficients to preserve space. OLS, ordinary least squares.

***p = 0.01. **p = 0.05. *p = 0.10.

SUMMARY

The overwhelming majority of the evidence available to date suggests that a nontrivial proportion of Wal-Mart's employees and their families receive antipoverty transfer payments. There is some evidence, derived primarily from my research, that Wal-Mart leads to higher levels of Medicaid expenditures (see Hicks, 2005b, 2007). What is far less clear is whether this presents a public policy problem or is merely evidence that the programs are providing antipoverty assistance to low-income workers who are commonly employed by retail firms.

Discussion of the policy innovations designed to remedy the high rates of Medicaid use by Wal-Mart employees will appear again in this book. Before shifting to more detailed policy analysis, I believe that a review of some of the more poignant social impacts (and by that I mean outside the more commonly analyzed economic issues) provides a good segue to understanding Wal-Mart's impact on local economies.

SECTION IV

SOCIAL IMPACTS OF WAL-MART

The impact of Wal-Mart goes beyond those associated with fiscal and commercial economic activity. Indeed, much of the criticism of Wal-Mart targets issues of wages, working conditions of suppliers, the strength of local communities, and environmental considerations. In this section I review existing studies and provide additional estimates of Wal-Mart's impact on poverty, mom-and-pop stores, ghostboxes, labor force participation, unionization, local philanthropy and social cohesion, and urban sprawl. I begin with a broad review of studies examining issues beyond the fiscal and commercial economic impacts of Wal-Mart.

One of the more ambitious studies (Shils, 1997) surveyed 6,000 local business owners in four states asking businesses their expectations regarding future stability of their enterprise when Wal-Mart or other big-box stores enter their markets. And, while the wisdom of asking about expectations in lieu of actual results in communities where Wal-Mart had located should be noted, the results aligned with the reported media concerns over big-box and chain stores that I reviewed at the outset of this book.

Lichtenstein (2005) published papers from a conference on Wal-Mart. This conference proceeding was argued to represent several important views on Wal-Mart, and Lichtenstein focused on describing Wal-Mart as the representative firm of a new type of capitalism. The papers are interesting and represent a very broad set of analytical approaches. Indeed, the papers included a review of Wal-Mart's legal troubles regarding employment law by one of the plaintiff's attorneys. The papers by historians, lawyers, anthropologists, and management scholars, ranging from undergraduate students to full professors, represent an unusually diverse set of academic specialties; unfortunately, the diversity of analysis on these economic issues did not extend to actual economists.

The majority of the inferences regarding Wal-Mart's social impacts are derived from generally accepted anecdote regarding chain store impacts on mom-and-pop stores, the role of larger retailers on local wages and employment conditions, the impact on job quality (part-time and unionization), the role of chain stores in community through philanthropy and social cohesion, and, perhaps most cited, impacts of big-box stores on sprawl. However, 'generally accepted anecdote' is a poor starting point from which to launch a policy debate; so I will attempt to attach some empirics to each of these issues, treating each in turn.

CHAPTER TEN

THE POOR, THE PHILANTHROPIST, AND THE MOM-AND-POP STORE

The three community factors that first entered into the Wal-Mart debate were the role of the retailer on poverty through wages and job conditions, the impact on local philanthropy, and, perhaps most importantly, the survival of the mom-and-pop store. Although all of these issues have diverse dimensions and are too extensive too treat fully in this book, there are some straightforward empirics that can lend significant understanding. My goal in this and the ensuing social impact chapters is to provide some isolated analysis to push forward an understanding of these areas.

WAL-MART'S IMPACT ON POVERTY AND INCOME DISTRIBUTION

Few researchers have attempted to link Wal-Mart directly to poverty. This research is far outside the scope of more common economic analysis, which focuses on market forces, not individual firms. Perhaps most importantly, researchers seem to have difficulty making convincing theoretical links to Wal-Mart's role in causing poverty. Most importantly, although Wal-Mart is a big firm and often the largest private sector employer in counties in which it is located (and several states), it employs less than 1% of the U.S. workforce. Indeed, I would be surprised if Wal-Mart accounted for even 25% of the retail workforce in any county in which it located (outside of Bentonville, Arkansas). These are small numbers with which to affect labor markets, as I have already indicated. However, there are other considerations, and one that is of the most immediate concern is the potential for Wal-Mart's geographic setting to influence access to retail for some consumers.

Concern over access to food is a recurring theme of poverty researchers, and at least two groups have examined this directly. Thomas, Martin, and Dai (2005), in the previously reviewed study on grocery store pricing in central New York State, found that prices in rural areas for food items were higher than in larger markets. Thomas et al. argue that this is a recurring rural problem. Blanchard and Lyson, two researchers at Mississippi State and Cornell Universities, respectively, examined grocery store access in Mississippi using Geospatial Information Systems to assign a market area (based on distance and road network) from existing supercenter-type stores, including more than Wal-Mart supercenters. By comparing the demographics of the locations served by these supercenter grocery formats, Blanchard and Lyson concluded that the poor and disadvantaged (e.g., older, less mobile) tend to have poorer access to the lower priced foods than their more affluent neighbors. They suggest that the location process of these stores has distanced themselves from the poorer regions and characterize this as the creation of "food deserts" (see Blanchard and Lyson, 2000). However, these concerns have not been an important element in the anti-Wal-Mart campaign probably because the most likely local policy solution is to permit a Wal-Mart to move into urban settings.

One very important paper by Stephan Goetz and Hema Swaminathan (2006) evaluates the role Wal-Mart plays in changing local levels of poverty. Using, as Basker (2005a) did, data drawn directly from commercial sources (the Rand McNally maps of Wal-Mart), these authors construct a model in which local poverty rates are influenced by Wal-Mart presence, initial levels of poverty, local labor force, and demographic and other variables drawn for a fairly extensive research stream by Goetz and others. They handle the endogeneity problem through instrumenting Wal-Mart's expected entrance based on a subset of the poverty-related variables, existing poverty, and the presence of a Wal-Mart store before the sampled period of 1987 to 1998.

The authors found a number of interesting results related to Wal-Mart. One was that Wal-Mart growth seemed to be unrelated to population growth, a finding that echoed that of Franklin (2001) and Hicks and Wilburn (2001). More central to the question of poverty, Goetz and Swaminathan found that Wal-Mart stores were associated with increases in the poverty rate or slower poverty reductions in counties in which they were located. This impact is small, with the incremental impact of a new store raising poverty to rates 0.204% higher than they would have been absent a store. Existing stores (those located before the sampled period) had an impact of a little less than half that magnitude.

Goetz and Swaminathan provided three causative factors for Wal-Mart's impact on poverty. They observe that displacement from existing mom-and-pop stores might lead to lower wages for some workers and hence higher poverty rates. They argue also that philanthropy may also suffer, leading to higher poverty rates. These are problems I will empirically address in this chapter. Finally, they suggest a more subtle impact may be that Wal-Mart store formats reduce the leadership class of counties and thus lead to higher poverty rates. They seem to imply that they believe this is the stronger of the forces at play.

This study has been criticized for its instrument choice, which, as I have discussed, is a convenient first target of all econometric studies. However, I believe that their results are likely quite robust. I believe that the more important weakness is not empirical, but, in the assertion by the authors, that the increased poverty rates are a Wal-Mart–specific externality.[1] However, these provocative results are not reliant on theory; the careful empirics and important policy question are the compelling parts of this paper.

A second study of the poverty question was performed by Keil and Spector (2005). These authors examined Wal-Mart's impact on unemployment rates and income differentials across ethnic groups in Alabama from 1980 to 1990. They constructed a model that accounted for the presence and entrance of a Wal-Mart, population and income growth rates, the retail share of income, the male-to-female ratio, and proportion of the population that was African-American. This model was constructed to explain unemployment and income differentials between White and Black residents at the county level.

These authors found that during the 1980s the presence of a Wal-Mart in a county reduced the White–Black unemployment rate differential, hence benefiting Blacks. They attribute this to a more competitive labor market. They found no closing of the White–Black income gap during this time period. They note that the long-run results may differ from those in this short-run analysis, meaning the income gap may close over time.

These authors offer some potential shortcomings of their analysis, in particular that intercounty labor flow may cloud some of the findings. They do not explicitly address the potential for endogeneity in the entrance decisions of Wal-Mart.[2] Clearly, Wal-Mart's entrance is exogenous with respect to ethnic mixes, but it may not be with respect to economic factors that have secondary impacts on White–Black income differentials. Importantly, the findings by Goetz and Swaminatham (2006)

---

[1] The authors suggest the poverty impact is a negative externality, like pollution. Economists have not made this type of link before, and I believe there are significant theoretical weaknesses in their case.

[2] Interestingly, there is widespread belief that ethnic or racial differences do matter in store or employment design. For example, one publication notes that "African-Americans place a much greater importance on stores being involved in the community and having black elements or cultural cures, things that make them feel more comfortable in a store" (Janice Jones, quoted in Joseph, 2005, p. 77).

and Keil and Spector (2006) are not inconsistent, because poverty rates could rise and unemployment rate differentials decline. In addition, although it is a matter of opinion, most would agree that increased poverty is an unfortunate result, whereas decreased unemployment rate differentials across ethnic or racial groups is a positive result.[3]

To extend this analysis I will examine the role of Wal-Mart stores in income distribution. To do so, I use the Gini coefficient, perhaps the best known measure of income inequality. The Gini coefficient is an index number that is bounded by 0 and 1, with 0 being perfect income equality (all persons receiving the same level of income) and 1 being the condition in which one person receives all the region's income. I use data from Nielsen (2002) for U.S. county Gini coefficients for 1970, 1980, 1990, and 2000. I choose Arkansas as the region of analysis because it has had the longest history of Wal-Mart presence (in each of the decades for which I have data). One concern with this choice is that Arkansas' long, and largely favorable, relationship with Wal-Mart may mean that its impact differs from that of other areas. Descriptive statistics appear in Table 10.1.

Using these data, I construct a model to test decennial impacts of Wal-Mart on the Gini coefficient. The specification of the model is

$$\ln(G_{i,t}) = c_i + \delta_1 WM_{1970} + \delta_2 WM_{1980} + \delta_3 WM_{1990}$$
$$+ \delta_4 WM_{2000} + e_{i,t}, \quad \text{where } e_{i,t} \rightarrow iidN(0,\sigma^2) \quad (10.1)$$

where the dependent variable is the natural log of the Gini coefficient, regressed on a common intercept and the number of Wal-Mart stores (regular and supercenters only) that entered a county in the previous decade. The use of the logarithm for the dependent variable (expressed as 0–100] is done for ease of interpretation and to smooth any potential

---

[3] This, of course, is not necessarily true, as increased poverty rates may subject unskilled workers to programs that boost their long-run productivity, and a 100% unemployment rate across all people is probably much worse than a small differential at a roughly 5% unemployment rate.

TABLE 10.1
Descriptive Statistics of Arkansas (Gini and Wal-Mart)

| | | Year | | | |
		1970	1980	1990	2000
GINI	M	40.44	39.26	40.04	40.76
	Mdn	40.27	38.99	39.68	40.09
	SD	3.21	2.97	3.06	2.84
	Minimum	33.20	32.06	33.32	33.65
	Maximum	50.32	49.4 5	49.26	47.96
Wal-Mart	M	0.11	0.67	0.93	0.95
	Mdn	0.00	1.00	1.00	1.00
	SD	0.35	0.78	0.79	0.80
	Minimum	0.00	0.00	0.00	0.00
	Maximum	2.00	4.00	4.00	4.00

nonlinearities in the relationship. The results of the log specification are almost identical to the estimate in levels (but levels are less easily explained than percent changes implied by the logarithm). I use the time-specific coefficients to evaluate whether or not different decades experience different effects, a matter of some importance. Also I treat this model for heteroscedasticity using White's (1980) method. Results appear in Table 10.2.

These results provide interesting insight into the issue of Wal-Mart and income distribution. Arkansas counties that experienced a Wal-Mart in the 1960s and 1970s saw declines in income inequality of between 2.8% and 2.5% for each Wal-Mart store that entered in these decades, respectively. In the 1980s, income inequality resulting from each additional Wal-Mart store decreased by less than 1%. In the 1990s, this impact dropped to a value statistically indifferent from zero. In essence, the early entrance of Wal-Mart clearly played a role in reducing income inequality in Arkansas counties, by 6.3% in the Gini Index. However, it is likely that this impact ran its course by the 1990s, as the market matured.

TABLE 10.2
Wal-Mart's Impact on the Gini Coefficient

	Coefficient (*t* statistic)
Intercept	3.693270
	(929.73)
No. Wal-Marts in 1970	−0.028437
	(−9.15)
No. Wal-Marts in 1980	−0.025569
	(−10.03)
No. Wal-Marts in 1990	−0.009271
	(−4.23)
No. Wal-Marts in 2000	0.002807
	(1.28)
Adjusted R^2	0.99
F statistic	128921.5
Durbin-Watson statistic	1.31

Note. The Durbin-Watson panel statistic reported is derived from Bhargava, Franzini, and Narendranathan (1982). I whitewashed the variance matrix using a version of White's (1980) heteroscedastic consistent variance–covariance matrix derived from Driscoll and Kraay (1998). As is common, I have not reported the values of the cross-sectional fixed-effects coefficients to preserve space.

Although my findings are not directly comparable to those of either Goetz and Swaminathan (2006) or Keil and Spector (2005), they are not inconsistent with either of these findings. My finding of reduced income inequality is technically not incompatible with the small poverty impacts found by Goetz and Swaminathan, although most economists would expect a different result, if only through a "gut" feel. However, if there were a broad reduction (or much slower growth) in incomes in Wal-Mart counties that also resulted in less inequality but pushed a small number of residents into poverty, then the two findings are not inconsistent. However, my findings are more suggestive of Keil and Spector, who argue that the reductions in the White–Black unemployment rate are likely to translate into reductions in the income differentials in these two groups in the long run.

In the final analysis, much additional work on the role of Wal-Mart in poverty and income distribution would be welcomed. I now turn my attention to the role of Wal-Mart on the presence of that favorite American institution: the mom-and-pop store and local philanthropy.

WAL-MART'S IMPACT ON PHILANTHROPY

A criticism of chain stores that dates back at least a century is that the putative loss of mom-and-pop stores to national chains would also remove from the local community the dedicated philanthropy emanating from the owners of these establishments. Appreciating the level of this concern from research is difficult. However, it is a persistent concern. Indeed, Nichols (1940) answered several chain store critics and cited a Senate document from the 73rd Congress (1933–34) in which charitable giving by chain stores and chain store managers was reported. Clearly, chain store impacts on philanthropic activity and social cohesion is an issue that warrants further examination.

I have not found any empirical analysis of the impact of a single firm, such as Wal-Mart, on local giving. There is considerable anecdotal information on the role that large corporations in general or Wal-Mart in particular may play in nonprofit growth. However, there is a growing body of research on the nonprofit sector that enlightens some of the issues purported by the popular literature to be affected by Wal-Mart. I review a few of these here.

Abzug and Galaskeiwizc (2001) examined the composition and role of nonprofit boards. This is relevant to Wal-Mart since the role of the retailer on weakening local institutions is a frequent refrain in the popular media (and by Goetz and Swaminathan, 2006, in the context of entrepreneurship). They do so empirically through an examination of boards in 1931, 1961, and 1991. Among the many interesting findings of this study is that the number of college-educated professionals and managers on boards grew dramatically during this period (as it did in the general population). The authors argue that board composition is designed to lend credibility to the organization and enhance its ability to procure resources. Obviously, the loss of locally based managers would dilute the pool of potential nonprofit board members.[4]

Twombly (2003), a researcher at the Brookings Institution, examined the entry and exit of nonprofit firms in the 1990s. His models of exit / entry were

$$\text{Prob}(Exit \,/\, Entrance) = f(\text{organizational, policy,}$$
$$\text{economic, demographic,}$$
$$\text{emergency services}) \qquad (10.2)$$

where an estimate of the probability of a firms exit was based on different measures within these broad areas.[5] The economic variables of government expenditures and poverty rate may, as other research suggests, be related to Wal-Mart. Twombly found that experimentation surrounding the 1996 Welfare Reform Act was a dominant cause of entrance–exit dynamics in the nonprofit sector.[6] This was also coincident with accelerating Wal-Mart growth in terms of the number of new stores.

Teihan (2000) estimates the relationship between higher female labor force participation rates and the decline of volunteerism. Using time-diary data, Teihan models volunteerism as a discrete choice by individuals that is conditioned on age, work (full- and part-time), demographics (e.g., age and number of children), and education levels for women in 1965, 1975, 1985, and 1993. She finds that volunteerism rates decline with labor market participation, but volunteerism hours

---

[4] This report is an especially interesting analysis. I served briefly on a nonprofit board of directors (Center for Economic Options, Inc., which won the 2000 President's Award for Microenterprise). The insights of the board role and composition that can be gleaned from this modest report are tremendous.

[5] This type of model, which estimates probability, is known as a limited dependent variable regression and possesses several distinct econometric features. This author reports the marginal impacts, making its interpretation similar to the traditional regression models discussed in this book.

[6] The Personal Responsibility and Work Reconciliation Act of 1996 (PRWORA).

donated by those who do participate is increasing. In a later chapter, I discuss Wal-Mart and labor force participation.

Grønbjerg and Paarlberg (2001) estimated a panel model of the nonprofit sector in Indiana's counties. The authors test nonprofit demand, supply, density, and community structure on a model of four different types of nonprofits. They find that community structure (e.g., religious affiliation and percent locally employed) and local resources are dominant explanations of nonprofit supply. They do not support the demand-side explanation for nonprofit growth.

These studies represent the whole of the serious analysis of philanthropic giving and nonprofit operations, which I deem as possibly related to the presence of a local Wal-Mart in a community. In addition, although these fine studies are important contributions to understanding nonprofit and charitable performance, I believe an additional estimate of Wal-Mart's impact is warranted. To perform this analysis, I focus on Michigan from 1988 through 2002, the period of Wal-Mart's entrance into the state. I use data from the Regional Economic Information System, which measures total charitable receipts by nonprofits from businesses. These series measure money, securities, and real property, of which money is by far the dominant component. These nonprofits are those that provide services to individuals. A second test is performed on the payments to membership organizations (their private earnings). These are essentially receipts by such organizations as the Optimists, Rotary, Junior League, Lions, and so on. Obviously, the first set of data tests the direct hypothesis that Wal-Mart is affecting lower local charity payments. The second series is a test of the indirect affect of Wal-Mart on local social cohesion as expressed by income received by employees of these organizations (presumably through member dues, although other revenue sources are also possible).

Other means available to measure charitable giving consist of reported giving by individuals as presented to the Internal Revenue Service (IRS). However, these are the only time-series data on actual business giving I can locate. These data are available at the county level from 1969 through 2004 but suffer from considerable suppression at this level, although most is in the early years and my sample includes data on all counties beginning 1995.

I choose Michigan to preserve some of the economic diversity in the regions I study, not for any particular charitable or nonprofit characteristics. Michigan is squarely in the middle of per capita charitable giving, with 36% of IRS filers giving an average of just over $2,800 to assorted charities.[7] A graph of real business payments to nonprofits and membership organizations (in $1,000s of 2000 constant dollars) from 1969 through 2000 is shown in Figure 10.1.

Using these two data series, I model the influence of Wal-Mart on them as follows:

$$\Gamma_{i,t} = \alpha + \alpha_i + \beta_1 WM_{i,t} + \beta_2 \tilde{W}\Gamma_{j,t} + \delta\phi_{t-1} + e_{i,t} \qquad (10.3)$$

where Γ is either charitable giving by businesses or membership organization receipts in county i, year t, which is a function of common and county-specific intercepts (the cross-sectional fixed effects) and the presence of Wal-Mart. I treat spatial concerns with

FIGURE 10.1   Business Charitable Giving and Membership Organization Receipts in Michigan (in $1,000s of constant 2000 dollars)

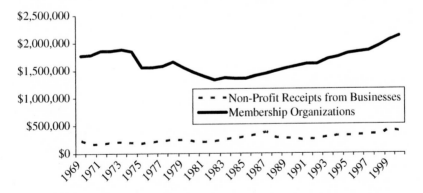

---

[7] These data are from the 2004 report produced by the Urban Institute on charitable giving.

the first-order spatial lag of the dependent variable Γ in county j, adjusted by the row-weighted first-order contiguity matrix $\bar{w}$. These data are stationary, and the fixed-effects model, as I have noted before, accounts for the cross-sectional characteristics that are fixed over the sample period (such as relative population position of counties). I assume Wal-Mart's entrance is exogenous with respect to charitable giving by businesses. Results appear in Table 10.3.

This model provides an estimate of Wal-Mart's impact on charitable giving by businesses and receipts by membership organizations. The first is a direct test of the hypothesized negative impact of Wal-Mart on local charities. The second is an indirect test on Wal-Mart's impact on the social cohesion of communities. The first test enjoys a solid

TABLE 10.3
Wal-Mart and Nonprofits in Michigan

	Charitable Giving by Businesses	Membership Organization
Intercept	−0.356542	−80.84620
	(−0.05)	(−0.17)
Wal-Mart	4.231119**	7.545875*
	(2.03)	(4.38)
Spatial lag	0.948362***	0.028803
	(5.82)	(0.13)
Autoregression ($t-1$)	0.754171***	1.025688***
	(5.04)	(23.40)
Adjusted R^2	0.99	0.99
Durbin-Watson	1.03	2.19
Observations	1,065	913

Note. The Durbin-Watson panel statistic reported is derived from Bhargava, Franzini, and Narendranathan (1982). I whitewashed the variance matrix using a version of White's (1980) heteroscedastic-consistent variance–covariance matrix derived from Driscoll and Kraay (1998). As is common, I have not reported the values of the cross-sectional fixed-effects coefficients to preserve space.
***$p = 0.01$. **$p = 0.05$. *$p = 0.10$.

direct linkage to the data, while the indirect test provides merely a proxy for a directly unobservable variable of participation in social organizations.

These results not only strongly reject the hypothesis that Wal-Mart is negatively affecting local business support of nonprofits, but it illustrates that Wal-Mart has a positive, and more than modest, impact. Indeed, for the average county in 2000, the presence of a Wal-Mart increased giving to nonprofits by 9.3%. This result is highly statistically significant. Second, these results also reject a hypothesis that Wal-Mart is negatively influencing social cohesion as measured by receipts to membership organizations. Indeed, I find that Wal-Mart actually increases receipts by membership organizations, with each new store leading to a roughly 2.8% increase in wages paid by these organizations. This finding is also quite statistically reliable. The study does have limitations, most specifically in that these data are not the whole of charitable giving (although I think this a mild critique). Also, my social cohesion measure is, like all proxies, merely a representation of an unobservable event, albeit among the better I have seen. In addition, the presence of a Wal-Mart store may affect the business contribution in a way that differs from local businesses. For example, if Wal-Mart chooses to provide direct financial support (instead of in kind gifts), these data may reflect that shift, when there may not be a real impact or even a negative result. These concerns warrant more comprehensive research on the way local giving is affected by Wal-Mart and by other similar businesses.

Wal-Mart stores report a high degree of charitable giving to a variety of local causes. As with their reporting of jobs and wages, this is a gross impact and does not account for potential net reductions. The enduring argument has been that local stores, notably mom-and-pop establishments, are more supportive of local charities. The results presented here—the first of their type—strongly reject this hypothesis and find that, within the arena in which this these data measure (business contributions to nonprofits and membership organization receipts), Wal-Mart has a strong positive and statistically meaningful impact across Michigan counties.

WAL-MART AND MOM-AND-POP STORES

Perhaps the greatest local criticism of chain stores over the past century is their purported negative impact on small businesses. Wal-Mart is the latest chain store to experience such criticism. At least one early study focuses on the response of incumbent firms (mostly small), finding that innovative or aggressive pricing, followed by targeted marketing and changes to product variety, dominated the response by firms following the entrance of a Wal-Mart (McGee and Rubach, 1996). Professors Thomas Harris and Scott Shonkwiler, in their study of the independence of retail businesses, found that the types of retail trade across subsectors are highly dependent. They indicate that the inter-action of these different sectors (e.g., general merchandising, eating and drinking establishments) is necessary for a trade area to grow. This interaction is important to Wal-Mart and mom-and-pop stores in that it may explain interaction between large stores like Wal-Mart and smaller retailers (Harris and Shonkwiler, 1997).

As I described in the chapters on commercial impacts, the existing literature on the impact of firms is mixed. The econometric studies performed by Hicks and Wilburn (2001) and Basker (2005a) both examine the impact of Wal-Mart on the number of retail firms. Kristy Wilburn and I examined total retail firms in separate retail subsectors in each of West Virginia's 55 counties from 1989 through 2000. We found that the number of firms increased by just under five per county when a Wal-Mart was present. Basker examines retail establishments, which she labels as small (fewer than 20 employees), medium (fewer than 100 employees), and large. She found a modest decline in the number of small firms (four over a 5-year period), a loss of less than one medium-size firm per county, and an increase (less than one) at the large retailer level. This final finding suggests that Wal-Mart is displacing some competing large retailers.

The difference in these findings may be attributable to the authors' differing treatment of endogeneity, or it could be the result of real economic differences on display in the two samples (55 West Virginia counties vs. the largest half of total U.S. counties).

Sobel and Dean (2006) assess directly the impact of Wal-Mart on entrepreneurship and mom-and-pop businesses in a nationwide sample. Using a spatial autoregressive model of Wal-Mart's presence in states from 1997 through 2003, the authors reject any impact (positive or negative) on the number of firms in these size categories. These three papers are the only empirical analysis of retail firm impacts, and, with divergent findings, additional analysis is warranted.

MOM-AND-POP STORES IN IOWA

To explicitly evaluate Wal-Mart's impact on small businesses, I examine the experience from one state that I have already reviewed in this book: Iowa. I begin with the familiar model of Wal-Mart's impact:

$$\Theta_{i,t} = \alpha + \alpha_{i,t} + \beta_1 WM_{i,t} + \beta_2 WM_{j,t} + \beta_3 \tilde{W}\Theta_{j,t} + \delta\phi_{i,t-1} + e_{i,t} \tag{10.4}$$

where the number of small retail businesses in each size category, Θ, is a function of a common and cross-sectional specific intercept, a Wal-Mart presence / count variable, the number of Wal-Mart's in j adjacent counties, a first-order spatial lag of the dependent variable, a first-order autoregressive variable, and a white noise error term. These data are stationary, so I estimate them in their actual values without any transformation. As with previous analyses of Wal-Mart's impacts, I am concerned about the potential for endogeneity. For example, if Wal-Mart is systematically entering markets with a growing number of retail stores, then my estimates will be biased toward finding a positive effect of Wal-Mart. Recall, however, considerable debate remains over the appropriate correction for this endogeneity bias. Recognizing this, I estimate the impact using the most accepted instrument, which was offered by Neumark, Zhang, and Ciccarella (2005). This takes the form

$$\Theta_{i,t} = \alpha + \alpha_i + \delta_1 DIST_i + \delta_2(DIST_i \cdot T) + e_{i,t} \qquad (10.5)$$

which is a familiar specification of the identifying equation. Using an instrumental variable approach estimated with two-stage least squares, and including lagged exogenous variables within the instrument to account for the contemporaneous relationship between Θ and its spatial lag, $\bar{w}\Theta$, I estimate the impact on Iowa's counties from 1989 through 2003. I use as my dependent variable the number of firms by firm size category as reported by the County Business Patterns data series. The Wal-Mart data are from the 2003 data release. Results appear in Table 10.4.

My study of Wal-Mart's impact on the number of small retailers in Iowa reveals no statistically meaningful estimates. In the one case in which statistical significance is close to accepted levels, the impact is positive. Interestingly, a Wal-Mart store in adjacent counties exerts a very weak negative, but not statistically meaningful, impact. In addition, although I do not report them, similar estimates in Maryland and Indiana show almost identical impacts. Also of interest is Wal-Mart's impact on large retailers. These results closely mirror those of Sobel and Dean (2006), who conclude, as do I, that there is no net impact of Wal-Mart on small retailers. In addition, although the literature reveals some disagreement, the impact of Wal-Mart on small retailers, even using the most negative estimates (Basker, 2005a), is remarkably modest.

Of similar interest is Wal-Mart's impact on large retailers. Basker reports that Wal-Mart's entrance leads to a net increase of less than one retailer on average in her sample. This, she argues, suggests that Wal-Mart is associated with the exodus of some larger firms. My analyses in Iowa, Maryland, and Indiana support these findings, although the impact is less than commonly held levels of statistical significance. One conclusion to be drawn is

TABLE 10.4

Wal-Mart's Impact on Iowa's Mom-and-Pop Retailers

	Employee Range		
	1–4	5–9	10–19
Common intercept	2.866587	1.383424	−3.483242
	(0.204)	(0.17)	(−0.10)
Wal-Mart	3.786541	9.894825†	42.26103
	(0.53)	(1.57)	(0.39)
Adjacent Wal-Mart	−7.418041	−8.599172	−31.81699
	(−0.58)	(−1.09)	(−0.50)
Spatial lag	0.991583***	0.960798***	0.998684***
	(8.59)	(6.64)	(3.65)
Autoregressive component	0.830817***	0.850836***	0.688254***
	(16.91)	(19.37)	(7.84)
Adjusted R^2	0.98	0.98	0.97
Durbin-Watson	2.26	2.40	2.00
Observations	1,485	1,485	1,485

Note. The Durbin-Watson panel statistic reported is derived from Bhargava, Franzini, and Narendranathan (1982). I whitewashed the variance matrix using a version of White's (1980) heteroscedastic-consistent variance–covariance matrix derived from Driscoll and Kraay (1998). As is common, I have not reported the values of the cross-sectional fixed-effects coefficients to preserve space.

***$p = 0.01$. †$p = 0.15$.

that it is the larger incumbent retailer, not the smaller one, that has most to fear from Wal-Mart's entrance. This lesson is likely abundantly clear to anyone who held Sears or K-Mart stock in the 1980s and 1990s.

CHAPTER ELEVEN

THE SOCIAL ASPECTS OF LABOR MARKET: UNIONS AND PARTICIPATION

In earlier chapters, I dealt with Wal-Mart's influence on labor markets, limiting the discussion to wages, employment, and industry mix. Here I delve deeper into labor market issues, namely the manner in which Wal-Mart affects the proportion of a county's available workers who actually work (labor force participation rates [LFPRs]). Further, I examine how Wal-Mart may be affecting union participation rates. The former issue is not often a policy issue but speaks to opportunity provided by the retailer. The latter is a very obvious source of tension between Wal-Mart and unions.

WAL-MART'S IMPACT ON U.S. LABOR FORCE PARTICIPATION

One clearly important aspect of Wal-Mart is its potential to offer additional employment opportunities through adjustments to the aggregate labor markets. Although I have reviewed this issue in an earlier chapter, here I offer evidence of Wal-Mart's impact on the LFPR.

Evaluating Wal-Mart's impact on the LFPR is useful in evaluating the counterfactual argument that the presence of Wal-Mart is extinguishing employment. It is also useful in providing evidence of greater labor market flexibility, which is widely believed by economists to accompany higher rates of labor force participation. Virtually all existing studies of labor force participation are focused on individual workers, not regions studies, so I do not review them here.

LFPRs are typically defined as the total number of those in the labor force (employment or unemployed) as a proportion of the entire population.[1] This is the approach used in this analysis, which constructs a purely empirical model of Wal-Mart's impact on LFPR. The model I use is similar to the basic Wal-Mart exposure model presented by Hicks (2005a), who estimated Wal-Mart's impact on anti-poverty programs.

The basic specification of the model is

$$
\begin{aligned}
LFPR_{i,t} = \alpha + \alpha_i + \beta_1(WM_{i,t}) \\
+ \beta_2 \tilde{W}(LFPR_{j,t}) + \delta\phi_{i,t-n} + e_{i,t}
\end{aligned}
\tag{11.1}
$$

where the LFPR (expressed in the range [0,100]) is a function of a common intercept and a state-level fixed-effects intercept and a Wal-Mart presence count variable, which comprises the annual sum of all Wal-Mart and supercenters in a state. To this I add a first-order spatial lag of the LFPR. This is the weighted value of the dependent variable in the contiguous counties.[2] To this I include the first-order time-autoregressive element and a white noise error term, e.

I further refine this model by identifying this equation using a time / distance from Bentonville function similar to Neumark, Zhang, and

---

[1] Some definitions further refine this definition to include only those potentially within the labor force.

[2] This is weighted by the now familiar row-standardized first-order contiguity matrix W.

Ciccarella (2005) and Dube, Eidlin and Lester (2005). The identifying equation is thus

$$LFPR_{i,t} = \alpha + \beta_1 DIST + \beta_2 T \cdot DIST + e_{i,t} \qquad (11.2)$$

where the estimated LFPR is a function of a common intercept, distance from the state capital to Bentonville, Arkansas, and a time variable, *T*, which is the number of years since the opening of Wal-Mart. To this equation I include the lagged dependent variables to correct for the endogeneity of the lagged spatial autoregressive variable in the basic equation.

This seemingly complex process of estimation is actually quite intuitive. I propose to test whether the LFPR is determined by the entrance of Wal-Mart stores within a state. To test this, I construct a measure of the number of Wal-Mart stores and then account for the effect of the greater region (adjoining states) on labor force participation and for the previous year's LFPR. This is the basic ordinary least squares (OLS) specification. However, because I am still concerned that Wal-Mart may be choosing locations based on the LFPR, I again use a statistical technique, known as an instrumental variable approach, which corrects for the potential relationship between the LFPR and Wal-Mart entrance, using a measurement that is related to Wal-Mart's entrance but not necessarily to the LFPR. This is the time / distance function mentioned previously. Both Neumark, Zhang, and Ciccarella (2005) and Dube, Eidlin, and Lester (2005) use the same approach but on county-level data, whereas I test on U.S. statewide data. I further refine the estimate by evaluating the period in which Wal-Mart had entered more than five states and splitting it into roughly three periods: 1975–1984, 1985–1994, and 1995–2004. Results appear in Table 11.1.

From a modeling standpoint, these regressions perform well and provide useful interpretation. Apart from the very obviously high correlation between current LFPR in a state and lags in time and space, Wal-Mart has no statistical effect prior to the most recent decade. Here, there is a small but statistically strong impact of Wal-Mart on the LFPR. In my estimates, each new Wal-Mart in a state is associated with a roughly one tenth of 1% increase in labor force participation.

TABLE 11.1

Wal-Mart's Effect on Labor Force Participation Rate

	1975–1984	1985–1994	1995–2004
Intercept	1.180688	8.410928	14.00935
	(0.26)	(0.54)	(1.05)
No. of Wal-Marts	0.002963	–0.010602	0.096906**
	(0.12)	(0.43)	(1.98)
Spatial lag	0.996952***	0.881862***	0.792147***
	(11.28)	(3.78)	(9.07)
Autoregression	0.829848***	0.881675***	1.020519***
	(32.89)	(38.18)	(26.37)
Adjusted R^2	0.99	0.99	0.99
Durbin Watson (panel)	1.29	1.49	1.42
Observations	490	490	441

Note. The Durbin-Watson panel statistic reported is derived from Bhargava, Franzini, and Narendranathan (1982). I whitewashed the variance matrix using a version of White's (1980) heteroscedastic-consistent variance–covariance matrix derived from Driscoll and Kraay (1998). As is common, I have not reported the values of the cross-sectional fixed-effects coefficients to preserve space.
***$p = 0.01$. **$p = 0.05$.

This is a small effect but, when translated into actual employment (either full- or part-time), results in a considerable number of workers nationwide. These results suggest that Wal-Mart, by the end of the 20th century and in the first part of the 21st century, was having some effect on labor markets. This finding is quite consistent with those of Keil and Spector (2007), who found that more competitive labor markets decreased unemployment rate disparities between Black and White citizens of Alabama. They are also consistent with the findings of Neumark, Zhang, and Ciccarella (2005) and Dube, Eidlin, and Lester (2005), whose analysis suggested increased overall employment attributable to Wal-Mart. My findings here are also reminiscent of those in Chapter 4 regarding aggregate employment impacts.

Resurrecting a limitation in the findings is the argument about job quality and type. The data cannot tell us enough about the job to speak earnestly about its quality. In addition, although the markets do suggest there are ample workers willing to work at Wal-Mart, what we don't know about them is important. Are they casual workers such as high school and college students, looking convenient hours with little regard for benefits? Are they senior citizens simply looking for income supplement or the satisfaction of working? Are the workers beleaguered single mothers in desperate need of full-time employment with health benefits? Are they women seeking to reenter the labor force and start a career as children grow older? Of course, some or all of these types of workers are at every Wal-Mart store on every shift. However, the share of each of these types of workers (and how much Wal-Mart permits workers to self-select among employment options) is a key policy concern that we simply do not know enough about.

The social impacts of Wal-Mart on such factors as LFPRs speak to labor market effects beyond those of pure employment and wages. However, policymakers and citizens interested in local economic performance will also be interested in other factors related to choices about work and wages, union membership, and rates of union participation in regions.

IS WAL-MART INFLUENCING UNION PARTICIPATION?

Among the chief critics of Wal-Mart's national presence are labor unions. The three major areas of concern over Wal-Mart are the lack of unions at Wal-Mart stores, the impact of Wal-Mart on unionized workers (primarily at grocery stores that are losing market share to the supercenters), and Wal-Mart's role in promoting international trade. I discuss these grocery store concerns and the international trade argument in other sections of this book. In addition, as I pointed out at the beginning, this is not a book that deals explicitly with such matters as the legal treatment of employees. That matter is simply better addressed in another venue. However, Wal-Mart's potential impact on national unionization is a matter of interest at the local level.

Research of the influence and cause of unionization is widespread and worthy of several other books. To highlight the role that unionization rates may play on local labor markets, I will briefly review the work on labor markets in the grocery store sector. Grocery stores are a useful place to consider unionization because they are densely unionized at about twice the retail trade average, and their wages are perhaps 60% higher than their nonunionized counterparts. For individual workers, Belman and Voos (1993) found that union participation had a very strong impact on individual wages. In an extension of this approach, Johannson and Coggins (2002) found that higher rates of unionization of grocery stores in local labor markets increased both unionized and nonunionized wages in these sectors. These studies supported other findings that union participation boosted own-wage effects, with some spillovers. However, this clear benefit to unionized workers is not the whole of the estimated effect of unions. Major criticisms of union impact on labor and goods markets have been provided by a number of researchers. These market-related criticisms include familiar market power-related criticisms such as implicit restraints on employment. Hirsch (2004) reviews some of the popular arguments and suggests that both the benefits and ills of unions are largely overstated, at least with respect to economists' ability to measure them.

For the purposes of this book, I would like to determine whether Wal-Mart's presence, either as a supercenter or as a discount store, influences the level of unionization in a state. I begin with estimates of total unionization in the 48 conterminous states provided by Hirsch, Macpherson, and Vroman (2001). The remaining data are from Wal-Mart's 2003 data release and the Regional Economic Information System. To measure the union effect, I construct a model of union participation:

$$
\frac{U_{i,t}}{\bar{U}_t} = \alpha + \alpha_i + \beta_1 WM_{i,t} + \beta_2 SS_{i,t} + \beta_3 T
$$
$$
+ \beta_4 \tilde{W} \frac{U_{j,t}}{\bar{U}_t} + \delta \phi_{t-1} + e_{i,t}
$$

(11.3)

in which the unionized share of total employment, U, in state i relative to the national average is a function of a common and state-specific intercept, the number of Wal-Marts and supercenters in each state in year *t*, a time trend, *T*, to account for the sectoral decline in union participation, a first-order spatial lag, and a time-autoregressive variable (with a 1-year lag). I assume the error term is white noise, an assumption that necessitated specifying the dependent variable as unionization relative to the nation.[3]

I am modestly concerned about endogeneity in Wal-Mart's entrance decision but feel that the time distance from Bentonville measure discussed earlier (see Chapter 3 and Neumark, Zhang, and Ciccarella, 2005) should prove adequate to identify this relationship.[4] I report both the estimation results in Table 11.2.

These results offer an interesting interpretation. Wal-Mart discount stores positively effect unionization, although the magnitude of the impact is very modest, with 100 additional Wal-Marts leading to a 10% increase in the rate of unionization in a state. Wal-Mart supercenters have a similarly small impact but the opposite sign (although its statistical significance drops to just greater than 10%). Thus, Wal-Mart supercenters actually reduce union participation rates, but modestly.

I limited the time span to honor the concerns of Neumark, Zhang, and Ciccarella (2005) over the time distance instrument's usefulness afterward. If I include the time period through 2004, the statistical strength of these relationships grows, but the magnitudes are largely unchanged. Similarly, I was worried about the influence of California on the sample, since supercenters had received considerable local opposition. If I exclude California from the sample, the magnitude of the impacts grows, with about a 60% rise in the impact of the discount store but only modest growth in the supercenter impact.

When treating Wal-Mart's discount stores and supercenters as homogeneous, the OLS estimate finds a statistically meaningful negative

---

[3] If I had left the dependent variable in its rate form, it would be effectively bound by 0 and 1. This presents some econometric concerns, since limitations on the range of the dependent variable lead to many well-known problems (primarily biased coefficient estimates). Thus, by scaling it, I am able to partially reconcile these problems in a panel model.

[4] Because this is a restatement of an equation earlier presented, I omit it here.

TABLE 11.2

Wal-Mart's Impact on Unionization Rates (1970–1995)

	OLS	2SLS
Intercept	0.786731***	–0.175688
	(10.85)	(–0.27)
Wal-Mart	0.001537***	0.001717*
	(2.69)	(1.80)
Supercenters	–0.001625***	–0.001108†
	(–4.08)	(–1.57)
Trend	0.000604	0.000325
	(0.71)	(0.71)
Spatial lag	0.213096***	1.178929*
	(2.93)	(1.83)
Autoregression	0.603002***	0.596527***
	(20.25)	(21.53)
Adjusted R^2	0.96	0.95
Durbin-Watson	2.02	2.04
Observations	1,248	1,248

Note. The Durbin-Watson panel statistic reported is derived from Bhargava, Franzini, and Narendranathan (1982). I whitewashed the variance matrix using a version of White's (1980) heteroscedastic-consistent variance–covariance matrix derived from Driscoll and Kraay (1998). As is common, I have not reported the values of the cross-sectional fixed-effects coefficients to preserve space. OLS, ordinary least squares; 2SLS, two-stage least squares.
***$p = 0.01$. *$p = 0.10$. †$p = 0.15$.

impact of Wal-Mart stores, whereas the two-stage least squares estimates drop from statistical significance. However, in both estimates, the magnitudes of the impacts are extremely small. Under these specifications, 100 new Wal-Mart stores would decrease unionization rates by one half of 1%. This is below the meaningful threshold of economic significance.

My findings here suffer the real concern that the level of aggregation (state unionization rates) may well be too high to fully capture the influence of Wal-Mart on unionization. Further, although the transmission mechanisms for Wal-Mart supercenter impacts on unionization are fairly clear (potential pressure on unionized grocery store competitors); these are not so clear for the basic discount stores.

However, these estimates do suggest that Wal-Mart is influencing total unionization. In addition, given the very rapid rate of supercenter conversion, the net impact of Wal-Mart on unionization in the United States is likely mildly negative. This result is sensitive to choice of time period analyzed. Also, whether these effects on unionization are important in magnitude is uncertain. Finally, the evidence regarding the net benefit of unions is not at all a settled matter, so whether this is a welcome finding or not is likely a very personal affair.

CHAPTER TWELVE

WAL-MART AND THE LOCAL ENVIRONMENT: GHOSTBOXES AND SPRAWL

At the local level, environmental issues are often the key components of land use, planning restrictions, and neighborhood concerns. However, these worries surrounding Wal-Mart are fairly narrow. Unlike the manufacturing or transportation sectors, a local Wal-Mart is unlikely to generate worrisome toxic emissions. Retailers just do not have these types of very large-scale environmental concerns. However, the aggregate impact of the retailer on energy and emissions may be a different story (and one for which Wal-Mart has garnered considerable praise as well as criticism). Since this book focuses on local issues, I will narrow my analysis to a few of the chief environmental concerns about Wal-Mart: (a) the potential for greyfields and ghostboxes as a result of closure of competing stores or relocation of the retailer and (b) urban sprawl. I assess impacts to farmland, land use, and incumbent retail structure, an admittedly narrow set of concerns. I focus on these issues not because others are less important but rather, because I am an economist and not a biologist, I intend to preserve the specialization of labor.[1]

GREYFIELDS AND GHOSTBOXES

Greyfields—lightly used or vacant retail facilities—present a long-standing concern for local communities. Despite the common appearance of empty big-box stores and nearly vacant main streets, little in the way of rigorous empirical analysis of the impact of vacant retail has been performed. Fortunately, there is voluminous descriptive analysis of the problem, especially that focusing on the practical matters of developing alternative uses for vacant retail centers.

Vacant buildings are not really a new phenomenon. The loss of population concomitant with the increase in agricultural productivity in the Midwest during the first half of the 20th century, culminating in the dustbowls of the plain states, provided the United States its first large-scale examples of redundant real estate. Big-box retail vacancies, often referred to as "ghostboxes," is merely the newer phenomenon on the economic landscape. Its reemergence is clearly worth investigation and analysis.

Wal-Mart potentially contributes to greyfields in two ways. First, if it relocates economic activity from one location (e.g., a city center) to another and the resulting facilities become vacant, then it indirectly contributes to greyfields as incumbent retailers close or relocate. Second, if a Wal-Mart store closes, consolidates, or relocates, then any remaining vacant facilities may become greyfields. The analysis reviewed and presented here should make clear that the loss or gain of retail establishments

---

[1] This approach is not always shared in the limited environmental literature on the subject. One study of the environmental concerns surrounding a potential Wal-Mart in Potsdam, New York, addresses the economic issues in the middle of what is otherwise a study of the local environment. Rather than insult biology as badly as these authors did economics, I will leave that type of analysis to those with at least minimal understanding of the subject.

as a result of Wal-Mart's entrance is not a resolved matter, and the impact probably varies considerably across regions. The movement of Wal-Mart from one facility to a newer one within a community is well documented (and has occurred in perhaps 15% of all Wal-Mart stores). The reasons for doing so are probably pretty simple. It is a profit-maximizing decision for the store to relocate activity either to take advantage of demand differences (population shifts or changes to traffic flow) or to exploit economies of scale.

The dearth of economic analysis of the issue of the economic impact of greyfields is exemplified by a mere two references to the problem in a 2001 report by Maryland's Department of Planning, which specifically addressed planning problems with big-box retail. This study compared local tax revenues lost because of a vacancy, assuming the loss has not been captured by some other entity (e.g., a competing establishment). The study also suggests that change due to retail "competition" is a loss (Perry, 2001). This analysis suffers some of the same conceptual weakness as studies that include all of Wal-Mart's employment as a net gain (without considering lost employment by competitors). The Maryland Department of Planning report also fails to acknowledge potential gains as a result of productivity growth, which are the sole source of per capita economic growth. However, this study is helpful in providing data and analysis of the question.

A far better study of greyfields and big-box stores was provided by the University of Wisconsin's Extension Office (Kures, 2003). The study identified changes to retail structure, population shifts, changing demographics, and consumer preferences and failure to reinvest by mall owners. Naming the vacant big-box stores as ghostboxes, the study notes especially the loss of Kmart's 600 stores nationwide from 2000 to 2003.

There are also many examples of revitalization programs and success stories. By far the most interesting is maintained by artist and academic Julia Christensen. Her Web site (http://www.bigboxreuse.com/) details types of reuse of vacant big-box stores, focusing on the aesthetic styles of architectural changes made to the facilities. This researcher is a critical source for any studies on ghostboxes.

Wal-Mart provides some data on vacancies, primarily as a method of selling or leasing the facilities through their realty service. To understand how turnover in their operations has occurred, I compare data obtained from their Web site in late summer 2004 with the same information from 2006. Virtually all of these were for Wal-Mart stores that were relocating within a community. This listing includes all sites that are available or are planned for relocation. In 2004, the site listed 379 properties with buildings. Of these, 68 were not yet available (planned relocation at some future date) and 13 were under contract or pending contract for sale or lease. The total available retail space was a whopping 29 million square feet. The average-sized facility was about 75,000 ft^2 (mean, 77,934; median, 74,779). The largest was 162,478 ft^2 and the smallest 1,453 ft^2 (assuming the 23 ft^2 location was a data entry error).

I compared the 2004 and the 2006 data to understand how rapid the turnover might be in these types of vacant big-box stores. Interestingly, by 2006, the total number of properties listed had fallen from 379 to 284, with only 108 of the original list still available. Of the 284 properties, 50 were not yet available (relocation plans were announced almost 2 years into the future) and 58 were under contract for sale or lease. Two were being used for Hurricane Katrina relief efforts, and about half of the remaining stores had some remaining tenants in the mall. The average size and range of store sizes were nearly identical to those of the 2004 vacancies. See Figure 12.1.

Interpretation of these data is not clear-cut, but a few tantalizing clues emerge. First, it seems that the ghostboxes themselves are smaller than the newer Wal-Mart discount stores or supercenters. Thus, it is likely that the relocation within a city is due to pursuit of scale economies or reconfiguration of a discount store into a supercenter. Second, the number of stores that appear for sale or lease 2 years later seem to have dropped by just under one third. There could be several explanations for this. First, it could be simply that Wal-Mart is doing a better job of choosing locations than in previous years. Second, the rate of relocation could have slowed because of either the most recent recession or inadequacy of demand for a new store or

FIGURE 12.1   Wal-Mart's Ghostbox Status for 2004 and 2006

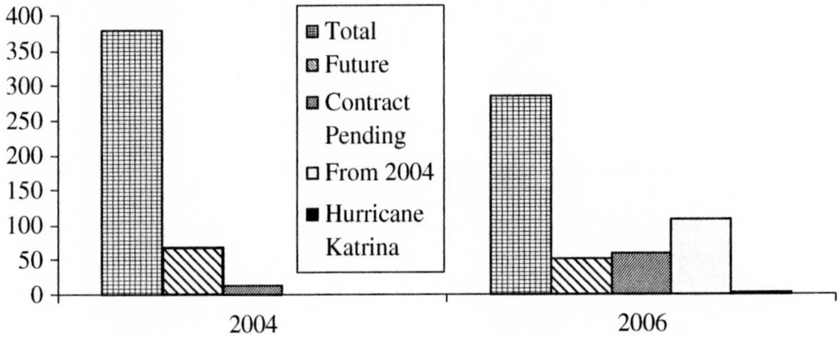

Source: Wal-Mart Realty.

supercenter. Third, the best locations for relocation were probably chosen first, with remaining sites less viable. For whatever reasons, it seems clear that the rate of relocation has slowed a bit. That condition could well change. Finally, the rate of lease or sale of these properties does not appear particularly untimely. I have been unable to locate any data on the duration of retail vacancies, but anecdote suggests that 2 years for a large vacant store (big-box or mall anchor) is not unusual.

What is not clearly understood is whether, as some have claimed, the creation of ghostboxes blights a community, causing economic decline that can be directly attributed to Wal-Mart. To test a hypothesis of ghostbox- or greyfield-related economic decline attributable to Wal-Mart, I tested the impact of ghostboxes on Ohio's retail sector. Using the existing Wal-Mart ghostboxes in 2003, I estimate a model that accounts for existing conditions and the decision by Wal-Mart to exit, the traditional endogeneity problem, here playing out in reverse. Thus, I posit the identifying equation as

$$\Omega_i = \alpha + \beta \left(\frac{dR_i/R_i}{dt} \right) + e_i \tag{12.1}$$

where Ω is the number of retail firms in county i in year 2003, which is a function of a common intercept, and the retail sector growth rate from 1990 to 2002. The error term, e, is assumed to follow a Poisson distribution as Ω is a count variable (the number of retail establishments). This equation gives an instrumental variable estimate of Ω for the second stage of the estimation. The second stage involved rounding the estimate of Ω to fit within the specifications of a Poisson count model. The estimated second stage is then

$$\Omega = \alpha + \beta_1 GB + \beta_2 FAM + e_i \tag{12.2}$$

where the number of retail stores is a function of vacant Wal-Marts or ghostboxes and the number of families to scale the estimate (the family data are from the 2000 U.S. Census release). The results appear in Table 12.1.

TABLE 12.1

The Impact of Ghostboxes on County-Level
Retail Establishments in Ohio

	Coefficient (z statistic)
Intercept	2.693045***
	(57.37)
Ghostbox	0.752637**
	(2.06)
No. of families	4.22E-06***
	(4.26)
Adjusted R^2	0.34
Likelihood ratio index (pseudo-R^2)	0.33
Log likelihood	−415.25
Observations	88

Note. Both stages were estimated using the traditional maximum likelihood estimator and do not appear to suffer from overdispersion. This estimate was corrected for heteroscedasticity using the Huber-White method. The Poisson distribution is a common estimation technique that accounts for nonnormally distributed errors. The equation was solved using the Berndt, Hall, Hall, and Hausman hill-climbing algorithm.
***$p = 0.01$. **$p = 0.05$. *$p = 0.10$. ††$p = 0.15$"

These regression results point to a modest increase in the number of retail establishments because of the presence of an empty big-box store, but the values are trivial (0.75 of a firm). These results are robust to alternative specifications, which include dropping the correction for endogeneity. One note of caution is important: These are county-level tests, and so the reordering of economic activity within a county is not visible. However, there is no evidence that the existence of an empty ghostbox negatively affects the number of retail establishments in a county.

Actual closing of Wal-Mart stores has been far rarer than their local relocation. In conjunction with the writing of this book, I asked Wal-Mart for several data elements, including the number of firms that were closed. They responded with a list of 14 closures and seven consolidations (involving 13 stores). I estimated the opening dates from the reported store numbers. The only media discussion I could find on these surrounded the North Little Rock closure, which was argued against by local leaders and the local newspapers. See Tables 12.2 and 12.3.

TABLE 12.2

Wal-Mart Closings

Store Number	City	State	Year Opened	Comment
110	North Little Rock	AR	1975	
191	Flat River	MO	1977	
202	Tulsa (Catoosa)	OK	1977/1978	
245	Jenks	OK	1979	
263	Charleston	MO	1979	
291	Hearne	TX	1980	
351	Kinder	LA	1980	
416	Nowata	OK	1982	Previously Bud's
455	Robstown	TX	1982	
496	Pawhuska	OK	1983	Previously Bud's
570	Dickinson	TN	1984	
679	Tuskegee	AL	1981	
920	Little Rock (Asher)	AR	1986	
2011	Kirksville	MO	1993	Farm store

TABLE 12.3

Wal-Mart Consolidations

From		To		
Number	City	Number	City	Opening Date
1145	McKenzie, TN	161	Huntington, TN	1977
187	Pacific, MO	295	Eureka, MO	1980
717	Avon Park, FL	666	Sebring, FL	1984
22	Allen, TX	1117	Plano, TX	1987
53	Broken Arrow, OK	1597	Tulsa (Bixby), OK	1990
367	Bixby, OK			
509	Douglasville, GA	1488	Douglasville, GA	1990

I have not been able to determine any real economic or demographic pattern of these closings or consolidations. Although many of the closed towns are small, rural, and frankly struggling, some of the locations are relatively vibrant (North Little Rock, Little Rock, and Tulsa, for example). Also, although Wal-Mart closed some of these stores, they also entered similar counties to include some of the most economically struggling locations in the nation (such as McDowell County, West Virginia). See Figure 12.2.

The consolidations do not seem to follow any real pattern. My supposition is that the decision to close a Wal-Mart or merge it with another nearby is probably very localized and may more likely be due to idiosyncratic factors such as store rent or traffic pattern changes than to any larger phenomenon.

Empty big-box stores have been a source of considerable angst for local planners but have attracted some surprisingly innovative local solutions. The presence of a ghostbox, however aesthetically unappealing, does not insinuate a net loss of economic activity at the county level.

WAL-MART'S IMPACT ON URBAN SPRAWL

The role of big-box retailers in urban sprawl is subject to the most emotional debates surrounding Wal-Mart. Web sites and books mimic

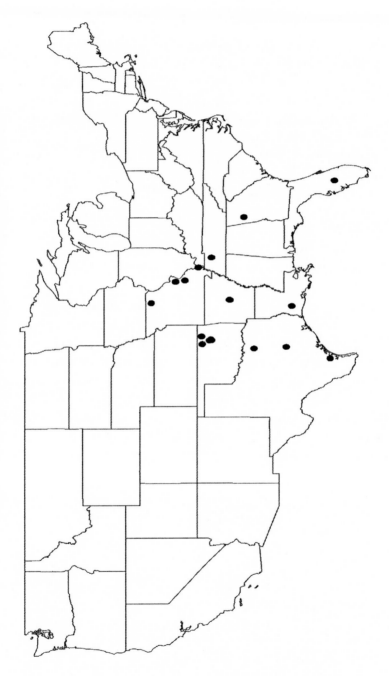

FIGURE 12.2   Closed and Consolidated Wal-Mart Stores, 1978–2004

the retailer with such monikers as "Sprawl-Mart," and numerous advocacy groups target Wal-Mart for its contribution to sprawl. Perhaps the most famous of these is a group headed by Al Norman, author of two books and several articles linking Wal-Mart to sprawl and other adverse local consequences. The numerous criticisms of Wal-Mart (and, for example, Target, Kmart, Lowe's, Home Depot) make very entertaining reading and are especially useful in understanding the dynamics of local governance and zoning. The one piece universally absent from these writings is empirical linkages, causal or otherwise, of Wal-Mart to urban sprawl. This can perhaps be forgiven since, even for those engaged in researching sprawl, its measurement remains a difficult subject.

Stephen Goetz, whose work on Wal-Mart and poverty was cited in both Chapters 4 and 10, has written a useful summary of many of the measurement and data issues regarding sprawl, and reviewed some of the analytical methods to account for the changes to land use patterns over time (Goetz, 2004). Among the types of measures he reviews, reductions in population density, increased spatial discontinuity, and use changes are the most common. I focus on the latter of these: the change in use mixes represented by loss of farmland.

Thus, I focus on what I believe is an effective measure of Wal-Mart's contribution to sprawl in the Midwest: its influence on the size of farms and total acreage farmed. To test this, I examine Wal-Mart's impact on the number of farmed acres in Ohio. I construct the model

$$FARM_{i,t} = \alpha + \alpha_{i,t} + \beta_1 WM_{i,t-1}$$
$$+ \beta_2 \tilde{W}(FARM_{j,t}) + \delta\phi_{i,t-1} + e_{i,t} \qquad (12.3)$$

in which farmland, *FARM*, in each county *i* in year *t* is a function of a common and county-specific intercept, a 1-year lagged Wal-Mart's presence (to account for pre-opening construction), a first-order spatial lag, and an autoregressive variable with a 1-year lag. The error term is assumed to be a white noise error term. Further, I assume that Wal-Mart's entrance is exogenous to farm acres and farm size in

Ohio's counties. I extend this assumption of exogeneity to the spatial lag, since the market factors that provide contemporaneous impacts for economic variables are unlikely to influence farm land. All data are from the U.S. Department of Agriculture reports on Ohio farmlands for various years, and the Wal-Mart data are from the 2003 data release.

Interpretation of these data is subject to one important caution. Although it is very likely that these data represent working farms (because of the average farm size of about 190 acres per farm), there are significant tax advantages to reporting and using land for farm purposes. This might influence the farm size in my sample. The data are stationary, and thus I estimate them in levels. The results appear in Table 12.4.

My findings point to a real, albeit statistically weak, contribution of Wal-Mart to the loss of Ohio farmland. The impact on average

TABLE 12.4
Wal-Mart's Impact on Ohio's Farmland

	Number of Acres	Acres per Farm
Common intercept	118001.4***	40.41548***
	(22.50)	(3.44)
Wal-Mart	−245.6793†	−0.722442**
	(−1.44)	(−2.43)
Spatial lag	0.278075***	0.788547***
	(8.95)	(13.69)
Autoregressive	0.904216***	0.904644***
	(56.85)	(49.87)
Adjusted R^2	0.99	0.98
Durbin-Watson (panel)	1408	1408
Observations	2.01	2.16

Note. The Durbin-Watson panel statistic reported is derived from Bhargava, Franzini, and Narendranathan (1982). I whitewashed the variance matrix using a version of White's (1980) heteroscedastic-consistent variance–covariance matrix derived from Driscoll and Kraay (1998). As is common, I have not reported the values of the cross-sectional fixed-effects coefficients to preserve space.
***$p = 0.01$. **$p = 0.05$. †$p = 0.15$.

farm size is statistically strong and accounts for about three quarters of an acre per farm. Overall, these results conform to observation, with Wal-Mart associated with the loss of roughly 0.15% of farmland in the average Ohio county. However, this is a small impact, at just under 25% of the annual average variability in farmland in Ohio (the number of acres farmed both rises and falls in the sample). The size of Wal-Mart's impact on farmland is more statistically meaningful but quite small; the average farm loses about three quarters of an acre. Thus, the entrance of a Wal-Mart is associated with the loss of about one and one third average-sized farms.

These results provide some empirical confirmation for the emotional debate over Wal-Mart and sprawl, but the size of the impact is far smaller than the level of angst within the debate. Further, although these findings represent the first real empirical support in the sprawl debate, I must emphasize that farmland is but a small part of the overall concern. In other areas, Wal-Mart may well reduce measures of sprawl. For example, the retail sales per square foot of building space is evidence of much more concentrated economic activity, which is sprawl reducing.

SUMMARY

The social impacts I review in this and previous chapters represent only a modest element of a broad set of the criticisms leveled against Wal-Mart. I find that, where research exists, there is significant disagreement among researchers as to the impact of Wal-Mart on issues of poverty and income distribution, mom-and-pop stores, labor force participation, unionization rates, philanthropy, and sprawl. In attempting to add to this research, I find that the presence of a Wal-Mart reduced income inequality in the early years, but that this impact has continued to dissipate so that in recent years there has been no effect. I find that there is no ill effect of Wal-Mart on mom-and-pop stores. My analysis of philanthropic and social cohesion suggests that Wal-Mart is actually increasing philanthropy revenues and revenues to membership organizations.

I estimate a very modest and only recent correlation between Wal-Mart and increasing labor force participation rates. I also find that Wal-Mart discount stores are not negatively influencing unionization rates, but supercenters are correlated with lower rates of unionization. This is presumably due to the loss of unionized grocery jobs that compete with supercenters, but my analysis cannot speak firmly on this matter. Finally, I find that each new Wal-Mart discount store or supercenter reduces farmland by about 250 acres, or less than half the space its store facilities are likely to inhabit in Ohio.

The analysis of Wal-Mart's impact on social forces lags far behind the pace of the policy debate. This is unfortunate because, as outlined in Section I, few of these are new concerns. In addition, although the estimates I review are solid scholarly works, they are lonely scientific voices in this debate, which is mostly ruled by emotion. The analysis I perform here is novel and, I believe, solid but far from complete in the sense that the full range of related issues, not to mention geographic variability, is underrepresented. It is my hope that this issue will gain considerable additional analysis. However, impacts that I review and those that I present as new do not speak strongly to real policy concern. With one exception, none of these impacts are particularly large, suggesting that for better or worse Wal-Mart's impact on this spectrum of social issues, with the exception of local philanthropy, is quite modest.

Section V

State and Local Public Policy and Wal-Mart

The intent of this book is to review and expand on the estimates of Wal-Mart's impacts, with a focus on the state and local levels. Thus far, I have reviewed the history of chain stores and their success, opposition, and regulation and the development of the big-box store (Section I). This was followed by a review of Wal-Mart's impact on commercial markets for labor, goods, and services in retail, whole-sale, and the aggregate economy (Section II). I then reviewed fiscal impacts associated with the retailer and described the mechanisms by which the entrance of Wal-Mart would influence tax collections and expenditures (Section III). I followed this with three chapters on some, but by no means all, of the social dimension of Wal-Mart's impact (Section IV).

In Section V, I turn my attention specifically to state and local public policy. In Chapter 13, I examine local zoning ordinances, which potentially affect Wal-Mart, providing an economic analysis of these laws. This is done with a critical eye toward some of the apparent intent of the legislation. I also describe and briefly assess the current impact of living wage ordinances on Wal-Mart and try to estimate the number of employees who are affected by these laws. I then turn my attention to antitrust laws and enforcement at the state level and end with a detailed examination of the Wal-Mart tax and an examination of the economic theory of regulation as it may pertains to this wave of legislation. In Chapter 14, I describe the myriad difficulties state and local policymakers face when examining Wal-Mart objectively through the media and popular writings. I follow this up with a restatement of the analysis reviewed and performed in this book. From this, I offer specific guidance on the type of research that should accompany public policy discussions on the matter. I also provide a caution toward activist policy targeting Wal-Mart, for or against.

CHAPTER THIRTEEN

STATE AND LOCAL RESTRICTIONS ON WAL-MART

Wal-Mart, like many firms, is faced with state and local legislation, ordinances, and policies designed to influence its behavior. In an earlier chapter, I reviewed the research on tax incentives and industry location decisions. I also provided new evidence of the impact of tax incentives on Wal-Mart's entrance decision and the impact the incentives generated on local economic conditions. In both instances, the results were not supportive of providing state or local economic development incentives to Wal-Mart, a finding that echoes the economic research on the issue.

The economic development incentives Wal-Mart has received include tax increment financing, property tax abatements, and job creation tax credits. There are certainly others, and as I noted earlier, Wal-Mart is not out of the normal range in acceptance of these types of local incentives. In addition, however lamentable economic development incentives targeting Wal-Mart may be, there are also significant restrictions on

Wal-Mart placed by local and, increasingly, state governments. These restrictions are designed to influence the physical structure of the store and its placement. The rules range from fairly benign aesthetic rules to efforts to intentionally limit the advantages of scale economies, thus protecting incumbent retailers (whether intentionally or not). In contrast to the quantity of research on Wal-Mart's impacts, policy guidance on mechanisms to thwart Wal-Mart's entrance is far too voluminous to review in a single book, much less a chapter. Fortunately, most of the rules and restrictions are simply variations on a common theme, so their generic treatment doesn't diminish an understanding of what is a growing trend in communities across the nation. I begin with local restrictions on Wal-Mart, moving to state-level legislation and some new analysis of the issues.

LOCAL RESTRICTIONS ON BIG-BOX STORES

Regulatory strategies toward limiting the entrance of big-box stores, with a clear focus on Wal-Mart, have become so common that the American Planning Association produced a report that detailed restrictions on Wal-Mart (Evans-Cowley, 2006). The regulatory descriptions provided as part of this and similar studies are usually exercised under state constitutions, which devolve zoning power to local communities (counties or municipalities). These laws have generally been upheld by courts as part of this permission granted by states. These restrictions have been limited, however, to basic principles (such as generic size caps and traffic restrictions), not direct targeting of an individual company.[1]

George Lefcoe, professor of real estate law at University of Southern California, categorizes municipal restrictions into three legal categories: absolute bans, conditional use permits (CUPs), and site-specific review. The absolute bans on big-box development are a result of legislation that focuses on size restrictions and limitations on sales

---

[1] See the *Great Atlantic & Pacific Tea Company v. Town of East Hampton.*

of nontaxed items (such as food). CUPs permit local planning boards to review projects on very narrow subjects such as aesthetics, proximity to roads, and traffic congestion. The final restriction involves the requirement of an individual new store review, which can extend analysis from the very narrow CUPs to such issues as economic impacts on competitors. These types of reviews are very costly endeavors for the store and, therefore, act as a deterrent to entrance in a market (Lefcoe, 2006). Some interpretations of these laws include requirements that companies provide estimate impacts from a single store. Some also require estimates of cumulative impacts from multiple chains (see discussion of *Bakersfield Citizens for Local Control v. City of Bakersfield* in Curtin, 2004).

The more famous anti-Wal-Mart legal victories have tended to focus on these specific store reviews. In a law journal article titled "Staving Off the Pillage of the Village," Sherry Dreisewerd (1998) describes the legal interpretation of Vermont's Land Use and Development Law (ACT 240), which mandated a case-by-case review.[2] In Wal-Mart's efforts to open a store in St. Albans, Vermont, Dreisewerd explains that the Vermont Supreme Court determined that the case-by-case

---

[2] Whatever else it has provided, the Wal-Mart research has given us some of the most entertaining set of academic paper titles available. Dreisewerd's "Staving Off the Pillage of the Village" is joined by "Belling the Box: Planning for Large Scale Retail Stores" by Duerkson and Blanchard and "The High Benefit of Low Prices" by Anderson. Great titles also are "From 'Mom and Pop' to Wal-Mart: The Impact of the Consumer Goods Pricing Act of 1975 on the Retail Sector of the United States" by Boyd, "Always High Land Rents? The Effect of Big Box Retail Development on a Productive Spatial Economy" by Curs Stater and Visser, who also give us "How Much Will Sam Pay for Land? The Locations of Big-Box Retailers and Local Land Values." And who could forget "CPI Bias From Supercenters: Does the BLS Know Wal-Mart Exists?" by Hausman and Leibtag and "Has Wal-Mart Buried Mom & Pop? The Impact of Wal-Mart on Self Employment and Small Establishments in the United States" by Sobel and Dean. "Thinking Outside the 'Big-Box'" by Villareal, "Making Wal-Mart Pretty: Trademarks and Aesthetic Restrictions on Big-Box Retailers" by McConnell, Basker's "Selling a Cheaper Mousetrap: Wal-Mart's Effect on Retail Prices" and, of course, my all-time favorite (and one of the best papers around), Basker and Van's "Putting a Smiley Face on the Dragon: Wal-Mart as a Catalyst to U.S. China Trade."

ruling allowed consideration of Wal-Mart's impact on local businesses since the city required their tax receipts for continued operation. This was decided in re *Wal-Mart Stores, Inc* (1998, p. 2). The ruling was not without criticism. Schneider (1996), in a law review article, clearly identified the focus of the ACT 240 ruling as designed to protect incumbent retailers. His argument is persuading, and he cited direct passages from the ruling that detail the protectionist concerns of the court. The ruling was later upheld by Vermont's Supreme Court. However, Wal-Mart found other locations in Vermont. This case spawned similar legislation in California, with predictable legal struggles over the equal protection clause.

These case-by-case reviews seem to have grown dramatically and provide a considerable bulk of the purported studies of Wal-Mart available on the World Wide Web or held by interest groups. They range in depth and quality and are often weakened by asking only very specific questions that the municipal government requested. My experience with two of these, which I performed in 2000 and 2001, was that the analysis was specifically limited to such factors as big-box store sales tax revenues. More ambitious studies were often specifically avoided, sometimes for very good reasons. It is difficult to criticize a consultant for meeting customer demand (often local elected officials) in these cases, although I know of few studies of this type that are really useful in explaining Wal-Mart's net impact (although they may be very good sources of information on gross employment flows, taxes, etc.).

The bulk of the planning guidance promulgated by such organizations as the American Planning Association and the National Trust for Historic Preservation focuses on specific CUP-type zoning rules. Detailed guidance on the architectural composition of new buildings, size, presence of awnings and window, paint color, pedestrian flows, minimum setback, and parking limits are all examples of the types of rule making that is designed to control development. An example of the specificity of the limitations constructed by one city is as follows:

> All sides of a principal building that directly face an
> abutting public street shall feature at least one customer

entrance. Where a principal building directly faces
more than two abutting public streets, this requirement
shall apply only to two sides of the building. (Duerkson
and Blancard, 1998, p. 2, describing Fort Collins,
Colorado)

These types of restrictions appear more often to survive legal review
than do the individual restrictions like the one in St. Albans, Vermont.
This is probably because some sort of land use planning or zoning is
ubiquitous and these types of rules have been in existence for some
time. Perhaps most importantly, there is little evidence that these types
of restrictions have substantially altered big-box behavior (with the
possible exception of Wal-Mart's growing neighborhood stores, which
should meet most restrictions). The reason these are not likely to matter much to big-box stores is that they are most often implemented
in places where Wal-Mart (or other large stores) are less inclined to
locate in the first place because of inherent restrictions on scale economies: available space. In contrast to the legally benign nature of many
of the restrictions, it is very likely that some aesthetic restrictions are
a violation of federal copyright protections (McConnell, 2004). That
they have not been challenged by retailers suggest they, like most other
CUP rules, are not focusing on geographic locations widely targeted
by big-box stores. Of course, this may well change as Wal-Mart pen-
etrates more communities.

Another argument for these CUP restrictions over other types of
restrictions is nicely captured by Denning and Lary (2005) in their
review of the constitutionality of absolute bans. They argue that "to
the extent that municipalities are pursuing legitimate land-use goals,
we would expect to see more regulations [CUPs] ... which seem to
us to be 'less discriminatory alternatives' to size-cap ordinances, which
are a comparatively blunt tool." (Denning and Lary, 2005, p. 44)

As the preceding passage suggests, the absolute bans present perhaps the greatest legal problems for municipalities. It is clear from the
structure of some of the absolute ban legislation that they are narrowly
tailored to exclude firms that enjoy economies of scale in the retail
delivery of goods. These are, in an economic sense, anticompetitive,

and the opposition to Wal-Mart is often led by incumbent merchants using legal recourse to prevent competition. Denning and Lary, in addressing the legality of absolute ban-type legislation, succinctly argue that

> Economic concerns of the large retailers' would-be local competitors feature prominently in debates over size-capping legislation, and are sometimes expressed in the legislation itself. Given that the desire to insulate existing local enterprises from competition—economic protectionism, in other words—motivates much of this legislation, size cap ordinances, we argue here, invite scrutiny under the dormant Commerce Clause doctrine (DCCD). (Denning and Lary, 2005, p. 3)

This triad of state restrictions on big-box development presents three approaches to limiting entrance by Wal-Mart and others. Most communities enact zoning of the type listed under the CUP. It is clear that voters, the legislators who enact the laws, and the courts that have upheld the bulk of these types of ordinances believe this is appropriate exercise of legitimate restrictions. I agree. Further, I do not believe that these laws much influence Wal-Mart's history of location choice and timing. The scale economies inherent in larger retail firms necessarily require structures that are larger than can typically be accommodated by small town centers. Thus, most of the restrictions will have little consequence on Wal-Mart's entrance decision, although admittedly many rules, particularly regarding aesthetics, facades, pedestrian flow, and parking, can usually be simply accommodated in new construction. Wal-Mart may even have introduced a new store type (the neighborhood market) to specifically comply with these types of ordinances.

Also, I want to be careful to clearly differentiate between what can be argued to be anticompetitive (the absolute bans and some forms of the site-specific review) and the relatively benign and unquestionably legitimate application of local zoning restrictions under CUPs. In addition, there are active, as opposed to restrictive, incentives to control Wal-Mart's location. For example, in efforts to incentivize firms to infill, or use existing space so as to mitigate sprawl, the village of Brady, Oklahoma (Tulsa) has developed more expeditious development permit processing, very targeted economic development incentives (targeting brownfields and greyfields), and infrastructure grants.[3]

Also, the greyfield and ghostbox issue I discussed earlier is addressed in many communities through the use of "white elephant" ordinances that effectively bond the company to finance demolition or reuse of vacant big-box stores (Evans-Cowley, 2006). These types of laws are very much like requirements on more intensive users of land (such as mining and manufacturing), which often make post-use plans and financing an integral part of the permitting process. This might not have been necessary a half century ago, when a small retailer, with a small footprint, opened a store. Today's much larger stores may well reach the level that requires this type of legislation.

It is useful to compare the types of rules promulgated by state and local governments using Professor George Lefcoe's classifications. These are derived from various sources already noted. I have not included proposed legislation, which has not been passed by a state or local legislature (e.g., a specific size tax of the type described by Jennifer Evans-Cowley, pp. 56–57). These are likely unconstitutional. A comparison of the types of ordinances and legislation that I have found affect Wal-Mart is provided in Table 13.1.

Local legislation of the type constructed under the CUP may be said to address a market failure (although much of the legal argument stems from nuisance laws). The aesthetics, land use patterns, and congestion affect property owners and residents even if they do not shop at Wal-Mart or other big-box stores. Thus, a third party bears some cost (just as it bore some benefit of lower prices because of

---

[3] See Brady Village Infill Development Design Guidelines, 2005: http://www. tulsadevelopmentauthority.org/brady_infill_pdf/section_3_purpose_intro_overview.pdf.

TABLE 13.1
State and Local Zoning Restrictions Affecting Wal-Mart

	Absolute Ban	Conditional Use Permit	Site-Specific Reviews	Local Only
Adaptive reuse		X		X
Aesthetic integration		X		X
Awnings / entrance restrictions		X		X
Building moratorium	X			X
Color / material restrictions		X		X
Common mall facade		X		X
Economic impact analysis		X	X	
Energy efficiency rules		X	X	
Environmental impact analysis		X	X	
Facade restrictions		X		X
Fair Share Health Care tax	X			
Fiscal impact analysis			X	
Individual design review			X	
Infill incentives		X	X	X
Landscaping design		X		X
Lighting design		X		X
Living wage ordinances	X			
Mixed transportation access		X		X
Mixed use requirements		X		X
Outparcel limitations		X		X
Parking lot design		X		X
Pedestrian flows design		X		X
Retail mix limits	X			X
Roofline limits	X	X		X
Setback restrictions		X		X
Sidewalk design (physical)		X		X

(*Continued*)

TABLE 13.1 (*Continued*)

	Absolute Ban	Conditional Use Permit	Site-Specific Reviews	Local Only
Signage design restrictions		X		X
Size caps (square footage limits)	X			X
Sublease reviews		X	X	X
Tract size limits	X			X
Traffic impact analysis		X	X	
Truck access		X	X	
Viewscape buffers		X		X
Watershed protection		X	X	
White elephant ordinances		X	X	X
Width restrictions		X	X	X
Window requirements		X		

Source: Evans-Cowley, 2006, and author's collection.

competition). Importantly, environmental protection rules such as watershed protection and parking lot design are designed to protect against damage to third parties, the well-known external cost problem. There is some debate over their effectiveness, however, especially when used to protect incumbent firms (see Mills, 1989).

It is not my intention to add substantially to the research on this matter, but I do want to clearly acknowledge that local land use planning and permits are well within the framework of controlling negative externalities or nuisances that could be generated by some land uses. More importantly than the economic suitability of zoning is an argument favoring local control over these types of decisions (with the hope that the argument is informed by quality analysis).

An additional type of local legislation that potentially affects Wal-Mart is state and local minimum wage laws. As I will illustrate, in terms of actual impact, these laws have almost no effect on Wal-Mart's employees and current operations. At the federal and state levels, where minimum wage laws affect retail occupations, the minimum wage laws probably play no role in setting Wal-Mart's wage. With perhaps a few exceptions, labor markets have set wages above the legal minimum, so Wal-Mart must pay more than the minimum wage to attract employees. However, there are perhaps 140 county and municipal governments that have established additional minimum wage laws (typically referred to as living wage ordinances).

Living wage ordinances are laws designed to establish wage floors (and often minimum health care benefits) for workers. Perhaps the strongest advocate of living wage ordinances is the Association of Community Organizations for Reform Now (ACORN), which operates the National Living Wage Resource Center. ACORN and other supporters (including the Economic Policy Institute [EPI], which has also provided very critical analysis of Wal-Mart) make two arguments in support of these laws. The first is essentially that the public subsidizes low-wage employers (often directly with economic development grants) but also indirectly through the provision of Medicaid, food stamps, and other public assistance. Thus, they argue, setting a wage floor will transfer the cost to the consumers of the good provided by the low-wage employer and away from the general taxpayer. The second argument addresses appropriately priced public sector activities by requiring wage and benefits floors for public sector employees and contracted workers. Here they argue that hiring low-wage workers for public activities may push these workers into Medicaid, food stamps, and other programs. The implication, quite rightfully, is that these programs are less efficient than private provision of health care and other services.

A perfect example is that, although a public university might save money by outsourcing cleaning services to a lower cost contractor, this would not necessarily save the state money. If the new, lower cost workers were also receiving state antipoverty benefits (that the university employee did not because of better benefits), the state might pay more for health care (and the worker might also be worse off). The perverse incentive here is clear. By outsourcing cleaning services, the university might save money but in doing so may actually cost the state more because of expansion of benefits.[4]

Of the two arguments offered by proponents of living wage ordinances, the first is far more compelling than the second, which is a bit too policy-wonkish for most folks. Unfortunately, the first argument has many more logical holes than the second. The greatest weakness in the first argument is that most low-wage workers are casual, or not prime, breadwinners and do not live with families in poverty. And because there will inevitably be some job losses associated with wage floors set above the market wage an individual could receive, someone is ill treated by the legislation (although the numbers might be quite low). To anyone who believes, like I do, that representative governments tend to cluster toward the better public policies, the evidence regarding the type of living wage ordinances will provide considerable gratification. Of the perhaps 140 living wage ordinances catalogued by ACORN, probably 125 are restricted to municipal or county workers and government contractors.

There are a number of studies of living wage ordinances, but by far the best work is by David Neumark (the same researcher who performed, with colleagues, the nationwide analysis of Wal-Mart I reviewed in Chapter 4 and elsewhere). In a very carefully crafted analysis, Neumark found that the poverty reduction goals of living wage ordinances are often modestly effective both in increasing low-wage earner incomes and in reducing poverty rates. He also found, as economic theory suggests, some employment reduction associated with the ordinances as well as some substitution of labor toward higher wage workers, which is again another prediction of economic theory and probably why unions strongly support the measures (Neumark, 2002).

The actual effect of living wage ordinances on commercial economic activity (beyond labor markets) is very thin. The most probable reason for this is that there are no more than a dozen or so active living

---

[4] Many thanks to Dr. Matt Murray at Tennessee for providing me this useful example.

wage ordinances in the United States; the impacts are likely quite difficult to disentangle from other factors, such as the very real possibility that policymakers enact living wage ordinances to achieve goals other than policy reduction (such as to increase their own political popularity). This shocking allegation is supported by measures such as those enacted in Madison and Eau Claire, Wisconsin. In both cities, the living wage ordinances established in the early part of the decade stand at about half the average wage for a retail salesperson in those cities. As noble as this ordinance sounds, it is as effective a policy measure as establishing a speed limit of 140 mph for my 1997 Honda Odyssey. Overall, the living wage ordinances passed since 2004 are, on average, 18% below the average wage for retail salespersons.

As of this writing, I can identify only 16 Wal-Mart stores that are potentially affected by living wage ordinances, and about half of them are in Chicago, in which the new rates have not yet gone into affect.[5] To compile this list, I applied the ordinances collected by ACORN and the EPI to the existing Wal-Mart and supercenter stores in each of these locations. I have assumed that Wal-Mart is not a local government contractor and so does not fall under the bulk of the provisions. However, a number of living wage ordinances also require any recipient of local aid through economic development programs to maintain a living wage.[6] Here I applied these rules to any Wal-Mart store in which I knew of economic development incentives provided under these rules. In this comparison, I used data collected by Mattera and Purinton (2004), which I discussed in the chapter on tax incentives. Only four stores in Los Angeles met this criterion, although these data are difficult to collect. Table 13.2 presents the Wal-Mart stores and local wages and living wage ordinance rates as of late summer 2006.

---

[5] As of this writing, the ordinance has been vetoed by Mayor Daley, and there is some uncertainty whether or not it will be overturned in the city county. This could affect two existing and some planned stores.

[6] This is probably a far more extensive policy outcome but one that is usually voluntarily agreed on by the employer and missed by the ACORN and EPI data.

TABLE 13.2

Wal-Mart Stores Facing Living Wage Ordinances

Municipality / County	Average Wage for Retail Clerk (2005)	No. Wal-Mart Stores	Living Wage Minimum	Existing State Minimum Wage
Los Angeles County	$11.91	4	$9.39	$6.75
Albuquerque, NM	$10.75	6	$6.75	$5.15
Milwaukee, WI	$11.5	4	$7.98	$5.70
Madison, WI	$11.15	2	$6.50	$5.70
Santa Fe, NM	$10.43	1	$9.50	$5.15

The very small number of Wal-Mart stores affected argues that the impact of living wage ordinances is not currently affecting the company in any real way except through their location decisions, which may explain why so few stores are involved. Further, although the data on wage distribution within Wal-Mart are simply unavailable for recent years, it is almost certain that the proportion of total workers affected is minimal. The living wage ordinances in Albuquerque, New Mexico, and Madison, Wisconsin, are both below what Wal-Mart likely pays for entry-level workers, and in Milwaukee, Wisconsin, the rate of $7.98 most likely affects less than a quarter of company's the labor force. In Santa Fe, New Mexico, and Los Angeles County, the rates may be higher but probably still affect less than one third of total Wal-Mart workers. Only in Chicago, where the final disposition is uncertain as of this writing, would as many as one third of Wal-Mart's employees be affected by the wage portion (the health care portion may affect 10% more, but that depends on some unresolved factors, such as whether the employee has coverage elsewhere). Extending this "back-of-the-envelope" calculation to total affected employees yields somewhere between 1,600 and 2,000 affected Wal-Mart workers at the very most. If the living wage ordinances raise salaries for these workers by an average of $1.50/hour, then the total wage impact is between $4.6 and $6.2 million annually for the company.

The wage portion of the living wage ordinances is, as they are currently implemented, no more than a modest nuisance for Wal-Mart. However, the health care component included in Chicago's new ordinance is far more problematic. The combined impact (estimated using the same "back-of-the-envelope" analysis) is just under $1 million per store. This would reduce profits by perhaps 10% for the retailer at those locations. My belief, although I am not a retail store operations expert, is that this is just about the threshold where the store becomes a minimally viable operation. This, combined with a potential need to establish a reputational effect at opposing these types of ordinances, may be sufficient to lead to the relocation or closure of stores if new ordinances are adopted. However, this is highly speculative.

In the final analysis, the most influential policy innovations involving Wal-Mart are not at the local level. I have argued that many local ordinances designed to keep Wal-Mart away may actually not matter, since many locations covered by this legislation are not suitable for a big-box store because of the absence of scale economies. Further, local ordinances are inherently local, and their passage is unlikely to extend so far as to prevent a Wal-Mart from locating a store close enough for most residents to visit (although poor residents are most ill affected by this policy). This also holds for the living wage ordinance. Further, it does not seem that Wal-Mart has had much difficulty in finding new locations for its stores. It is at the state level that we must turn to evaluate legislation that might affect Wal-Mart.

STATE-LEVEL RESTRICTIONS ON WAL-MART

States generate three types legislation that potentially affect Wal-Mart. One involves requirements for types of local zoning rules, which are then operated at the substate level. For example, a state might require a watershed protection assessment, which is then reviewed by local authorities, although review by state environmental protection departments often accompanies this type of rule. I have already discussed these rules. The second type of restriction includes extensions to federal antitrust legislation, primarily those involving predatory pricing. Wal-Mart has faced minimal antitrust litigation, and I will very briefly review this. The final restriction facing Wal-Mart includes types of "Wal-Mart tax" or the Fair Share Health Care Acts. This is the newest and very rapidly spreading policy innovation, and I shall provide considerable analysis of its causation. First, however, I will briefly review antitrust legislation and Wal-Mart's experience.

The Robinson-Patman Act, which I described briefly in Chapter 1, provides the chief source of federal antitrust legislation that affects chain stores. The Robinson-Patman Act requires that any local pricing difference by retailers be due to demonstrable cost differentials. Without these cost differences between local areas, the law proscribes setting different prices. This law, an extension of the Clayton Act (and ultimately the Sherman Act), is an attempt to prevent predatory pricing. Predatory pricing, as distinct from run-of-the mill competition, occurs when one firm reduces prices beneath its costs to drive a rival from the market. This standard is known as the Areeda-Turner standard for predatory pricing, which is an economic definition recognized by the courts. The motivation for driving a rival from the market is that the lost profits can be later recouped through the exploitation of monopoly pricing after the rival firm fails. Not surprisingly, this phenomenon has enjoyed extensive economic research, including game theoretic analysis, which resulted in the award of a Nobel Prize.[7]

The Robinson-Patman Act establishes a lower legal threshold for this second step (the possibility of recouping lost profits) than does interpretation of other restrictions on predatory pricing (i.e., the Sherman Act). Importantly, within the case law surrounding both the Robinson-Patman Act and the Sherman Act, the operative costs are those of the offending firm, not the rival.

---

[7] Professor Selten received a Nobel Prize in part for his game theoretic explanation of the chain store paradox.

Wal-Mart has not been successfully challenged on antitrust grounds at the federal level. Because the heavy weight of evidence is that its prices are lower than the competition's (even following putative exit by rivals), Wal-Mart is unlikely to face federal antitrust charges on this issue. However, a number of states have enacted antitrust laws, which have a lower threshold on intent to injure rivals or on the ability to recoup lost profits. This is what Professor Norman Hawker calls the "divergence of federal and state antitrust laws." In a 1996 paper, he describes the legal circumstances surrounding Wal-Mart's loss of a case involving pharmaceutical sales, which were a violation of the Arkansas Unfair Practices Act. He is very critical of the court in this case, which is not surprising, since the case was overturned on appeal to the Arkansas Supreme Court (*American Drugs v. Wal-Mart, Inc.*).

The case itself is of only minor interest, but the paper is very important since Hawker very cleverly evaluated state laws and the resulting interpretation of the purpose or intent behind below-cost pricing. His review of state predatory pricing restrictions found 26 states with definitions of intent similar to the standard set forth under the Robinson-Patman Act and Sherman Act (although these two interpretations differ slightly). He found another 23 states with legislation that softened the intent requirement (recoupment of lost profits) that were part of the case law surrounding the Sherman Act. Eight of the 23 states that outlawed below-cost pricing without regard to intent had objective standards. These are like the Areeda-Turner standards, which effectively require a very strict below-cost pricing, with production or sales at a level greater than the competitive level. The remainder had subjective interpretations, and at least two states have some ambiguity across intent. See Table 13.3.

In the end, Wal-Mart seems unlikely to suffer much risk of losing antitrust litigation given the absence of examples of it increasing prices consistent with monopolization at any time in its 44-year history. The greatest legal difficulty facing Wal-Mart at the time of this writing (and I predict for at least several more years) is the enactment of state-level Wal-Mart taxes or the Fair Share Health Care Acts.

TABLE 13.3
State Antitrust Law Intent Definition

State	Subjective Intent	Objective Intent	No Federal State Divergence	Statute
Alabama			X	
Alaska			X	
Arizona			X	
Arkansas	X			AR Code Ann. §4-75-209
California	X			CA Bus. And Prof. Code Ann. §17043
Colorado	X			CO Rev. Stat. §6-2-105
Connecticut			X	
Delaware			X	
Florida			X	
Georgia			X	
Hawaii	X			HI Rev. Stat. §481-3
Idaho		X		ID Code §48-104
Illinois			X	
Indiana			X	
Iowa			X	
Kansas			X	
Kentucky	X			KY Rev Stat Ann §365.030
Louisiana	X	X		LA Rev. Stat. Ann §41.422
Maine	X			ME Rev. Stat. Ann Title 10, §1204
Maryland	X			MD Code Annot. Com. Law §11-404
Massachusetts	X			MA Gen L ch 93 §14F
Michigan			X	
Minnesota	X	X		MN Stat Ann. §325.04
Mississippi			X	
Missouri			X	
Montana	X			MT Code Ann. §30-14-209
Nebraska	X			NE Rev. Stat. §59-905

(Continued)

TABLE 13.3   (*Continued*)

State	Subjective Intent	Objective Intent	No Federal State Divergence	Statute
Nevada			X	
New Hampshire			X	
New Jersey			X	
New Mexico			X	
New York			X	
North Carolina	X	X		NC Gen. Stat. §75-5(b)(4)
North Dakota	X			ND Cent. Code §51-10-03
Ohio			X	
Oklahoma	X	X		OK Stat. Ann. Title 7 §598.3
Oregon			X	
Pennsylvania	X	X		PA 73 Stat. §213
Rhode Island	X			RI Gen Laws §6-13-3
South Carolina	X			SC Code Ann. §39-13-1-150
South Dakota			X	
Tennessee	X	X		TM Code Ann. §47-25-203
Texas				
Utah	X			UT Code Ann. §13-5-7
Vermont			X	
Virginia			X	
Washington			X	
West Virginia	X		X	WV Code §47-11A-2
Wisconsin	X	X	X	WI Sta. Ann. §100.30(3)
Wyoming	X			WY Stat. §40-4-107

Source: Adapted from Hawker and Petty (1996).

WAL-MART AND THE FAIR SHARE HEALTH CARE TAX

Sometime between 2001 and 2004, a proposal known as the Wal-Mart tax appeared on Internet sites hosted by the AFL-CIO, the UFCW, and a few other labor sites. In mid-2004, Arin Dube and Ken Jacobs at Berkeley's Center for Labor Research published a report, which focused on California's experience with Wal-Mart and antipoverty programs. Later that year, Congressman George Miller (D-CA) had the Democratic Staff of the Committee on Education and the Workforce prepare a report that provided some estimates of the public funding received by Wal-Mart's workers. The report was not the least bit unbiased; nevertheless, it described the upper limit on antipoverty transfers paid to Wal-Mart employees. The following spring, Sonya Carlson, an undergraduate student at Lewis & Clark College (now a consultant for corporate social responsibility), performed the same analysis for Oregon, expanding on the analyses by Miller's staff and by Dube and Jacobs. Of course, none of these studies reflect the actual experience of Wal-Mart employees and antipoverty programs; they are, rather, simulations based on analysis of wage rates, eligibility, and family structure. This is not a criticism of these studies, merely a fact of the data limitations that this type of research faces.

That summer I wrote two papers analyzing Wal-Mart's impact on Medicaid expenditure at the federal level and for a single state (Hicks, 2005a, 2007). My point estimates for Medicaid costs attributable to Wal-Mart at the national level were $898 per worker; the 90% confidence interval was about $400 above and below that estimate (which, for policy purposes, could be interpreted as a potential range of the impact). My Medicaid estimates for Ohio were $651 per worker, making both my estimates higher than those estimated by Dube and Jacobs, Miller, or Carlson. I also examined several reports of administrative data on Medicaid expenditures associated with Wal-Mart employees and their families. My estimates, which required some normalization across other studies, ranged from $175 to $580 per worker in the half dozen states that then collected the data.

I presented these findings at the November 2005 Wal-Mart Conference, and, despite my estimates of relatively large impacts, I was far less critical of Wal-Mart than any of the proceeding authors. My reasoning, which was later far more effectively described by Jason Furman, a former Clinton Administration economist and New York University professor, hinged on the role the 1996 Welfare Reform Act played in providing health care access to low-wage workers.

Much to the dismay of many of Wal-Mart's critics, Furman called Wal-Mart a "progressive success story" (Furman, 2005).

As I detailed earlier, the Welfare Reform Act (formally the Personal Responsibility and Work Opportunity Reconciliation Act of 1996) allowed, for the first time, low-income workers to receive Medicaid. Before the Welfare Reform Act, only recipients of Aid to Families of Dependent Children (more frequently called welfare) could receive these health care benefits. From 1996 through 2001, the welfare rolls (now renamed Temporary Assistance to Needy Families) dropped by half. In two papers written shortly after the law was enacted, I estimated that a large percentage of the decline was attributable to economic conditions (Hicks, 1999; Hicks and Boyer, 1999). This was likely largely due to the possibility of welfare recipients having portable health care. Professor Furman calls this a progressive success story (although its bipartisan passage really makes the 1996 Welfare Reform Act a policy success story, not a political one). I personally believe that this single piece of legislation is likely to be remembered as President Clinton's most important policy achievement.

One result of the success of this legislation has been the growth of available workers, which is probably a boon to many firms across several industries. This result is also good for the overwhelming majority of workers who are employed. The rising Medicaid costs for the state and federal governments, which are due to some early profligacy by states combined with rapidly rising health care costs, has made those with short memories uneasy about the role of employers whose workers receive this benefit.

On its surface, the Fair Share Health Care Act is an effort to force employers to shoulder more of the direct health care burden of their workers. As such, the law has been proposed in about half the states (although it exited committee only in Maryland). The law passed in Maryland, was vetoed by Governor Ehrlich, the veto was overridden, and the law was overturned based on an interpretation of the Employee Retirement Income Security Act. The case is pending appeal. Table 13.4 contains the summer 2006 status of what is a fluid situation with respect to these laws.

TABLE 13.4

Fair Share Health Care Tax Laws

State	Bill Number	Minimum Number of Employees	Health Care Benefits (% total wages or hourly expenditures)	Disposition of Legislation
Alaska	HB 449	10,000	8%	
Colorado	HB 1316	3,500	11%	
Florida	HB 813	10,000	9%	
	SB 1618			
Kansas	HB 2579	10,000	8%	Committee on Insurance
Kentucky	HB 98	10,000	8%	Committee hearings
	HB 493	10,000	10%	Committee hearings
Maryland	HB 1284	10,000	8%	Fair Share Health Care Act, passed, vetoed, overridden, overturned (pending appeal, MD Supreme Court)
	S 790	10,000	8%	
Massachusetts	SB 695	99		Pending Joint Committee hearings
	HB 4479	11		
Michigan	SB 734	10,000	8%	Committee on Labor and Finance

(Continued)

TABLE 13.4 (*Continued*)

State	Bill Number	Minimum Number of Employees	Health Care Benefits (% total wages or hourly expenditures)	Disposition of Legislation
Minnesota	HF 2573	10,000	10%	Committee on Health Policy and Finance
Mississippi	SB 2684	10,000	8%	
Missouri	SB 944	10,000	10%	
New Hampshire	HB 1704	1,500	10.5%	Committee on Commerce
New Jersey	SB 1320	10,000	8%	
New York	AB 2513	10,000	8%	
	SB 6472	500	$3 per hour	
	A 9776	500	$3 per hour	Assembly Committee on Labor
Ohio	A 9534	10,000	8%	Assembly Committee on Labor
	HB 471	30,000	8%	Committee on Insurance, Commerce and Labor
	SB 256	10,000	8%	Committee on Insurance, Commerce and Labor
	SB 258	1,000	8%	Committee on Insurance, Commerce and Labor
Oklahoma	HB 2678	3,000	9%	
Rhode Island	HB 6984	1,000	8%	Committee on Finance

State	Bill			Committee
Washington	HB 6917	1,000	8%	Committee on Finance
	S 2201	1,000	8%	
	HB 2517	5,000	9%	Committee on Labor, Commerce, Research and Development
West Virginia	S 6356	5,000	9%	Committee on Labor, Commerce, Research and Development
Wisconsin	SB 147	10,000	8%	Committee on Labor
	HB 4024	1,000	8%	Committee on Health and Human Resources
	AB 860	10,000		
	SB 440	10,000		

Source: Herrera, 2006, with author's updates.

The intent of these laws, however, does not easily align with the supposed motivation of their strongest proponents: the labor movement. The reason is simply that there are no union workers at Wal-Mart, and so no one currently represented by the major proponents of the Fair Share Health Care tax actually works at Wal-Mart. Of course, this is exactly why Wal-Mart has been overtly targeted by these unions and their supporters. The absence of unionization at Wal-Mart stores, most especially supercenters, which compete with the heavily unionized grocery store chains, make Wal-Mart a prime target for unions, most especially the United Food and Consumers Workers Union. This is not a criticism of unions or union practices. However, a realization that the Wal-Mart Tax might be motivated for purposes other than those surrounding Medicaid is useful in economic analysis.[8] In the next section, I propose and test a model that examines the potential motivations behind the Wal-Mart Tax. This is a test of the political economy of the Wal-Mart Tax.

THE LAW AND ECONOMICS OF THE WAL-MART TAX

In Chapter 1, I reviewed a paper by Professor Thomas Ross that examined the chain store taxes of the 1920s and 1930s. This report provides an important framework for evaluating the genesis of the Wal-Mart tax proposals. Recall that Ross suggested that the chain store tax may be for purposes other than restricting trade. He suggested that the populist feelings at the time may have led legislatures to pass laws that were carefully written so as to fail constitutional muster. He implies that, through this process, they receive the political support for passing popular legislation without suffering the consequences of its implementation. He cites Kentucky and Virginia in particular, and there is considerable support for the role of populist

---

[8] For purposes of full disclosure, I am currently an associate member of a union (through which I and my family receive federal health care benefits) and belong to at least two professional organizations that behave much like trade unions (albeit fairly weak ones).

feelings as a mechanism for motivating political action (Schragger, 2005). I believe much of the same dynamics are currently at play in the debate over the Wal-Mart tax. I have two arguments, the first anecdotal and the second empirical.

The structure of the Fair Share Health Care tax outlined in Table 13.4 is very similar to documents produced by the AFL-CIO and circulated by other unions. Indeed, the draft Wal-Mart tax prescribes employment limits and health care expenditure percentages, which are almost exactly replicated by over half the laws described in the preceding table. With the exception of the Massachusetts legislature, which seems to be serious about the issue, the only real changes to the AFL-CIO plan are those that adjust the employment minimum to meet local conditions. For example, Ohio House Bill 471 adjusted its threshold up to 30,000 employees to exclude several other major companies in the state. Rhode Island, New Hampshire, and Washington all reduced their limits to levels that would primarily target Wal-Mart in their states. This strict adherence to a plan earlier labeled a Wal-Mart tax should suffice as Exhibit A in an equal protection clause challenge to these laws. With the exception of two of Massachusetts' proposals and one in New York, these look like the carefully crafted chain store taxes of Kentucky and Virginia of the 1930s, intentionally doomed to judicial rejection.

Another mechanism of analyzing the path of proposed legislation is to develop the type of model that tests the economic theory of regulation. Recall that the economic theory of regulation proposes that policymakers act on incentives, among which is the quest for political influence. These empirical models are notoriously difficult to design and are constructed through description of the process. I argue three major hypotheses. First, if Wal-Mart is indeed a problem in states, then exposure to Wal-Mart will be more likely to lead to a Wal-Mart tax. Second, if state legislatures are attempting to placate union concerns, then the proportion of union workers in the state will increase the probability of a Wal-Mart tax proposal in the legislature. Third, I expect that the history of enacting a chain store tax would influence the probability of a Wal-Mart tax. The direction of the impact here might explain how the success of the chain store tax was perceived, even though this stretches memory in these states. This last element is the weakest of the three arguments. I include a population control and in one specification a variable that accounts for the state's vote in the 2004 presidential election (1 if for Senator John Kerry), which I label a DEM variable. This latter variable is likely highly correlated with the union density variable (which is why, for technical reasons, I omit it from one specification); however, the 2004 presidential election experienced an unusually strong focus on nondomestic issues that should be controlled for in this type of model.

Thus, I estimate a model known as a Probit, which estimates the probability that a state will propose a Wal-Mart tax as a function of the dependent variables. The model is then

$$Prob(WMT = 1 | XB) = \alpha + \beta_1 WM + \beta_2 UD + \beta_3 CST \\ + \beta_4 POP + \beta_5 Dem + e_i \qquad (13.1)$$

where the probability of a Wal-Mart tax proposal is a function of exposure to Wal-Mart (which I calculated as the sum of the number of years each store was opened in 2005, or store years), union density in 2003, the enactment of a chain store tax between 1929 and 1940, and whether or not the state's electoral votes were Democratic in the 2004 presidential elections. The Huber / White standard errors (corrected for heteroscedasticity) were used. Results appear in Table 13.5.

These results support part, but not all, of the hypothesis that the economic theory of regulation explains the introduction of the Wal-Mart tax. Exposure to the 1920s and 1930s chain store tax and a Democratic vote in the 2004 presidential election have the expected signs but do not enjoy statistical significance. The union density variable also has the correct sign but does not achieve acceptable levels of statistical significance. Thus, union density is not influencing the introduction of a Wal-Mart tax. Interestingly, the exposure to a Wal-Mart as measured in store years of presence by the end of 2004 is negatively correlated with the probability that a state legislature

TABLE 13.5
The Economic Theory of Regulation and the
Wal-Mart Tax

	Model 1	Model 2
Intercept	−0.755360	−0.604369
	(−0.90)	(0.48)
Wal-Mart exposure	−0.000493*	−0.000627**
	(−1.79)	(−2.34)
Union density	0.030824	0.035669
	(1.03)	(1.20)
Chain store tax	−0.440584	−0.465022
	(−1.03)	(−1.09)
Population	−2.83E-08	−8.44E-09
	(−0.72)	(−0.24)
Democratic 2004	0.593896	***
	(1.27)	
McFadden's R^2	0.18	0.16
Log likelihood	−23.8	−24.6

***$p = 0.01$. **$p = 0.05$. *$p = 0.10$.

will introduce a Wal-Mart tax. Oddly then, the less exposure a state has to Wal-Mart, all things being equal, the more likely it is to introduce a Wal-Mart tax. This is consistent with the economic theory of regulation, suggesting that the Wal-Mart taxes are part of a political, not policy, process. Policymakers have explored a number of options to address Wal-Mart stores in their communities. These include three broad types of zoning ordinances, economic development incentives, living wage ordinances, antitrust legislation, and the Wal-Mart tax. Whether or not any particular piece of legislation is effective or appropriate is another matter.

CHAPTER FOURTEEN

ON LOVING AND HATING WAL-MART: A SUMMARY AND POLICY RECOMMENDATIONS

Local and state policymakers who are interested in objectively understanding Wal-Mart's impact on their community face a daunting task. Researchers themselves are, at a very tentative best, only beginning to come to some agreement on Wal-Mart's impact on local communities. If serious researchers do not yet broadly agree, then policymakers cannot be expected to receive the clear guidance they deserve. Further, the limited accessibility of much of the truly scholarly research on Wal-Mart compounds the difficulty for policymakers.[1] The problem

---

[1] Much research is available on the World Wide Web, but even in these forms information about peer review is difficult for someone unfamiliar with the research to conclude. Apparently because of demand, the Review of Economics and Statistics has just made Emek Basker's paper available on-line. My paper at the Review of Regional

of disentangling effects is made more awkward by the abundance of truly bad analysis of Wal-Mart's impact.

The early research I discussed in Chapter 4 was designed to understand Wal-Mart's impact without advancing any particular agenda. Although a good bit of it, including the best known of the early studies, was considerably worse methodologically than was really appropriate at the time, most of the early studies show the continual advance of knowledge, as research ought to do. I am also quite proud that the research by economists on this matter is almost wholly free of ideological bias. This is not so of many other fields. Economists might be faulted for not demonstrating a passion for cause that many of our colleagues do, but at least one result is a growing body of research that is reliably free of bias. One telling bit of evidence of the way economists have approached the problem is that empirical researchers ranging from a mildly vocal Wal-Mart supporter (Jerry Hausman) to a more vocal critic (Arin Dube) have both acknowledged important benefits and costs attributable to the retailer.

Currently available books on Wal-Mart range from seriously scholarly compendiums (Brunn, 2006; Vedder and Cox, 2006) to a rambling, self-published treatise that argues Wal-Mart is part of a large federal conspiracy. Both Brunn's and Vedder and Cox's works are soon to be in print, so I have little to comment on in either. I will stay clear of the conspiracy theorists. In between are several books that beg discussion.

A number of books herald Wal-Mart's success, business practices, innovation, and benefit to society. Some, like Slater (2002), outline how the company became successful, with much emphasis on individual achievement and insight. This book is far and away the most honest of the journalistic attempts to explain Wal-Mart. However, it is of little use in understanding Wal-Mart's local impacts. Firm biographies tend to find that which is novel in a company and attribute its great success to individuals. This is a good read but usually misses the possibility that the successful firm is simply the most recent to

---

Studies requires a subscription or interlibrary loan usually only available to professors and graduate students.

implement an existing idea. The scale economies in retail are not Wal-Mart's invention; neither are scale economies in distribution. They were just enormously successful at them. This observation by no means diminishes the achievement of Sam Walton or employees at Wal-Mart; it simply suggests that someone else would have figured out these benefits absent Wal-Mart (although some, like Kmart, seem not to have been watching). In the end, Sam Walton and his colleagues at Wal-Mart may be geniuses and fine men and women. But they did not invent any of the business practices that made them so successful. They just executed them better than anyone else. Being best is worthy of praise, but no one credits Michael Jordan with founding the NBA.

Unlike happy firm biographies that tend to find something unusual about a firm and laud it, firm antagonists tend more often to find something that is common across an industry and attribute it to an individual company. Al Norman, who is often referred to as the guru of the anti-Wal-Mart movement, has two books in print: *Slam Dunking Wal-Mart* (1999) and *The Case Against Wal-Mart* (2004). Both books describe successful anti-Wal-Mart efforts but are really emotional treatises, nothing more. Even in the one area in which my analysis suggests his opinions may be correct—the contribution of Wal-Mart to sprawl—Norman refuses to consider any analysis that is not anchored in emotion. He has posted two of my publicly available research papers on his Web site, Sprawlbusters, with a small synopsis (you can get them for a $3 donation or for free from a half dozen other Web sites). His description of one paper, which found that Wal-Mart increases commercial property values, is that it is an undesirable side effect of the retailer. And just to be clear, increased commercial (or residential) property values are a good thing since they represent the very human belief that something has become more valuable, in this case because Wal-Mart is nearby. He also criticizes Wal-Mart in an oft-delivered PowerPoint presentation for having fewer workers per dollar of sales. Again, just to be clear, this is economic growth: How could the world be better if it took more of us to do less? These silly interpretations really capture well much of the discussion about Wal-Mart that passes for analysis.

One fairly common argument against Wal-Mart appears in almost all discussions: that a corporate retailer is worse for a local economy than a local merchant. While I believe that the concerns about local entrepreneurship and philanthropy are legitimate (which is why I reviewed them in Chapter 8), that is not the source of the argument. The argument, most visibly made in several publications by the New Rules Project, is the tired mercantilist belief that preventing outflows of currency will lead to prosperity. It is unfortunate that policymakers are still confronted with this argument in the 21st century. Prosperity for a community does not come from eschewing trade or preventing commercial interaction with neighbors. The sole source of increasing prosperity comes from one ultimate source: productivity growth. For us as individuals, families, communities, states, and nations of the world to be better off, we must experience productivity growth, or, more simply, we must produce more goods and services (in value or quantity) with less material. Happily that is exactly what the world (and the United States in particular) has been doing for the past two to three centuries. To deny this transparent truth is to both misapprehend the simplest laws of economics and to simultaneously, if inadvertently, acclaim King George III an economic genius.

Yet another type of popular book is one I have reviewed already and I call the wary antiglobalist tract. These books, most notably by Charles Fishman (2006) and Anthony Bianco (2006), detail both the way Wal-Mart interacts with its suppliers and how this relationship is increasing global trade. Using anecdote (and in Fishman's case distorting research when it conveniences his argument), these types of books describe a very potentially serious decline in the nation's prosperity. I say "potentially" because the great fears they exploit will only come to pass if the laws of economics are repealed. To be sure, producers who engage in trade with Wal-Mart may lose some profit and may even have to relocate economic activity. However, by focusing on the anecdote and ignoring reams of available data, both authors entirely miss (or studiously avoid) the truth of American prosperity in the 21st century. Standards of living are growing both for Americans and our trading partners. They have been growing for generations and will continue to do so for the foreseeable future. Indeed, to most macroeconomists, the one looming concern is the impact of a widespread reversal of the gains of trade (due perhaps to a major war) and its effect on the standard of living of most of the world's population. Fishman's and Bianco's arguments are not really different than those of Al Norman or Stacey Mitchell at the New Rules Project or, for that matter, King George III. They just approach the same discredited myth from a different direction.

In my estimation, the most empirically supportable of the popular criticisms of Wal-Mart are offered by Barbara Ehrenreich and Liz Featherstone. Ehrenreich writes about her experiences performing low-wage work in three occupations, among them a Wal-Mart position. Featherstone criticizes Wal-Mart for its alleged unequal treatment of women. And although neither of these two issues is directly related to local economic impacts I discuss, these critics' arguments are not without foundation.

Ehrenreich describes the multiple difficulties of low-wage work and the challenges of maintaining a household at these wages. Her belief that the correction of this lies in motivating change at Wal-Mart is not clearly developed. To be sure, surviving with a family on $9.00 an hour is difficult, but the policy innovations most likely to mitigate this outcome are as varied as abstinence education in high schools, college vouchers, and extensions of the earned income tax credit. Targeting employers is likely to be the least effective technique to help the poor (and may be counterproductive).

Featherstone's critique of Wal-Mart's treatment of women enjoys some empirical support. And despite the fact that she called me and the other participants of the Wal-Mart economic conference "eggheads," it is impossible to dismiss her argument. In a 2003 study prepared in support of *Dukes v. Wal-Mart*, a discrimination case, Professor Richard Drogin details a very uncomfortable set of comparisons of Wal-Mart's pay differentials between men and women at all levels. Although his study does not provide any of the type of causative analysis of gender wage gaps that a labor economist would use, the stark comparisons are troubling. While I am far from convinced by his study that Wal-Mart is systematically biased against women, Drogin's report, combined with anecdote, makes a powerful case, and Featherstone's argument cannot be summarily dismissed (despite her calling me names). However, the remedy here is not public policy adjustment but legal action (the outcome of which is far from certain). In the end, though, both Ehrenreich's and Featherstone's concerns are far more valid than Fishman's and Bianco's. However, there is just not a serious public policy component, especially at the state and local levels, to any of these arguments.

One argument not made, perhaps because there is no convenient corporate villain, is that the persistence of adults who cannot command a living wage in a free market is a strong critique of our educational system, which invested at least $65,000 on each worker. Ehrenreich's argument in particular would be helpful in explaining the low returns to public education that are seemingly the root cause of her concern for low-wage working adults.[2]

Policymakers who are concerned with Wal-Mart better serve their constituents with a reasoned and considered evaluation of the giant retailer. The findings reviewed and presented in this book suggest a range of estimated impacts. In Figure 14.1 and the following discussion, I review and compare findings in this book from my and others' research that consider the more modern technical concern of estimation that accounts for Wal-Mart's entrance decision perhaps being influenced by local conditions. This endogeneity issue and some appropriate treatment are still matters of academic concern. However, what is not at issue is the importance of considering endogeneity, so studies that do not even acknowledge the problem are not included.

These economic (as opposed to fiscal) impacts suggest that changes in the order of one half of 1% or more occur in only 11 of the 20 issues I explored in this book. Of these, the impact can be construed as

---

[2] It is important to remember that many, if not most, Wal-Mart employees are casual workers (students, part-time parents, and older workers) who are looking for exactly the type of job Wal-Mart offers (today's Wal-Mart jobs are better than any summer employment I ever held!).

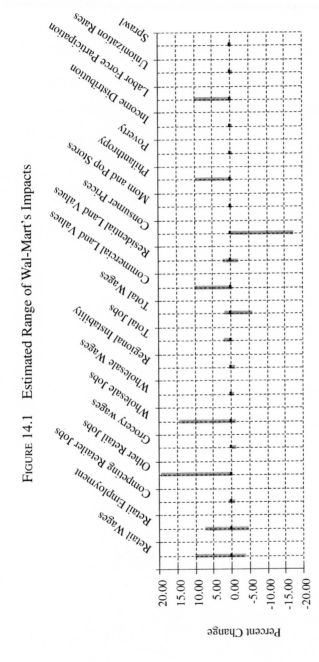

FIGURE 14.1   Estimated Range of Wal-Mart's Impacts

potentially unhappy in only four remaining areas: retail wages, retail employment, total wages, and residential land values. In each case, the estimated impacts are both positive and negative, depending on the study methodology, time, and location of analysis.

In six of the 20 issues presented here, the influence of Wal-Mart should be construed as unambiguously good. These are in competing retail jobs, wholesale jobs, commercial land values, consumer prices, philanthropy, and labor force participation rates. The fiscal impacts are similarly arrayed, with clear revenue increases associated with Wal-Mart, which are offset with some expenditure increases (although the bulk of these are self-inflicted wounds of state economic development incentives).

Although these finding suggest that a fairly narrow set of concerns ought to dominate local public policy discussions, they are not a cost–benefit analysis of Wal-Mart. Nor is it clear that a cost–benefit analysis is appropriate for policy decisions regarding a commercial economic activity. Allowing commerce to occur based on job accounting is shortsighted and most likely unconstitutional in most cases. Public policy should instead be directed at mitigating the short-run ill effects of markets. For example, if Wal-Mart's entrance leads to unemployment among competing retailers, an appropriate policy response is not to prevent Wal-Mart's entrance but rather to mitigate the ill effects of transitory unemployment (and more broadly to address structural weakness in labor markets). We need often be reminded that these are difficult matters; otherwise, relative poverty and want would long ago have been remedied.

Thus, the research findings in this book inform a wide range of existing public policy innovations. For example, if the entrance of a Wal-Mart in a local community creates congestion, reduces retail employment, and reduces consumer prices, then public policy can clearly mitigate these ill effects. Appropriate zoning regulations can mitigate congestion with improvements such as streetlights and pedestrian bridges financed through impact fees or public private partnerships. Displaced workers can receive unemployment benefits and be provided access to the local workforce investment board for a suite of services designed to improve human capital. Finally, city buses might be rerouted to provide access to the lower priced store for inner city residents without shopping alternatives. Each of these policies is consistent with the impact findings reported in this book and generate no obvious unintended consequences.

In the end, I am drawn to three strong conclusions about Wal-Mart. With one exception, these are not novel. The first is that there are clear benefits to consumers by having access to Wal-Mart. These benefits are large, nontransient, and clearly welcomed by the majority of American families. Further, they are likely to have the biggest benefit on the most needy among us. Second, the entrance of a Wal-Mart has the potential to change a local community through movement of retail centers, changes in local employment mixes, changes to local fiscal conditions, and alterations in the physical landscape surrounding a community. However, few of these changes are clearly for the worse and many, perhaps most, are for the better. Finally, policymakers and citizens are ill served by the quality of analysis in the debate over Wal-Mart.

Insofar as we face economic policy challenges, especially regarding the persistence of low-wage, low-skilled adult workers, Wal-Mart's critics do little to advance the cause of effective public policy in this arena. The many fierce opponents of Wal-Mart would better serve their community by focusing policy attention on remedying the low returns to our public investment in education that is experienced by those with low skills (and, therefore, low wages) or through easing the market transition's ill effects on workers. In the end, the hard work of seeking policy innovations that increase worker productivity, which might generate real economic gains for low-skilled workers, is probably a lot less fun than beating up Wal-Mart. But it just might make a difference in the lives and wellbeing of these workers.

REFERENCES

Abowd, John M., Robert H. Creecy, and Francis Kramarz. 2002. "Computing Person and Firm Effects Using Linked Longitudinal Employer-Employee Data." Cornell University Working Paper.

Abzug, Rikki, and Joseph Galaskeiwizc. 2001. "Nonprofit Boards: Crucibles of Expertise or Symbols of Local Identities." *Nonprofit and Voluntary Sector Quarterly*, 30(1): 51–73.

AFL-CIO. 2005. "Wal-Mart Imports from China, Exports Ohio Jobs." AFL-CIO Wal-Mart Campaign, pp. 1–8.

Anderson, William L. 2006. "The High Benefit of Low Prices." Maryland Policy Report 2006-4.

Andersson, Fredrik, Harry J. Holzer, and Julia I. Lane. 2003. "Worker Advancement in the Low-Wage Labor Market: The Importance of Good Jobs." Longitudinal Employment and Household Dynamics Technical Paper TP-2003-06.

Arnold, Stephen J, Jay Handelman, and Douglas J. Tigert. 1998. "The impact of a market spoiler on consumer preference structures (or, what happens when Wal-Mart comes to town)." *Journal of Retailing and Consumer Services*, 5(I): 1–13.

Artz, Georgeanne M. 1999. "The Impact of Wal-Mart on Retail Market Structure in Maine." Thesis. University of Maine, Orono.

Artz, Georgeanne M., and James C. McConnon. 2001. "The Impact of Wal-Mart on Host Towns and Surrounding Communities in Maine." Unpublished.

Barnes, Nora Ganim, Allison Connell, Lisa Hermenegildo, and Lucinda Mattson. 1996. "Regional Differences in the Economic Impact of Wal-Mart." *Business Horizons*, 39(4): 21–26.

Basker, Emek. 2005a. "Job Creation or Destruction? Labor Market Effects of Wal-Mart Expansion." *Review of Economics and Statistics*, 87(1): 174–183.

Basker, Emek. 2005b. "Selling a Cheaper Mousetrap: Wal-Mart's Effect on Retail Prices" *Journal of Urban Economics*, 13(52): 4–27.

Basker, Emek, and Pham Van. 2005. "Putting a Smiley Face on the Dragon: Wal-Mart as a Catalyst to U.S. China Trade." University of Missouri Working Paper.

Beaumont, Constance, and Leslie Tucker. 2002. "Big-Box Sprawl (and How to Control It)." *Municipal Lawyer*, 43(2).

Becker-Posner Blog. 2005. "Wal-Mart and Employee Health Insurance." http://www.becker-posner-blog.com/archives/2005/06/wal-mart_and_em.html. (accessed November 16, 2006).

Belman, Dale A., and Paula Voos. 1993. "Wage Effects of Increased Union Coverage: Methodological Considerations and New Evidence." *Industrial and Labor Relations Review*, 46(2): 368–380.

Bernstein, Jared, Josh Bivens, and Arindrajit Dube. 2006. "Wrestling With Wal-Mart: Tradeoffs Between Profits, Prices and Wages." Economic Policy Institute Working Paper 276.

Bhargava, A., Franzini, L., and Narendranathan, W. 1982. "Serial Correlation and the Fixed Effects Models." *Review of Economic Studies*, 49(4): 533–549.

Bianco, Anthony. 2006. *The Bully of Bentonville*. New York: Doubleday.

Bivens, Josh. 2004. "Shifting Blame for Manufacturing Job Loss: Effect of Rising Trade Deficit Shouldn't Be Ignored." Economic Policy Institute Briefing Paper 149.

Blair, John P., Thomas Traynor, and Manjiang Duan. 2004. "Retail Development in Rural Counties: Evidence from the Upper Midwest." *Journal of Regional Analysis and Policy*, 34(1): 69–85.

Blanchard, Troy, and Thomas Lysons. 2000. "Access to Low Cost Groceries in Nonmetropolitan Counties: Large Retailers and the Creation of Food Deserts." University of Mississippi, unpublished.

Bloom, Paul, and Vanessa Perry. 2001. "Retailer Power and Supplier Welfare: The Case of Wal-Mart." *Journal of Retailing*, 77: 379–396.

Boarnet, Marlon G., and Randall Crane. 1999. "The Impact of Big Box Grocers on Southern California: Jobs, Wages and Municipal Finances." Irvine, CA: Orange County Business Council.

Boarnet, Marlon G., Randall Crane, Daniel G. Chatman, and Michael Manville. 2005. "Emerging Planning Challenges in Retail: The Case of Wal-Mart." *Journal of the American Planning Association*, 71(4): 433–449.

Bohlin, Nils. 2001. "Clustering and Joint Marketing in Retail." Unpublished.

Boyd, David W. 1997. "From 'Mom and Pop' to Wal-Mart: The Impact of the Consumer Goods Pricing Act of 1975 on the Retail Sector of the United States." *Journal of Economic Issues*, 31(1): 223.

Brauer, David. 2004. "What Accounts for the Decline in Manufacturing Employment?" *Economic and Budget Issue Brief, Congressional Budget Office*, February 18. http://www.cbo.gov/showdoc.cfm?index=5078&sequence=0.

Brennan, David P., and Lorman Lundsten. 2000. "Impacts of Large Discount Stores on Small US Towns: Reasons for Shopping and Retailer Strategies." *International Journal of Retail and Distribution Management*, 28(4/5): 155.

Brennan, David P., Kevin Rowekamp, and Pamela M. Flottemeach. 2001. "An Analysis of the Impact of Discounters on Retail Mix in Small Towns in Minnesota." *Papers and Proceedings of Applied Geography Conferences*, 24: 115–120.

Brenner, Aaron, Barry Eidlin, and Kerry Candaele. 2006. "Wal-Mart Stores, Inc." *International Conference, Global Companies, Global Unions, Global Research, Global Campaigns* February 1, 2006, pp. 1–159.

Brunn, Stanley. 2006. *Wal-Mart World: The World's Biggest Corporation in the Global Economy*. Oxford, UK: Routledge.

Brock, W., W. Dechert, J. Scheinkman, and B. LeBaron. 1996. A Test for Independence Based on the Correlation Dimension. *Econometric Reviews*, 15: 197–235.

Bureau of Business and Economic Research. Florida Price Level Index. Gainesville, FL: University of Florida. 1980 through 2004.

Bureau of Economic Analysis, Regional Economic Information System. Database.

Burton, Mark L., Calvin A. Kent, and Michael J. Hicks. 1999. "Evaluating Comprehensive Tax Reform: Lessons From West Virginia." *State Tax Notes*, 17(19).

Buss, Terry F. 2001. "The Effect of State Tax Incentives on Economic Growth and Firm Location Decisions: An Overview of the Literature." *Economic Development Quarterly*, 15(1): 99.

Carlson, Sonya. 2005. "Is Wal-Mart's 'Efficiency' Based on a Government Subsidy: A Case Study of Oregon?" Thesis Lewis & Clark College, unpublished.

CBO. 2005. Changes in Participation in Means-Tested Programs Congressional Budget Office, pp. 1–6.

Chang, Myong-Hun, and Joseph E. Harrington, Jr. 1998. "Organizational Structure and Firm Innovation in a Retail Chain." *Computation & Mathematical Organization Theory*, 3(4): 267–288.

Chen, Zhiqi. 2003a. "Dominant Retailers and the Countervailing-Power Hypothesis." *Rand Journal of Economics*, 34(4): 612–625.

Chen, Zhiqi. 2003b. "Countervailing Power and Product Diversity." Unpublished.

Chiou, Lesley. 2005. "Empirical Analysis of Retail Competition: Spatial Differentiation at Wal-Mart, Amazon.com, and Their Competitors." Unpublished.

Corlija, Melvin, Emilian Siman, and Michael S. Finke. 2006. "Longitudinal Analysis of Big Box Store Construction on Nearby Home Values." *Consumer Interests Annual*, 52: 187–197.

Courtemanch, Aly, and Lani Bensheimer. 2005. "Environmental Impacts of the Proposed Wal-Mart Supercenter in Potsdam." Unpublished.

Coyne, William, and Environment Colorado Research and Policy Center. 2003. "The Fiscal Cost of Sprawl: How Sprawl Contributes to Local Governments' Budget Woes." http://www.environmentcolorado.org/envcogrowth.asp?id2=11566

Curs, Bradley, Mark Stater, and Michael Visser. 2005. "Always High Land Rents? The Effect of Big Box Retail Development on a Productive Spatial Economy." Unpublished.

Curtin, Daniel J. 2004. "Regulating Big Box Stores: The Proper Use of the City or County's Police Power and its Comprehensive Plan - California's Experience." *Vermont Journal of Environmental Law*, vol 6. pp. 1–37.

Curs, Bradley, Mark Stater, and Michael Visser. 2004. "How Much Will Sam Pay For Land? The Locations of Big-Box Retailers and Local Land Values." Unpublished.

Cutler, D., and Gruber, J. 1996. "Does Public Insurance Crowd Out Private Insurance?" *Quarterly Journal of Economics*, 111(2): 391–430.

Dahl, Molly. 2005. "Changes in Participation in Means-Tested Programs." *Economic and Budget Issue Brief, Congressional Budget Office*, April 20. http://www.cbo.gov/ftpdocs/63xx/doc6302/04-20-Means-Tested.pdf.

Dalgliesh, Scott. 2004. "Costs and Quality of Life the Wal-Mart Way." *Quality*, 43(3): 20.

Davidson, Sharon M., and Amy Rummel. 2000. "Retail Changes Associated With Wal-Mart's Entry Into Maine." *International Journal of Retail & Distribution Management*, 28(4/5): 162–172.

Davis, Elizabeth. 2005. "Product Market Competition and Human Resource Practices: An Analysis of the Retail Food Sector." Unpublished.

Davis, Elizabeth, Matthew Fredeman, Julia Lane, Brian BcCall, Nicole Nestoriak, and Timothy Park. 2004. "How Do Industry Human Resource Practices Change? The Impact of Competition on the Retail Food Sector." Paper presented at the NBER Conference on Research on Income and Wealth, Vancouver.

Davis, Stephen J., John C. Haltiwanger, and Scott Schuh. 1996. *Job Creation and Destruction*. Cambridge, MA: MIT Press.

Denning, Branonn P., and Rachel M. Lary. 2005. "Retail Store Size-Capping Ordinances and the Dormant Commerce Clause Doctrine." *The Urban Lawyer*, 37(4): 907–955.

Dobson, P. W., and M. Waterston. 1997. "Countervailing Power and Consumer Prices." *Economic Journal*, 107: 418–430.

Douglas, Edna. 1962. "Size of Firm and the Structure of Costs in Retailing." *The Journal of Business*, 35(2): 158–190.

Dreisewerd, Sherry K. 1998. "Staving Off the Pillage of the Village: Does in re Wal-Mart Stores, Inc [702 A.2d 397 (Vt. 1997)] Offer Hope to Small Merchants Struggling for Economic Survival Against Box Retailers?" *Washington University Journal of Urban and Contemporary Law*, 54: 323–343.

Driscoll, J., and A. Kraay. 1998. "Consistent Covariance Matrix Estimation With Spatially Dependent Panel Data." *Review of Economics and Statistics*, 80(4): 549–560.

Drogin, Richard. 2003. "Statistical Analysis of Gender Patterns in Wal-Mart Workforce." Dukes v. Wal-Mart.

Dube, Arindrajit, and Ken Jacobs. 2004. "Hidden Cost of Wal-Mart Jobs Use of Safety Net Programs by Wal-Mart Workers in California." Berkeley: University of California Berkeley Center for Labor Research and Education, Institute of Industrial Relations.

Dube, Arindrajit, and Steve Wertheim. 2005. "Wal-Mart and Job Quality—What Do We Know, and Should We Care?" Unpublished.

Dube, Arindrajit, Barry Eidlin, and Bill Lester. 2005. "Impact of Wal-Mart Growth on Earnings throughout the Retail Sector in Urban and Rural Counties." Berkeley: University of California Berkeley Center for Labor Research and Education, Institute of Industrial Relations.

Duerksen Chris, and Robert Blanchard. 1998. *"Belling the Box: Planning for Large-Scale Retail Stores"*, 1998 National Planning Conference.

Ehrenreich, Barbara. 2001. Nickel and Dimed On (Not) Getting By in America Published by Metropolitan Books, New York.

Eppli, Mark J., and John D. Benjamin. 1994. "The Evolution of Shopping Center Research." *The Journal of Real Estate Research*, 9(1): 5–32.

Evans, Joel. 2005 "Are the largest public retailers top financial performers? A longitudinal analysis." *International Journal of Retail & Distribution Analysis*, 33(11): 842–867.

Evans-Cowley, Jennifer. 2006. "Meeting the Big-Box Challenge: Planning, Design, and Regulatory Strategies" (Planning Advisory Service Report 537). Chicago: American Planning Association.

Featherstone, Liza. 2005. Wal-Mart Woos the Eggheads, *The Nation*, August 15, 2005.

Federation of Tax Administrators, March 2006.

Fernie, John, Barbara Hahn, Ulrike Gerhard, Elke Ploch, and Stephen Arnold. 2006. "The Impact of Wal-Mart's Entry into the German and UK Grocery Markets." *Agribusiness*, 22(2): 247–266.

Feltman, C. E. 1938. "Location Selection—The Basis of Successful Business." *Chain Store Age*.

Finn, Adam, and Harry Timmermans. 1996. "A Wal-Mart Anchor as a Repositioning Strategy for Suburban Malls." *Journal of Shopping Center Research*, 3(2): 23–43.

Fishman, Charles. 2006. *The Wal-Mart Effect*. New York: Penguin Press.

Fox, Mark A. 2005. "Market Power in Music Retailing: The Case of Wal-Mart." *Popular Music and Society*, 28(4): 501–519.

Franklin, Andrew W. 2001. "The Impact of Wal-Mart Supercenters on Supermarket Concentration in U.S. Metropolitan Areas." *Agribusiness*, 17(1): 105–114.

Franz, L., and E. Robb. 1989. "Effect of Wal-Mart Stores on the Economic Environment of Rural Communities." University of Missouri, unpublished.

Franzese, R., and J. Hays. 2005. *Spatial Econometric Models for Political Science*. (Available at www.personal.umich.edu/ franzese/FranzeseHays.SpatialEcon. Book.pdf.)

Furman, Jason. 2005. "Wal-Mart: A Progressive Success Story." Unpublished.

Gabe, Todd M., and Kraybill, David S. 2002. "The Effect of State Economic Development Incentives on Employment Growth of Establishments." *Journal of Regional Science*, 42(4): 703.

Global Insight. 2005. *The Economic Impact of Wal-Mart*. Boston: Global Insight.

Goetz, Stephan J. 2004. "Big-Boxes and Economic Development." Network04, 19(4). http://www.nercrd.psu.edu/Newsletter/Dec04/network.pdf

Goetz, Stephan J., and Hema Swaminathan. 2006. "Wal-Mart and County-Wide Poverty." *Social Science Quarterly*, 87(2): 211–226.

Graff, Thomas O. 1998. "The Locations of Wal-Mart and Kmart Supercenters: Contrasting Corporate Strategy." *The Professional Geographer*, 50(1): 46.

Graff, Thomas O. 2006. "Unequal Competition Among Chains of Supercenters: K-Mart, Target and Wal-Mart." *The Professional Geographer*, 58(1): 54–64.

Grønbjerg, Kirsten, and Laurie Paarlberg. 2001. "Community Variations in the Size and Scope of the Nonprofit Sector: Theory and Preliminary Findings." *Nonprofit and Voluntary Sector Quarterly*, 30(4): 684–706.

Grosenbaugh, Richard. 2006. Richard's Journal. http://richgros.com/

Gross, Randall. 2004. "Understanding the Fiscal Impacts of Land Use in Ohio." Washington, DC: Development Economics. http://www.regionalconnections.org/documents/pdf/fiscalimpacts.pdf

Gruidl, J., and S. Kline. 1992. "The Impact of Discount Stores on Retail Sales in Illinois Communities." Rural Research Report, Western Illinois University.

Gruidl, John J., and Dimitri Andrianacos. 1994. "Determinants of Rural Retail Trade: A Case Study of Illinois." *The Review of Regional Studies*, 24(1): 103–118.

Guyer, Jocelyn, and Cindy Mann. 1998. "Taking the Next Step: States Can Now Take Advantage of Federal Medicaid Matching Funds to Expand Health Care Coverage to Low-Income Working Parents." Washington, DC: Center on Budget and Policy Priorities.

Hadsell, Lester. 2002. "Large Retailers, Economic Development, and the Local Property Tax Base: Evidence From Wal-Mart in New York State." *New York Economic Review*, 32: 27–42.

Hanauer, Amy. 2004. "Taking Credit: Boosting Participation in the Earned Income Tax Credit in Greater Cleveland." *Policy Matters Ohio*. http://www.policymattersohio.org/eitc/eitc_04.htm

Hawker, Norman W, and Ross D. Petty. 1996. "Wal-Mart and the divergence of state and federal predatory pricing law," *Journal of Public Policy & Marketing*, 15(1): 141–148.

Harris, Thomas R., and J. Scott Shonkwiler. 1997. "Interdependence of Retail Business." *Growth and Change*, 28(4): 520–533.

Hausman J., and E. Leibtag. 2004 "CPI Bias from Supercenters: Does the BLS know that Wal-Mart Exists" National Bureau of Economic Research working paper 10712.

Hausman J., and E. Leibtag. 2005. "Consumer Benefits From Increased Competition in Shopping Outlets: Measuring the Effect of Wal-Mart." National Bureau of Economic Research working paper 11809.

Hernandez, Marco, and Tony Biasiotto. 2001. "Retail Location Decision-Making and Store Portfolio Management." *Canadian Journal of Regional Science*, 24(3): 399–418.

Herrera, Christie Raniszewski. 2006. "Fair Share Health Care' May Pose Threat to Fiscal, Physical Health." Chicago: Heartland Institute.

Hicks, Michael J. 1999. "A Dynamic Analysis of West Virginia's Cash Assistance Programs, 1978–1998." Marshall University Working Paper 99-03-A.

Hicks, Michael J. 2005a. "Does Wal-Mart Cause an Increase in Anti-Poverty Program Expenditures?" Unpublished.

Hicks, Michael J. 2005b. "What Do Quarterly Workforce Dynamics Tell Us About Wal-Mart? Evidence from New Stores in Pennsylvania." http://econpapers. repec.org/paper/wpawuwpur/0511010.htm; see also, Hicks, Michael J. 2007b. "Job Turnover and Wages in the Retail Sector: The Influence of Wal-Mart" *Journal of Private Enterprise*, VolXXIII(3) forthcoming.

Hicks, Michael J. 2005c. "Does Wal-Mart Cause an Increase in Medicaid Expenditures?" Marshall University, Center for Business and Economic Research. http://www.businessweek.com/pdfs/2005/michael_hicks.pdf

Hicks, Michael J. 2005d. "Wal-Mart and Urban Sprawl in Colorado." Unpublished.

Hicks, Michael J. 2006a. "What Do We Know About Wal-Mart's Local Impact, and Why Is It Important." *Economic Development Journal*, 5(3): 23–31.

Hicks, Michael J. 2006b. "Transportation Infrastructure, Retail Clustering and Local Public Finance: Evidence from Wal-Mart's Expansion." *Regional Economic Development*, 2(2).

Hicks, Michael J. Forthcoming-a. "Estimating Wal-Mart's Impacts in Maryland: A Test of Identification Strategies and Endogeneity Tests." *Eastern Economic Journal*.

Hicks, Michael J. 2007. "The Impact of Wal-Mart on Local Fiscal Health: Evidence From a Panel of Ohio Counties." *Atlantic Economic Journal*, 35(1).

Hicks, Michael J., and Mark Boyer. 1999. "What Caused the Decline in Welfare Caseloads in the 1990's: Evidence From a State AFDC Program." *Journal of Applied Social Sciences*, 24(2).

Hicks, Michael J., and Kristy Wilburn. 2001. "The Regional Impact of Wal-Mart Entrance: A Panel Study of the Retail Trade Sector in West Virginia." *Review of Regional Studies*, 31(3): 305–313.

Hirsch, Barry T. 2004. "What Do Unions Do for Economic Performance?" *Journal of Labor Research*, 25(3): 415–455.

Hirsch, Barry T., David A. Macpherson, and Wayne G. Vroman. 2001. "Estimates of Union Density by State." *Monthly Labor Review*, 124(7): 51–55.

Hollander, Stanley C. 1960. "The Wheel of Retailing." *The Journal of Marketing*, 25(1): 37–42.

Holmes, Thomas J. 2006. "The Diffusion of Wal-Mart and the Economics of Density." Federal Reserve Bank of Minneapolis, unpublished.

Hoopes, James. 2006. "Growth Through Knowledge: Wal-Mart, High Technology and the Ever Less Visible Hand of the Manager." In *Wal-Mart The Face of 21st Century Capitalism*, ed. Nelson Lichtenstein, pp. 83–106.

Hornbeck, J. F. 1994. "The Discount Retail Industry and Its Effect on Small Towns and Rural Communities." CRS Report for Congress, Library of Congress.

Jencks, Christopher. 2002. "Liberal Lessons From Welfare Reform: Why Welfare Reform Turned Out Better Than We Expected." *The American Prospect*, 13(13): A9(4).

Jia, Panle. 2005. "What Happens When Wal-Mart Comes to Town: An Empirical Analysis of the Discount Retailing Industry." Unpublished.

Johannson, Robert C., and Jay S. Coggins. 2002. "Union Density Effects in the Supermarket Industry." *Journal of Labor Research*, 23(4): 673–685.

Joseph, Marc. 2005. *The Secrets of Retailing, or: How to Beat Wal-Mart!* Hong Kong: Silverback.

Kazee, Nicole D. 2006. "Medicaid for the Working Poor: Policy Preferences and Political Strategy in the Business Community." Paper presented at the Yale University Department of Political Science, Inequality and American Democracy Graduate Student Conference, University of Minnesota, Minneapolis, April 7–8, 2006.

Keil, Stanley R., and Lee C. Spector. 2007. "The Impact of Wal-Mart on Employment and Wage Differentials in Alabama." *Review of Regional Studies*, 35: 336–355.

Kentucky Long-Term Policy Research Center. 2004. "Visioning Kentucky's future: Measures and Milestones." Frankfort: Kentucky Long-Term Policy Research Center.

Keon, T., E. Robb, and L. Franz. 1989. "Effect of Wal-Mart Stores on the Economic Environment of Rural Communities." University of Missouri Working Paper.

Ketchum, B. A., and J. W. Hughes. 1997. "Wal-Mart and Maine: The Effect on Employment and Wages." University of Maine, unpublished.

Khanna, Naveen, and Sherry Tice. 2005. "Pricing, exit, and location decisions of firms: Evidence on the role of debt and operating efficiency." *Journal of Financial Economics*, 75: 397–427.

Kiser, Brad, and William Fox. 2005. "The Impact of TennCare: A Survey of Recipients." Knoxville: University of Tennessee, Center for Business and Economic Research.

Klimek, Shawn D., Ron S. Jarmin, and Mark E. Doms. 2002. "IT Investment and Firm Performance in U.S. Retail Trade." Center for Economic Studies, U.S. Census Bureau FRB of San Francisco Working Paper 02-14.

Konishi, Hideo. 2005 "Concentration of Competing Retail Stores." *Journal of Urban Economics*, 58: 488–512.

Kures, Matt. 2003. *Greyfields and Ghostboxes: Evolving Real Estate Challenges.* Madison: University of Wisconsin-Extension, Center for Community Economic Development.

LaFaive, Michael, and Michael Hicks. 2005. "MEGA: A Retrospective Assessment." Mackinac, MI: Mackinac Center for Public Policy.

Lane, Julia, Simon Burgess, and Jules Theeuwes. 1998. "The Uses of Longitudinal Matched Employer / Emploee Data in Labor Market Analysis." In *Proceedings of the American Statistical Association*, pp. 249–254.

Lebhar, Godfrey. 1952. *Chain Stores in America 1859–1950.* New York: Chain Store Publishing.

Lefcoe, George. 2006. "The Regulation of Superstores: The Legality of Zoning Ordinances Emerging From the Skirmishes Between Wal-Mart and the United Food and Commercial Workers Union." *Arkansas Law Review*, 58: 1–27.

Lichtenstein, Nelson. 2005. "Wal-Mart—Yesteryear's GM?" *The Globalist.*

Lichtenstein, Nelson. 2006. *Wal-Mart: The Face of 21st Century Capitalism.* New York: The New Press.

Laulajainen R. 1987. *Spatial Strategies in Retailing.* Dodrecht, The Netherlands: D. Reidel.

Laulajainen R., and Gadde, L.-E. 1986. "Locational Avoidance: A Case Study of Three Swedish Retail Chains." *Regional Studies*, 20: 131–140.

Mann, Lawrence B. 1923. "The Importance of Retail Trade." *The American Economic Review*, 13(4): 609–617.

Mattera, Philip, and Anna Purinton. 2004. "Shopping for Subsidies: How Wal-Mart Uses Taxpayer Money to Finance Its Never-Ending growth." *Good Jobs First*, pp. 1–64.

McConnell, Ankila Sankar. 2004. "Making Wal-Mart Pretty: Trademarks and Aesthetic Restrictions on Big-Box Retailers." *Duke Law Journal*, 53: 1537–1567.

McCraw, Thomas K. 1984. *Prophets of Regulation.* Cambridge, MA: Harvard University Press.

McGee, Jeffrey E. 1995. "When Wal-Mart Comes to Town: A Look at How Local Merchants Respond to the Retailing Giant's Arrival." *Journal of Business and Entrepreneurship*, 8(1): 43–52.

McGee, Jeffrey E., and George G. Gresham. 1995. When Wal-Mart Comes to Town: A Look at the Retailing Giant's Impact on Rural Communities. *Frontiers of Entrepreneurship Research*.

McGee, Jeffrey E., and M. J. Rubach. 1996. "Responding to Increased Environmental Hostility: A Study of the Competitive Behavior of Small Retailers." *Journal of Applied Business Research*, 13(1): 83–94.

McKinsey Global Institute. 2002. *Reaching Higher Productivity Growth in France and Germany* Washington, DC: McKinsey & Company.

Mehta, Chirag, Ron Baiman, and Joe Persky. 2004. "The Economic Impact of Wal-Mart: An Assessment of the Wal-Mart Store Proposed for Chicago's West Side." Chicago: University of Illinois at Chicago, Center for Urban Economic Development.

Mikelson, Kelly S., and Robert I. Lerman. 2004. "Relationship Between the EITC and Food Stamp Program Participation Among Households With Children, Economic Research Service." Washington, DC: U.S. Department of Agriculture.

Miller, George. 2004. "Everyday Low Wages: The Hidden Price We All Pay for Wal-Mart." Report of the Democratic Staff of the Committee on Education and the Workforce. Washington, DC: U.S. House of Representatives.

Mills, David E. 1989. "Is Zoning a Zero-Sum Game?" *Land Economics*, 65(1): 1–12.

Mitchell, Preston W., Derek H. Alderman, Jeffrey T. Webb, and Dustin W. Stancil. 2004. "When Wal-Mart Doesn't Come to Town: Competititve Responses of Established Retail Merchants in Edenton, North Carolina." *The Geographical Bulletin*, 46(2): 15–24.

Mitchell, Stacy. 2000. *The Home Town Advantage*. Minneapolis, MN: The New Rules Project.

Molho, Ian, and Michael Waterson. 1989. "Modeling Supermarket Store Locations." *Scottish Journal of Political Economy*, 36(4): 375–385.

Moreton, Bethany. 2006. "It Came From Bentonville: The Agrarian Origins of Wal-Mart Culture." In *Wal-Mart The Face of 21st Century Capitalism*, ed. Nelson Lichtenstein, pp. 57–82.

Munroe, Scott. 1999. "How to Solve Multi-Facility Location Problems." *National Petroleum News*, August.

Myrer, Anton. 1968. *Once an Eagle*. Harper Collins.

Neumann, Todd C. 2004. "Endogenous Entry and Competition in the Retail Market during the Early 20th Century" mimeo.

Neumann, Todd C. 2005. "Specialization of Retail Labor: Evidence From Population Census Data." University of Arizona, unpublished.

Neumark, David. 2002. *How Living Wage Laws Affect Low-Wage Workers and Low-Income Families*. San Francisco: Public Policy Institute of California.

Neumark, David, Junfu Zhang, and Stephan Ciccarella. 2005. "The Effects of Wal-Mart on Local Labor Markets." Unpublished.

Nichols, John P. 1940. *The Chain Store Tells its Story*. New York: Institute of Distribution.

Nielsen, Francois. 2002. "Income Inequality in U.S. Counties (Gini Coefficients)." http://www.unc.edu/nielsen/data/data.htm

Norman, Al. 1999. *Slam Dunking Wal-Mart*. Atlantic City, NJ: Raphel Marketing.

Norman, Al. 2004. *The Case Against Wal-Mart* Atlantic City, NJ: Raphel Marketing.

Ozment J., and Martin, G. 1990. Changes in the competitive environment of rural retail trade areas. *Journal of Business Research*, 21: 277–287.

Perry, Theodis L. 2001. *Managing Maryland's Growth: Models and Guidelines "Big-Box" Retail Development*. Baltimore: Maryland Department of Planning.

Peters, Alan, and Fisher, Peter. 2004. "The Failures of Economic Development Incentives." *Journal of the American Planning Association*, 70: 27.

Petrovic, Misha, and Gary G. Hamilton. 2006. "Making Global Markets: Wal-Mart and Its Suppliers." In *Wal-Mart: The Face of 21st Century Capitalism*, ed. Nelson Lichtenstein, pp. 107–142.

Ratcliff, R. U. 1939. *Problem of Retail Site Selection*. Ann Arbor: University of Michigan Business Studies.

Ross, Thomas W. 1986. "Store Wars: The Chain Tax Movement." *Journal of Law and Economics*, 29: 127.

Rukeyser, Merryle Stanley. 1928. "Chain Stores: The Revolution in Retailing." *The Nation*, 127(3308): 568–570.

Ryan, Bill, Tim Filbert, Jim Janke, and Aaron Brault. 1998. "Retail Mix in Wisconsin's 'Tiny Towns' How Distance From a Major Discount Store Impacts Local Retail Availability." University of Wisconsin–Madison, Center for Community and Economic Development.

Ryant, Carl G. 1973. "The South and the Movement Against Chain Stores." *The Journal of Southern History*, 39(2): 207–222.

Schiller, Zach. 2002. *Ohio's Vanishing Corporate Franchise Tax*. Policy Matters Ohio.

Schneider, James H. 1996. *County and Local Government Land Use Planning and Regulation*, Madison: University of Wisconsin-Extension, Local Government Center.

Schonberger, Richard J. 2006. "Lean Extended." *Industrial Engineer*, 37(1): 26–31.

Schragger, Richard C. 2005. "The Anti-Chain Store Movement, Local Ideology, and the Remnants of the Progressive Constitution, 1920–1940." University of Virginia Law School, Public Law and Legal Theory Working Paper Series No. 21.

Sharkey, Todd, and Kyle Steigart. 2006. "Impacts of Nontraditional Food Retailing Supercenters on Food Price Changes." Food Systems Research Group, FSRG Monograph Series, No. 20.

Sheridan, Richard G., David A. Ellis, and Richard Marountas. 2003. Adequacy of Ohio's Tax Structure to Support Essential Government Services." *Taxing Issues*, 1–20.

Shils, Edward B. 1997. "The Shils Report: Measuring the Economic and Sociological Impact of the Mega-Retail Discount Chains on Small Enterprise in Urban, Suburban and Rural Communities." Philadelphia: Wharton Entrepreneurial Center.

Shore-Sheppard, L., T. C. Buchmuller, and G. A. Jensen. 2000. "Medicaid and Crowding Out of Private Insurance: A Re-Examination Using Firm Level Data." *Journal of Health Economics*, 19(1): 61–91.

Singh, Vishal, Karsten T. Hansen, and Robert C. Blattberg. 2004. "Impact of Wal-Mart Supercenter Entry on Consumer Purchase Behavior: An Empirical Investigation." Unpublished.

Slater, Robert. 2002. *The Wal-Mart Triumph*. New York: Penguin Group.

Sobel, Russell S., and Andrea Dean. 2005. "Has Wal-Mart Buried Mom & Pop? The Impact of Wal-Mart on Self Employment and Small Establishments in the United States." Morgantown: West Virginia University, Entrepreneurship Center.

Social Security Administration. 2005. *OASDI Beneficiaries by State and County, 2005*. Washington, DC: Social Security Administration.

Stone, Ken E. 1989. "The effects of Wal-Mart stores on businesses in host towns and surrounding towns in Iowa." Iowa State University, Ames, unpublished.

Stone, Ken E. 1995. *Competing With the Retail Giants.* New York: Wiley.

Stone, Ken E. 1997. "Impact of the Wal-Mart Phenomenon on Rural Communities." In *Increasing Understanding of Public Problems and Policies.* Chicago: Farm Foundation.

Stone, Ken E., S. C. Deller, and J. McConnon, Jr. 1992. "The New Retail Environment in Maine." *The Maine Business Research Report*, 3:1.

Stone, Ken E., G. Artz, and K. Myles. 2002. "The Economic Impact of Wal-Mart Supercenters on Existing Businesses in Mississippi." Unpublished.

Teihan, Laura. 2000. "Has Working More Caused Married Women to Volunteer Less? Evidence From Time Diary Data, 1965 to 1993." *Nonprofit and Voluntary Sector Quarterly*, 29(4): 505–529.

Thomas, Alexander R., Sherry Martin, and Peter Dai. 2005. "Rural Retail Redux: Supermarket Pricing in Rural Central New York." Oneonta: State University of New York College at Oneonta, Center for Social Science Research.

Tischler and Associates. 2002. "Fiscal Impact Analysis of Residential and Nonresidential Land Use Prototypes Prepared for Town of Barnstable, Massachusetts." Bethesda, MD: Tischler and Associates.

Twombly, Eric C. 2003. "What Factors Affect the Entry and Exit of Non-profit Human Service Organizations in Metropolitan Areas? *Nonprofit and Voluntary Sector Quarterly*, 32(2): 211–235.

Vance, S., and R. V. Scott. 1992. "Sam Walton and Wal-Mart Stores, Inc.: A Study in Modern Southern Entrepreneurship." *The Journal of Southern History*, 58: 231–252.

Vance, S. 1994. *Wal-Mart: A History of Sam Walton's Retail Phenomenon.* New York: Twayne, Inc.

Van Heerde, Harald J., Els Gijsbrecht, and Koen Pauwels 2005 "Price War: What is it good for? Store choice and basket size responses to retailing price wars" mimeo.

Vedder, Richard, and Wendell Cox. 2006. *The Wal-Mart Revolution: How Big Box Stores Benefit Consumers, Workers, and the Economy.* Washington, DC: AEI Press.

Villareal, Pam. 2005. "Thinking Outside the 'Big Box'." National Center for Policy Analysis Brief Analysis no. 501.

Villianatos, Shaffer, Beery, Gottleib and Wheatley (2004). Price Study.

Waddoups, C. Jeffrey. 2004. "Health Care Subsidies in Construction: Does the Public Sector Subsidize Low Wage Contractors." In *The Economics of*

Prevailing Wage Laws, ed, Hamid Azari-Rad and Mark J. Prus. London: Ashgate Publishing.

Wal-Mart Alliance for Reform Now. 2005. "Wal-Mart Real Wage and Turnover Study." http://warnwalmart.org/index.php?id=24.

Walton, Sam. 1992. *Made in America*. New York: Doubleday.

Wassmer, Robert W. 2004. "Fiscalization of Land Use, Urban Growth Boundaries, and Non-Central Retail Sprawl in the Western United States." *Urban Studies*, 39: 1307–1327.

Wasylenko, Michael. 1997. "Taxation and Economic Development: The State of the Economic Literature." *New England Economic Review*, pp. 37–52.

Wheaton, William C., and Raymond Torto. 1995. "Retail Sales and Retail Real Estate." *Real Estate Finance*, 12(1): 22–33.

White, Halbert. 1980. "A Heteroscedasticity-Consistent Covariance Matrix Estimator and a Direct Test for Heteroscedasticity" *Econometrica*, 48(4): 817–838.

Whitely, A. S. 1936. "Retail Trade in the United States and Canada." *Journal of Political Economy*, 44(1): 54–69.

Wilburn, Kristy. 1999. "The Effect of Wal-Mart Stores in Southern West Virginia." *Regional Economic Review*.

AUTHOR INDEX

SUBJECT INDEX

A&P (see also Great Atlantic & Pacific Tea Company), 7, 8, 10f, 11, 23, 122, 128, 161
A. L. Duckwall, 8t
A. S. Beck, 8t
Absolute bans (see zoning, Conditional Use Permits, Site Specific Review), 268, 271, 272
ACCRA, 127, 131
ACNielson, 126
ACT 240, 269, 270
Adaptive Reuse, 274t
Aesthetic Integration, 274t
AFL-CIO, 158, 211, 212t, 284, 291
Agglomeration, 34, 35n5, 86, 91, 95, 100, 101, 102t
Aid to Dependent Children, 206
Aid to Families with Dependent Children (AFDC), 205–207, 213
Akaike Information Criterion (AIC), 187
Alabama, 175t, 178t, 180t, 226, 244, 283t
Alaska, 66, 67, 175t, 178t, 283t, 287t
Albuquerque, New Mexico, 279
Allegheny County, Maryland, 16
Allen, Texas, 258t
Amarillo, Texas, 18
American Drugs v. Wal-Mart, Inc., 282
American Planning Association, 268, 270
American Retail Federation, 17
Anti-Chain Store, 14, 15, 17, 18, 19, 21
Anticompetitive, 24, 101, 271, 272

Antipoverty, 3, 4, 169, 205, 210, 213, 218, 242, 276, 285
Antitrust, 20, 122, 266, 281, 282, 283t, 293
Apparel sales, 108t, 109t, 113t, 115t
Areeda-Turner, 281, 282
Arizona, 22, 175t, 178t, 212t, 283t
Arkansas, 45, 60, 76t, 81, 88, 104, 105, 175t, 178t, 180t, 212t, 224, 227, 228, 243, 283t
Arkansas Supreme Court, 282
Arkansas Unfair Practices Act, 282
Association of Community Organizations for Reform Now (ACORN), 276, 277, 278
Atlanta, 77t
Atlantic Economic Journal, 162
Autocorrelation, 80, 89, 91n5, 92, 94t, 97, 104, 106t, 110, 140, 182
Automobile, 54
Avon Park, Florida, 258t
Awnings / Entrance Restrictions, 274t

Baby-boom, 22
BadgeCare, 212t
Bakersfield Citizens for Local Control v. City of Bakersfield, 269
Barnstable, Massachusetts, 189, 190
Bentonville, Arkansas, 45, 60, 63, 81, 88, 104–107, 112t, 154, 157, 217, 224, 242, 243, 247
Big-Box, 3–5, 21, 23–25, 54, 58t, 76t, 77t, 99, 100, 119, 120f, 162, 181, 190, 221, 222, 252–255, 257, 258, 265, 268–273, 280